Geology of the Kirkcudbright–Dalbeattie district

The area described in this memoir extends northwards from the low cliffs, beaches and estuaries along the Solway Firth to the gently undulating moorland between Gatehouse of Fleet and Castle Douglas. Although much of the ground is still devoted to the traditional uses of sheep and cattle rearing together with some arable farming on the lower ground, there are now also extensive areas of coniferous forest plantation. Geological factors relevant to land use planning are reviewed and key issues discussed.

Geologically, the district forms part of the Southern Uplands Terrane and consists mainly of wacke sandstones and shales of the Gala, Hawick and Riccarton groups, all of Silurian age. These sedimentary rocks are of marine origin and were laid down in an elongate basin trapped between the colliding continental masses of Laurentia and Avalonia. As the two continents moved together, the sedimentary strata were folded and sequentially thrust beneath the margin of Laurentia (the northern continent), eventually forming a thrust belt which prograded southwards and over-rode the leading edge of Avalonia which was approaching from the south. This tectonic episode was followed by intrusion of the extensive late Silurian to early Devonian syn- and post-tectonic dyke swarms, associated subvolcanic vent complexes (such as Black Stockarton Moor) and the two major post-tectonic granitic plutons of Criffel–Dalbeattie and Cairnsmore of Fleet. Much of the known disseminated (Cu) and vein-type (Cu, Ba, Fe, U) mineralisation within the district was associated in space and time with this igneous episode.

The Silurian rocks are overlain unconformably by an Upper Devonian to Lower Carboniferous terrestrial to shallow marine succession of sandstones and limestones. The district also includes part of the Dumfries Basin with its Permian red-bed succession of desert sandstones and breccias.

Superficial deposits of Quaternary age are mainly found in the eastern part of the district, in lower-lying areas in the valleys and along the coast. They include a complex sequence of boulder clay (till), moraine, meltwater and raised beach deposits formed during and following the Devensian glaciation, as well as more recent deposits of peat and alluvium.

The district is covered by Sheets 5W (Kirkcudbright) and 5E (Dalbeattie) of the 1:50 000 geological map of Scotland. Both sheets are available as separate solid and drift editions.

D1514282

Cover photograph
View of Kirkcudbright Harbour, looking south-west, showing part of the scallop fishing fleet [NX 687 515] (D 4377).

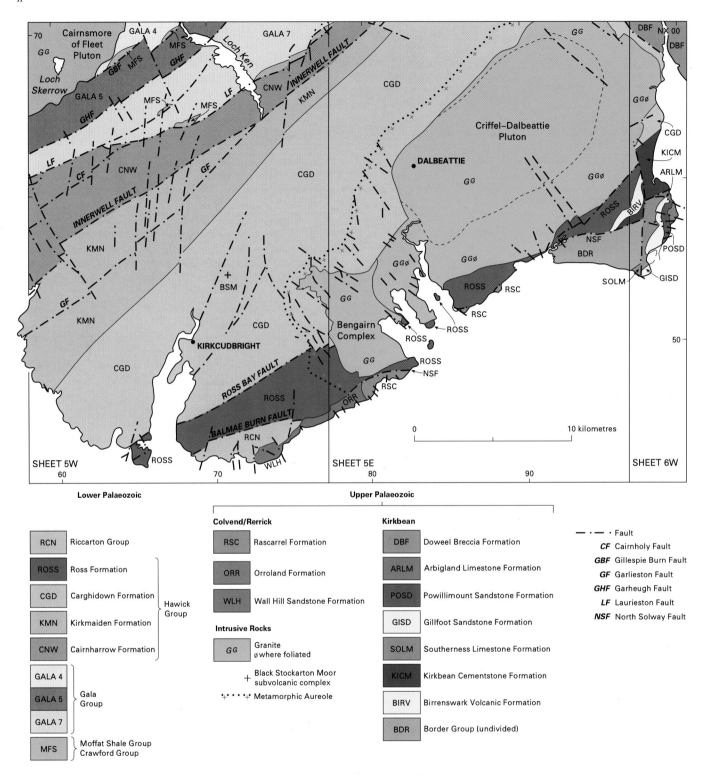

Figure 1 Summary geological map of the Kirkcudbright – Dalbeattie district.

BRITISH GEOLOGICAL SURVEY

B C LINTERN AND
J D FLOYD

Geology of the Kirkcudbright–Dalbeattie district

Memoir for 1:50 000 Geological Sheets 5W, 5E and part of 6W (Scotland)

CONTRIBUTORS
D F Ball
R P Barnes
P J Brand
D J Fettes
M J Gallagher (deceased)
P J Henney
S R Hirons
G S Kimbell
A A McMillan
R J Merriman
E R Phillips
B Roberts
A W A Rushton
S P Tunnicliff

London: The Stationery Office   2000

Bibliographical reference
LINTERN, B C, and FLOYD, J D. 2000.   Geology of the Kirkcudbright–Dalbeattie district.   *Memoir of the British Geological Survey*, Sheets 5W, 5E and part of 6W (Scotland).

Authors/compilers
B C Lintern, BSc, PhD (deceased)
J D Floyd, BSc, PhD, CGeol
British Geological Survey, Edinburgh

Contributors
D F Ball, BSc
R P Barnes, BSc, PhD
P J Brand, BSc
D J Fettes, BSc, PhD, CGeol
M J Gallagher, BSc, PhD (deceased)
A A McMillan, BSc, CGeol
E R Phillips, BSc, PhD
British Geological Survey, Edinburgh

P J Henney, BSc, PhD
G S Kimbell, BSc
A W A Rushton, BA, PhD
S P Tunnicliff, BSc
R J Merriman, BSc, CGeol
British Geological Survey, Keyworth
B Roberts, BSc, PhD
S R Hirons, BSc
Birkbeck College, University of London

Acknowledgements

The bulk of the mapping on Sheets 5W and 5E and much of this Memoir text was the work of the late Dr Byron C Lintern who worked in this area from 1986 until his untimely death in January 1993. The compilation of the Memoir was subsequently undertaken by Dr J D Floyd, with the assistance of the numerous other contributors. All would like to record their respect and appreciation for the outstanding contribution that Byron Lintern made to the geological understanding of the Kirkcudbright–Dalbeattie district in particular and the Southern Uplands in general.

Chapter 1 Introduction was written by B C Lintern and J D Floyd, Chapter 2 Applied Geology by J D Floyd and D F Ball, Chapter 3 Concealed geology by G S Kimbell, Chapter 4 Ordovician and Silurian by B C Lintern, J D Floyd, S P Tunnicliff and A W A Rushton, Chapter 5 Caledonian structure and metamorphism by R P Barnes and R J Merriman, Chapter 6 Caledonian intrusive rocks by D J Fettes, E R Phillips and P J Henney, Chapters 7 Upper Palaeozoic and 9 Quaternary by A A McMillan, Chapter 8 Tertiary and Information sources by J D Floyd, and Chapter 10 Mineralisation by M J Gallagher and J D Floyd.

The authors/compilers and contributors extend their thanks and appreciation to numerous colleagues both in BGS and academia for assistance in the field and for access to unpublished data. Particular thanks are extended to Dr A E S Kemp for allowing free access to unpublished field maps and for field demonstration of localities studied during postgraduate research at the University of Edinburgh, and to C Cooper who provided similar assistance for the Black Stockarton Moor subvolcanic complex which was the subject of his research at Imperial College, University of London. The Lower Palaeozoic biostratigraphy was reassessed and revised with the assistance of Dr D E White (formerly BGS) and the Upper Palaeozoic by P J Brand (formerly BGS). Dr B Roberts and Mr S R Hirons of Birkbeck College, University of London collaborated in the section on low-grade metamorphism.

Structural and stratigraphical interpretations benefited from extended discussion with colleagues, especially Dr P Stone and numerous participants on the various Southern Uplands Field Workshops. The text was edited by Dr P Stone and Mr A D McAdam and was produced under the programme management of Dr D J Fettes. Diagrams were produced in the Drawing Office of the BGS, Edinburgh.

Notes

The word district is used in this memoir to denote the area included in the geological 1:50 000 Series sheets 5W Kirkcudbright and 5E Dalbeattie with part of 6W Annan. National Grid References are given in square brackets throughout the memoir. Unless otherwise stated, all lie within the 100 km square NX.

CONTENTS

TABLES

PLATES

PREFACE

Geology underpins a wide range of activities vital to the creation of wealth, particularly in relation to the exploration for and exploitation of resources. It is also important that we have the best possible understanding of the geology of the United Kingdom if we are to maintain the quality of life whether through the identification of potential hazards prior to development or helping to ameliorate the problems created by earlier developments. The British Geological Survey is funded by Government to improve our understanding of the three-dimensional geology of the UK through a national programme of geoscience surveying, data collection, interpretation, publication and archiving. One aim of this programme is to provide coverage of the UK land area by modern 1:50 000 geological maps, together with explanatory memoirs, by the year 2005. This memoir on the Kirkcudbright–Dalbeattie district of the Southern Uplands of Scotland is part of the output from that programme.

The Kirkcudbright–Dalbeattie district in south-west Scotland lies almost entirely within the former county of Kirkcudbright, apart from a tiny area on the east bank of the River Nith which was formerly in Dumfriesshire. Topographically, the district varies between the elevated country around Criffel, to the cliffs, beaches and estuaries along the Solway Firth. Apart from the principal towns of Kirkcudbright, Castle Douglas, Gatehouse of Fleet and Dalbeattie, the district is essentially rural, with numerous small picturesque inland and coastal villages. Agriculture and forestry remain the principal land uses, though tourism is now a major contributor to the local economy, supported by the growing number of visitors attracted by the relatively peaceful and unspoiled scenery of the Galloway hills and Solway coast.

Notable topographical features within the district include the granite peaks of Criffel and Airie Hill, together with the lower reaches and estuaries of the rivers Fleet, Dee, Urr and Nith. There are also numerous small and medium-sized lochs, the principal one being Loch Ken, now part of the only substantial hydroelectric scheme in Scotland outwith the Highlands.

The district includes an excellent cross section through the southernmost (Silurian) part of the Lower Palaeozoic succession in the Southern Uplands and contains several notable geological localities which are critical to the interpretation of this major Caledonian terrane. These also confirm the now well-established along-strike tectono-stratigraphical continuity which is such a characteristic feature of the Southern Uplands. The combination of biostratigraphy, petrography and sedimentology together with new structural data has contributed to the ongoing debate on the overall tectonic interpretation for the Southern Uplands, principally centreing on a back-arc/foreland basin versus forearc (accretionary prism) model. The memoir also deals with the major granitoid pluton of Criffel–Dalbeattie as well as touching on the Cairnsmore of Fleet Pluton (described more fully in the Memoir for the adjacent Carrick–Loch Doon district). These plutons, together with their associated dyke swarms, provide critical geochemical and geochronological evidence for the understanding of important Caledonian events in the south of Scotland.

The Silurian rocks are unconformably overlain by an Upper Devonian to Lower Carboniferous terrestrial to shallow-marine succession, which crops out as a number of outliers along the Solway coast, and shows clear evidence of active tectonic control on sedimentation by the North Solway Fault. The district also includes a small part of the Dumfries Basin which contains a Permian red-bed succession of sandstones and breccias.

Extensive till, glaciofluvial sand and gravel, raised beach deposits, peat and alluvium provide plentiful evidence for the Quaternary glaciation and Recent geological history of the district.

The 1:50 000 map has been published in two sheets, 5W and 5E (including a small part of 6W), with separate drift (published 1980 and 1981 respectively) and solid (published 1993) editions.

David A Falvey, PhD
Director

British Geological Survey
Kingsley Dunham Centre
Keyworth
Nottingham
NG12 5GG

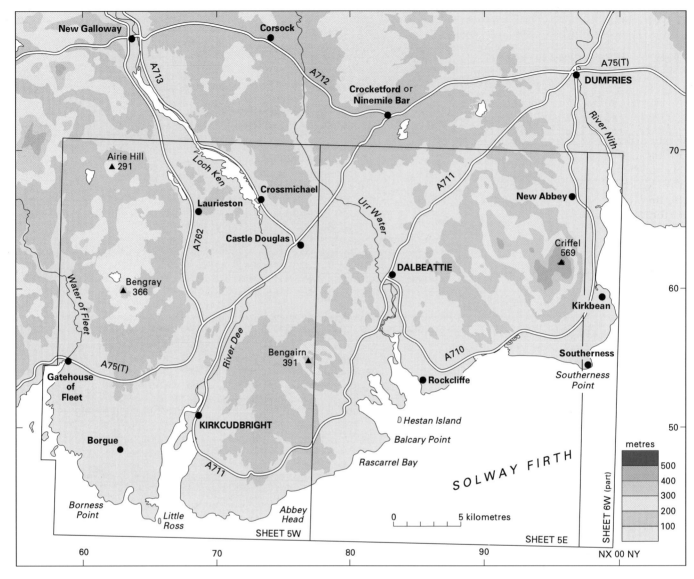

Figure 2 Principal physical features of the district and its regional setting.

ONE

Introduction

This memoir describes the geology represented on the Kirkcudbright (5W), Dalbeattie (5E) and part of Kirkbean (6W) sheets of the 1:50 000 geological map of Scotland; an area of 850 km² subsequently referred to as the Kirkcudbright–Dalbeattie district (Figure 1). Bounded on the south by the Solway Firth, the district extends from Gatehouse of Fleet in the west to the mouth of the River Nith in the east and includes the lower reaches of the Water of Fleet, River Dee and Water of Urr (Figure 2).

Geologically, the district forms part of the Southern Uplands Terrane and is underlain for the most part by a thick succession of sedimentary rocks deposited, during Silurian times, as vast submarine fans of sand/silt turbidites on the floor of a long-vanished ocean. As this ocean closed, the sedimentary rocks were folded and deformed into their present-day subvertical attitude and were subsequently, during the late Silurian/early Devonian, intruded by granitic plutons and suites of basic to intermediate dykes. The main geological points of interest include sections through these Lower Palaeozoic wackes and siltstones, well displayed in excellent coastal exposures, and the large granitic plutons of Criffel–Dalbeattie and Cairnsmore of Fleet with their associated dyke swarms. Carboniferous rocks, deposited near the northern shoreline of a marine basin centred along the Solway Firth, crop out along the coast in the southern part of the district with good exposure of fossiliferous strata not seen elsewhere in the region. Permian rocks of terrestrial facies crop out in the extreme north-east of the district but are generally poorly exposed hereabouts and are best examined in the Dumfries district further to the north-east.

Topography

The highest ground in the district occurs in the east and is formed by the Criffel–Dalbeattie Pluton and associated hornfelsed country rocks, with a maximum height of 569 m on Criffel [957 619] itself. In the north-west, the Cairnsmore of Fleet Pluton forms ground of more subdued relief (maximum height of 291 m on Airie Hill [621 686]), although further to the west, in the Wigtown district, the summit of Cairnsmore rises to 711 m. The topography in the intervening area varies from hilly to low-lying, drumlin-dominated ground, with a well-defined north-east–south-west grain reflecting the regional strike of the underlying turbidite sequences. This linear topography is particularly well developed on the ridge of higher ground (up to 366 m on Bengray [631 599]) which stretches north-east from Gatehouse of Fleet to Bargatton Loch [693 618] and also in the series of low linear ridges inland of the shoreline between Borgue and Gatehouse of Fleet.

The main centres of population are Dalbeattie, Castle Douglas, Kirkcudbright and Gatehouse of Fleet. Tourism is an important part of the economy of the district which overall presents a tranquil mix of coastal and inland scenery.

Previous research

The earliest recorded geological research on the Lower Palaeozoic rocks of the district was carried out by Professor Jameson who, as early as 1814, reported on the nature of some of the intrusive igneous rocks of Criffel–Dalbeattie to the Wernerian Natural History Society. In 1843, Thomas Stevenson, a civil engineer who had supervised the building of the lighthouse on Little Ross Island in the mouth of Kirkcudbright Bay, noted that the rocks consisted of a sequence of steeply dipping and cleaved wackes and slates. In the same report, Stevenson also recorded the presence of graptolites in finer-grained wackes. Cunningham (1843) published a description of the general geology of the district but the first systematic geological work in the area was undertaken in the 1850s by Professor Harkness who, in a series of publications (1850; 1853; 1856) described the lithologies, fossils, structures and minor igneous intrusions from the coastal sections. The Geological Survey of Scotland first mapped the district in the 1870s. Based on the 1:10 560 (6 inch to 1 mile) scale maps produced by D K Irvine and J Horne, a 1:63 360 (1 inch to 1 mile) scale map was published in 1879 but the accompanying Sheet Explanation was not available for another 17 years (Horne et al., 1896). The reason for this delay lay in the fact that the mapping in the Southern Uplands had proceeded in parallel with the work of Lapworth who, in 1878, published his paper on 'The Moffat Series'. This seminal work elucidated the zonal distribution of graptolites which was essential to an understanding of the structure of the Southern Uplands. Subsequent research by Lapworth (1889) and the Geological Survey resulted in the monumental memoir of Peach and Horne (1899), in which the tectonostratigraphical framework of the Southern Uplands and contiguous areas was established.

In this century, the region has attracted a wide range of academic workers from a number of earth science disciplines and their detailed studies of various aspects of the geology will be reviewed in detail in the appropriate chapters of the memoir. However, in order to provide at this stage an indication of the scope of the previous research, brief reference will be made to the more significant contributions from the considerable body of work available.

Craig and Walton (1959) used the structural section from Fleet Bay to Meikle Ross to demonstrate that the simplistic anticlinorium/synclinorium model of Lapworth (1889) was inconsistent with the evidence of predominantly northward-younging strata within the turbidite sequence. Subsequent biostratigraphical data (Kemp and White, 1985; White et al., 1992) has confirmed this relationship. The structural model of the region has been further refined by Stringer and Treagus (1980; 1981) and Knipe et al. (1988) while new tectonostratigraphical research has been carried out by Kemp (1986; 1987a), and Barnes et al. (1989).

Among the igneous suites, the granitoid intrusion of Cairnsmore of Fleet has been described by Parslow (1968; 1971) and the Criffel–Dalbeattie Pluton by Phillips (1955; 1956a), following the earlier work of Macgregor (1937; 1938). More recently the geochemistry and petrogenesis of the Criffel–Dalbeattie Pluton has been discussed by Stephens and Halliday (1980) and Stephens et al. (1985), while Henney (1991) paid particular attention to the suite of minor intrusions associated with the pluton. Courrioux (1987) used a study of the foliation trajectories in the pluton to develop a model for oblique intrusion. Bott and Masson Smith (1960) analysed the Bouguer gravity data for Criffel–Dalbeattie and the surrounding area and proposed models for the granite intrusion which required steeply dipping contacts. Kafafy and Tarling (1985) have measured the magnetic fabric in the aureoles and marginal phases of the granites of the Cairnsmore of Fleet and Criffel–Dalbeattie plutons. The isotopic ages of the Cairnsmore of Fleet (392 ± 2 Ma) and Criffel–Dalbeattie (397 ± 2 Ma) plutons have been determined by Halliday et al. (1980) using the Rb–Sr method. The distribution, geochemistry, petrogenesis and isotopic ages of the various dyke suites and volcanic vents of the district have been discussed by Rock et al. (1986b). The Black Stockarton Moor subvolcanic complex has been described by Leake and Cooper (1983) and the mineralisation associated with the intrusive phases of the complex was investigated by the British Geological Survey as part of the Mineral Reconnaissance Programme (Brown et al., 1979). In an earlier phase of mineral exploration by BGS, Miller and Taylor (1966) examined the uranium mineralisation associated with veins cutting the aureole of the Criffel–Dalbeattie Pluton. More recently the mineralogy of these veins has been studied in detail by Basham et al. (1989).

The Upper Palaeozoic sequences of the Kirkcudbright–Dalbeattie district have also received a good deal of attention over the years. In 1869, W Jolly outlined the geology of the Carboniferous rocks at Southerness and provided a list of fossils collected from Arbigland shore. More recently, the lithological, sedimentological and biostratigraphical details of the Southerness–Kirkbean area and the related Carboniferous outliers which occur along the Solway coast have been described by Craig (1956), Craig and Nairn (1956) and Deegan (1970; 1973). Ord et al. (1988) have used a study of the structural, sedimentological and diagenetic relationships of the rocks of the outliers to demonstrate syn-sedimentary faulting on extensional structures at the northern margin of the Solway Basin.

Geological history

Geologically the district is part of the extensive outcrop of Lower Palaeozoic strata which forms the Southern Uplands of Scotland, a terrane bounded to the north by the Southern Upland Fault and to the south by faulted and unconformably overlying Upper Palaeozoic strata (Figure 3). The general stratigraphical framework was established by Peach and Horne (1899) who subdivided the sequence into the three strike-parallel **Northern, Central** and **Southern 'belts'**, which coincided with the boundaries of the Ordovician, Llandovery and Wenlock age turbidite sequences. In the Northern and Central belts, fault-bounded, strike-parallel tracts of wacke, siltstone and shale (turbidite sequence), commonly with distinctive petrography (Walton, 1955; Kelling, 1961; Floyd, 1982), form steeply dipping, northward-younging sequences. These tracts are commonly separated by narrow, discontinuous and deformed outcrops of basic volcanic rocks and chert (Crawford Group) and fossiliferous black mudstone (Moffat Shale Group), which are interpreted to form the loci of strike-parallel faults. These thin Moffat Shale Group successions are usually interpreted as the imbricated repetitions of a pelagic sequence which Peach and Horne (1899) recognised as the local base of the stratigraphical sequence. The Moffat Shale Group is overlain by thick sequences of turbidites (alternating wacke, siltstone and mudstone) which rarely include thin beds of fossiliferous black shale. These graptolite-bearing horizons are important in providing well-constrained biostratigraphical dating of turbidite deposition. On a regional scale, the base of the wacke sequences is diachronous and becomes progressively younger southwards in successive fault-bounded tracts (Figure 4). This structural configuration has now been generally accepted as representing a south-east-verging imbricate thrust stack (McKerrow et al., 1977; Stone et al., 1987).

Over the past 20 years, several plate tectonic models of the Southern Uplands have been proposed. Following the initial model of Dewey (1969), subsequent workers have argued that the Southern Uplands Terrane developed above a north-west-directed subduction zone active during the Ordovician and Silurian. This was situated near the southern margin of a continental landmass (Laurentia) and on the northern side of the Iapetus Ocean. In the 1970s, McKerrow et al. (1977) and Leggett et al. (1979) interpreted the Southern Uplands as an accretionary prism in which the turbidites were deposited in a trench and the pelagic sequences represent contemporary oceanic deposits. In this model, although subduction was continuous, the sediment pile deposited on the descending oceanic crust was scraped off at intervals and stacked against the continental margin in a series of fault-bounded slices. This model elegantly explained the tectonostratigraphical relationships and gained widespread acceptance. However, since the mid-1980s this interpretation has been challenged and in the alternative models (Murphy and Hutton, 1986; Stone et al., 1987; Morris, 1987) the northern portion of the Southern Uplands and its along-strike

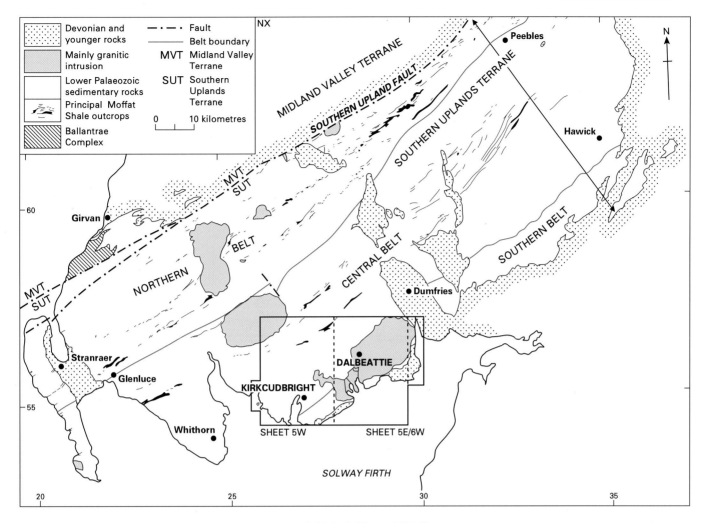

Figure 3   The Kirkcudbright–Dalbeattie district (1:50 000 Sheets 5W, 5E and part of 6W) in its regional context within the Southern Uplands and Midland Valley terranes.

equivalent in Ireland (Longford-Down) have been interpreted as parts of a back-arc basin. Following closure of Iapetus and collision between Laurentia and the southern continental mass of Eastern Avalonia, the back-arc basin was deformed into a south-east-propagating thrust stack which overrode the eroded remnants of the volcanic arc and provided detritus to a prograding foreland (or successor) basin.

The Kirkcudbright–Dalbeattie district falls within the southern part of the Central Belt and the Southern Belt of Peach and Horne (1899). An outline geological map of the district is shown in Figure 1. In the accretionary prism model, the Lower Palaeozoic rocks of the district were deposited during the waning of subduction while in the alternative model of Stone et al. (1987) the district records the change from back-arc to foreland basin.

The oldest rocks proved in the district are from the narrow, discontinuous Moffat Shale Group (and minor Crawford Group) inliers of the Laurieston [681 648] — Crossmichael [731 668] line. These include graptolite-bearing black shales as well as minor volcaniclastic units,

cherts and metabentonites. The oldest recorded graptolite fauna is from Tottlehams Glen [7769 6985] and indicates a Caradoc (*gracilis* Biozone) age. Throughout the district, the Moffat Shale Group is succeeded by thick sequences of interbedded wacke, siltstone and mudstone (turbidites) ranging in age from Llandovery (*cyphus* Biozone) to mid-Wenlock (*lundgreni* Biozone). Based on a variation in the lithological, petrographical and structural characteristics, the turbidite sequences have been divided into three main tectonostratigraphical units (Figure 4): the Gala, Hawick and Riccarton groups; these have been further sub-divided into both formal formations and informal sub-units.

The turbidite sequences which make up the Gala Group are compositionally uniform and consist of medium- to thickly bedded predominantly quartzose wacke, locally with thin silty mudstone interbedded with and passing laterally into very thickly bedded coarse-grained (gritty) wacke. Three informal formations (**Gala 4, 5 and 7**) of the Gala Group have been mapped in the district being equivalent to the Sinniness,

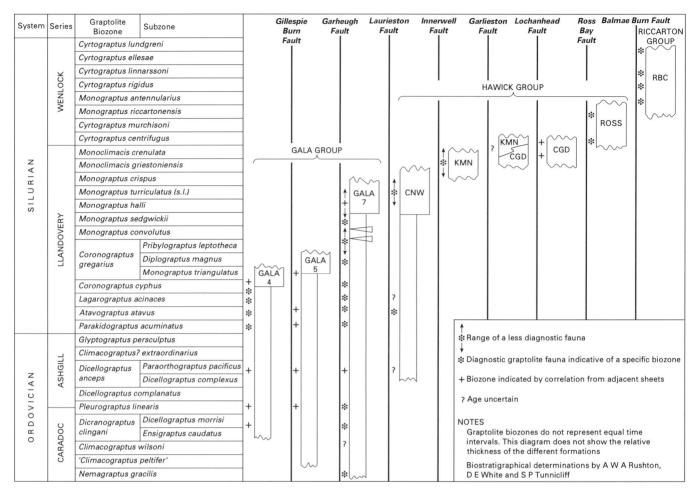

Figure 4 Biostratigraphical correlation diagram for the tectonostratigraphical units in the district. For key to stratigraphical units see Figure 1.

Garheugh and Mull of Logan formations, respectively, in Wigtownshire. Variably deformed Moffat Shale Group successions occur locally at the diachronous base of the turbidites in the Gala Group and each of the formations occur within a discrete fault-bounded tract (Figure 4). Since the formations are fault-bounded, of uniform composition and are primarily distinguished on biostratigraphical and structural grounds, they have not been allocated formal lithostratigraphical names within the district. Gala 4 rests on Moffat Shale Group with a *cyphus* Biozone fauna and also contains interbeds of the same age; the younger Gala 5 in the next tract to the south overlies Moffat Shale Group of *triangulatus* Biozone age, whereas Gala 7 rests on black shales with a *sedgwickii* Biozone fauna and has interbeds with a *turriculatus* Biozone fauna (Figure 4).

To the south of the Gala Group, the turbidite sequences of the southern part of the Central Belt (and part of the former Southern Belt) form the Hawick Group, previously termed the 'Hawick Rocks' (Lapworth and Wilson, 1871) and recently redefined with four formations by White et al. (1992). The Cairnharrow Formation (CNW) is transitional between the Gala and

Hawick groups and consists of medium- to thinly bedded quartzose and calcareous wacke with packets of interbedded mudstone up to 40 m thick. A sparse graptolite fauna from thin black shale interbeds within the Cairnharrow Formation suggests a *turriculatus* to *crispus* Biozone age. The Kirkmaiden Formation (KMN) is characterised by medium- to thickly bedded calcareous wacke with thinly bedded silty mudstone. White et al. recorded a *griestoniensis-crenulata* Biozone age from graptolites found in an interbedded mudstone unit. The Carghidown Formation (CGD) is similar to the Kirkmaiden Formation but, in addition to the medium- to thickly bedded wacke and thinly bedded silty mudstones, it also includes red mudstone beds and disrupted (?slumped) zones. No graptolites have so far been recorded from the Carghidown Formation of the district, though similar rocks along strike to the northeast have yielded a *crenulata* Biozone fauna (White et al., 1992). The Ross Formation, originally part of the Southern Belt, is of Wenlock age and comprises medium- to thickly bedded calcareous wacke with thinly bedded silty mudstone, thin but distinctive horizons of fossiliferous laminated carbonaceous siltstone (hemipelagite) and disrupted zones, the latter thought to have originated as soft-sediment slumping. Abundant graptolites constrain the age of the formation to between the *centrifugus* and mid-*riccartonensis* biozones of the early Wenlock.

The Riccarton Group is represented by the Raeberry Castle Formation which consists of thin- to medium-bedded wacke and siltstone with rare coarse channelised sandstone and hemipelagite beds up to 25 m thick. An abundant graptolite fauna from the hemipelagites indicates a mid-*riccartonensis* to *lundgreni* Biozone age. In contrast to the Gala and Hawick groups, in which the relatively uniform sequences were deposited from medium- to high-density turbidity currents as sheet flows, lobes and meandering channel systems, the Raeberry Castle Formation comprises a much more diverse facies association. Turbidite sequences record the development of meandering channel/overbank complexes and coeval channel-mouth, depositional lobe and fan-fringe facies.

The coastal exposures of the Lower Palaeozoic turbidites of the Kirkcudbright–Dalbeattie district reveal some of the most spectacularly folded sequences in the Southern Uplands. Although some boudinage and shearing effects seen in the Carghidown Formation are interpreted as synsedimentary, in general three main phases of tectonic folding can be identified. The first is diachronous and is associated with the development of the imbricate thrust-stack which produced upright, north-east-trending folds. The fold hinges have variable plunge, ranging from shallow to steep, some hinges being markedly curvilinear. The overall vergence is predominantly towards the south-east. The cleavage is also variable and may be either axial planar or clockwise transecting, spaced to penetrative. The second phase folds are also north-east-trending but are distinctly domainal, primarily occurring adjacent to the early thrusts. Geometrically, their axial planes are horizontal to shallow dipping with an axial planar crenulation cleavage. No regional-scale second phase folds have been recognised. The third phase comprises steeply plunging sinistral folds formed in narrow zones of shearing adjacent to the tract-bounding faults. The three phases may overlap in space and time. Sporadically developed conjugate north-north-west- and north-north-east-trending kink bands represent a weak late phase of folding in the lower Palaeozoic sequences. The pronounced north-east-trending Caledonoid grain of the district is disrupted by a conjugate system of cross-cutting north-north-west- and north-north-east-trending dextral and sinistral wrench faults. However, despite the complex deformation history, outwith the thermal aureole of the igneous intrusions the metamorphic grade of the sedimentary sequences is uniformly low, varying from the diagenetic to high anchizone facies.

Suites of syn- and post-tectonic igneous rocks were intruded into the turbidite sequences over an extended period (c.430 to 390 Ma) from the late Silurian (Wenlock) to the early Devonian. The earliest phase includes rare foliated syn-tectonic lamprophyre dykes which were emplaced late in the local expression of the diachronous D_1 deformation and were coeval with turbidite sedimentation in the younger tracts to the south. These early dykes were followed by the main post-tectonic suite of volcanic vents and dykes including the important Black Stockarton Moor subvolcanic complex of lamprophyres, felsites and porphyritic microdiorites. Following the initial phases of dyke emplacement, the plutonic phase began with the intrusion of the Bengairn Complex which was intruded in turn by the composite Criffel–Dalbeattie Pluton. The Gala and Hawick groups and the Black Stockarton Moor, Bengairn and Criffel–Dalbeattie intrusions are all cut by a regional swarm of microdiorite dykes. A small but significant number of minor volcanic vents are also preserved, apparently coeval with the dyke swarms. The youngest major intrusion in the region is the relatively unzoned Cairnsmore of Fleet Pluton, dated about 392 Ma, only the south-east segment of which lies within the district. The most recent igneous activity in the region is represented by a number of west-north-west-trending dolerite dykes of presumed Tertiary age and thought to be members of the Mull or Arran swarms.

Upper Palaeozoic sedimentary sequences within the district comprise rocks of Upper Devonian and Lower Carboniferous (Dinantian) age, which occur in a series of fault-bounded outliers along the Kirkcudbrightshire coast. Rocks of Upper Old Red Sandstone facies lie unconformably on the Lower Palaeozoic turbidites as a thin sequence of alluvial red mudstones and sandstones with cornstone nodules. This is conformably overlain by a sequence of olivine-basalt lavas (Birrenswark Volcanic Formation) assigned to the early Carboniferous Border Group. The remaining Upper Palaeozoic rocks consist of a discontinuous sequence of coarse-grained sandstones, siltstones, mudstones and limestones of alluvial, fluvial and shallow-marine origin also assigned to the Border Group. These lithologies preserve a record of early Carboniferous sedimentation controlled by syn-depositional movement on the North Solway Fault which forms the northern margin of the Solway Basin. The fault was probably generated by reactivation of an existing north-east-trending Caledonoid structure. A small part of the Permian Dumfries Basin occurs in the north-east corner of the district. This is a north-west-oriented half-graben, with the main fault on the north-east margin, filled with a thick red-bed succession of terrestrial sandstones and breccias.

Quaternary deposits are widespread and of varied facies suggesting that most of the district was covered by ice during one or more of the Pleistocene glaciations from about 1.6 Ma, and certainly during the last major glacial event, the Dimlington Stadial (26 000–13 000 years BP). Deposits of locally derived till or boulder clay deposited during this period are mostly concentrated in the broad valleys and lower-lying areas near the coast. During the temperate conditions of the following Windermere Interstadial (13 000–11 000 years BP), the glacial meltwaters laid down moundy deposits of sand and gravel along the coast and within the main valleys. Sequences of peat and fluvial sediments were deposited on the lower-lying ground and raised beaches developed along the Solway coast during periods of higher sea level. The brief return to an arctic climate during the Loch Lomond Stadial (11 000–10 000 years BP), though not resulting in a renewed ice sheet cover, did give rise to periglacial conditions as evidenced by frost wedges in the fluvioglacial sediments and solifluction deposits on the hillslopes. When climatic conditions finally ameriorated, the sea level was initially lower than at present but rose rapidly during the post-glacial marine transgression before falling intermittently to the present level. During this period of higher sea level, the marine and estuarine sediments of the so-called 'carse deposits' were laid down in embayments along the Solway and are now located well inland of the present-day coastline.

TWO

Applied geology

In this chapter the geological factors relevant to land-use planning and development within the district are reviewed and key issues identified. Some, such as groundwater and hard-rock quarrying, have a close geological link and could have considerable economic impact. With other issues, however, the geological connection is less direct and potential difficulties can, in such a rural environment, usually be accommodated by a combination of careful site investigation and minor re-siting of developments.

KEY ISSUES

- *planning and conservation:* recent and current development, SSSIs

- *agriculture and forestry:* type and extent of land use, soil conditions

- *ground stability and foundation conditions:* potential foundation stability problems

- *water resources and pollution potential:* groundwater potential of various solid rocks units and from superficial deposits, mineral content of groundwaters

- *flooding and land drainage:* natural flooding of the Nith and other main rivers, run-off from forested areas

- *mineral resources, quarrying and mining:* existing hard rock quarrying resources, granite, wacke, sand and gravel, copper mineralisation

Planning and conservation

With a relatively small and stable population in the district, there is generally little development pressure for new building, with only minor housing, farm and light industrial units to be considered. The major construction work in the district in recent years has been associated with the various road re-alignment, bridge rebuilding and by-pass schemes forming part of the long-term plan to upgrade the A75 'Euroroute' from Dumfries to Stranraer. This work has greatly improved the quality of life in those towns, such as Castle Douglas, which previously straddled the trunk road. The trackbed of the former railway line between Dumfries and Glenluce traverses the north-western part of the district and includes an attractive legacy of stone bridges and other engineering works. The newly constructed natural gas pipelines from Scotland to Ireland cross the district from north-east to south-west. The pipeline to Dublin enters the sea at Brighouse Bay, 5 km south-west of Kirkcudbright, while the branch to Belfast heads off westwards towards the Rhins of Galloway and the North Channel.

A few geological Sites of Special Scientific Interest (SSSIs) lie within the district, mostly on the coast south of Kirkcudbright. A list is given in Stone, 1996, appendix 2.

Agriculture and forestry

Between them, these two activities account for by far the largest proportion of land use in the district. Agriculture is quite extensive in the lower lying western parts of the district, near the coast and along the broad river valleys, where the soils are underlain by boulder clay or alluvium resting on Lower Palaeozoic wackes. In these areas, the land is generally of good quality and is mostly used for dairy and beef cattle production, with a certain proportion devoted to arable use. In the more elevated areas, mostly underlain by the large granitic plutons of Cairnsmore of Fleet and Criffel, the soils are generally thin, acidic and poor in nutrients, forming moorland which mainly supports sheep farming and an expanding forestry sector.

Ground stability and foundation conditions

Bedrock or boulder clay usually form good-bearing ground in the Southern Uplands region. The main stability problems are likely to occur on steep slopes or within the alluvium- or peat-covered areas, where soft or otherwise unpredictable ground conditions may prevail. Site investigation by trenching will usually be sufficient to establish the actual conditions at any particular location. With only very minor upland vein mining, no underground mining for bedded deposits, nor known evaporite deposits in the district, there are unlikely to be any subsidence problems from the collapse of underground cavities, A possible exception could be rare subsurface structures of a more archaeological nature dug in the superficial deposits (old cellars, brandy holes etc.).

Water resources and pollution potential

Water is one of the main natural resources of the region and is utilised for electricity generation in the Galloway Water Power Scheme, the lowermost station of which is located within the district at Tongland, near Kirkcudbright.

Groundwater resources

Traditionally, groundwater in the district has not been exploited on a large scale except where shallow wells and springs provide domestic supplies. There are many old records of wells less than 10 m deep in the Castle Douglas, Dalbeattie and Kirkcudbright areas, the original public supply for the latter coming from springs on Angel Hill [690 511] to the east of the town. The lack of large-scale development is partly due to the ready avail-ability of surface water from upland streams, but also to the lack of underground sources of suitable scale. Owing to their lack of primary porosity and permeability, the Lower Palaeozoic rocks of the district do not, in general, have the capacity to store and transmit large quantities of groundwater. Users requiring large volumes of water have, therefore, turned to surface sources for their supplies and, as a consequence, very few boreholes have been drilled into the Silurian strata. However, experience from other parts of southern Scotland indicates that the Silurian rocks do have the potential for providing reliable supplies of good quality groundwater to farms and houses through the use of boreholes up to 30 m in depth. All groundwater within such rocks moves via joints and fissures and the chances of drilling a successful borehole depend entirely on encountering these discon-tinuities below the water table. Suitable sites for drilling tend to be within valleys, commonly eroded along fault-lines, where the water table is high and groundwater is naturally discharging into surface watercourses. The hydraulic properties of the Criffel Pluton are unknown since there are no records of any boreholes having been drilled within the granite. However, it is likely to form a poor aquifer, suitable only for small domestic supplies.

Superficial deposits probably have greater groundwa-ter resource potential than bedrock sources. Dumfries and Galloway Regional Council have carried out exploratory drilling at several localities in the district with a view to using shallow groundwater for public supply. Groundwater from superficial deposits has many advan-tages for small rural supplies. It can be a reliable source of good-quality water and is commonly located close to the community, so minimising pipeline lengths and other capital costs such as reservoir construction.

The Regional Council has acted on the results of their exploratory programme and constructed a well field for public supply near the village of Ringford [682 579]. Here, alluvial deposits on the floodplain of the Tarff Water are flanked by fluvioglacial sand and gravel. The aquifer comprises 6 m of medium- to coarse-grained gravel beneath 4 m of silt and peat. Two boreholes presently supply over 1000 m^3/day of very high quality water, requiring only precautionary chlorination, to the village and surrounding area. The well field has the capacity to produce double the current abstraction, and its use during recent dry summer periods has helped to avoid cuts in supply over a wide area.

There are several localities in the district where valley deposits might be developed for both domestic supplies and industrial/agricultural/fish farm use. The broad spread of alluvial and glacial deposits to the north-west of Castle Douglas, as well as those farther downstream in the Dee valley, contain useful thicknesses of water-bearing gravel that warrant further investigation. Additionally, the floodplains of the Urr Water to Dalbeattie and the Water of Fleet north of Gatehouse of Fleet appear to be good groundwater prospects. At Dildawn [724 588], a trial borehole located on the floodplain of the River Dee encountered only 2.7 m of coarse gravel beneath 2 m of alluvial clay. However, this limited deposit demonstrated

the potential of thin alluvial aquifers by yielding 1300 m^3/day of good quality groundwater which was replenished by rainfall on surrounding land and by induced leakage from the River Dee. Closer to the sea, the valley deposits near Kirkcudbright have been shown to contain brackish groundwater and, in general, raised beach deposits within 2 km of the coast do not form exploitable aquifers owing to problems with water quality.

The use of agricultural fertilisers on farmland within many of the valleys has resulted in the presence of elevated concentrations of nitrate in the groundwater. In future, careful selection of drilling sites, along with the establishment of source protection zones around well-fields will be necessary in order to prevent derogation of water quality. From their location, commonly underlying built-up areas and arable farmland, valley gravels can be susceptible to pollution from surface sources. At Mollance [721 593], a trial borehole encountered groundwater that was mineralised to a greater degree than other waters in the area. This has been tentatively attributed to the presence of a nearby landfill site holding shellfish waste. High manganese concentrations from naturally occurring sources have been measured in shallow groundwaters in surrounding districts and their apparent absence from the present district may be ascribed to the current lack of comprehensive data on the chemical quality of groundwaters.

Groundwaters are, on the whole, weakly mineralised across the district within Silurian rocks and superficial deposits. They are, nevertheless, capable of resisting acidification from rainfall containing acidic pollution. Weakly buffered groundwaters in granitic rocks and some isolated superficial deposits may be prone to acidification.

As with groundwaters, the chemistry of surface waters also shows a close relationship with the local bedrock/ superficial geology. This is well demonstrated in Plate 1 which illustrates the acidity (pH) of stream water in the district recorded as part of the BGS Regional Geochem-istry Programme (BGS, 1993a). The pH has a negative correlation with the available Ca, Mg and total carbonate content of bedrock and shows strongly acidic drainage (pH 5–6) over the granite areas which are poor in these factors, broadly neutral conditions (pH ~ 7) over the Gala Group rocks and mildly alkaline surface waters (pH ~ 8) over the carbonate-rich Hawick and Riccarton groups.

Flooding and land drainage

Local flooding may occur from time to time during periods of spate in low-lying areas adjacent to the main lochs and rivers. There is a long history of flooding associ-ated with the River Nith, in the eastern part of the district, though the worst effects are generally seen further upstream in the immediate vicinity of Dumfries. Loch Ken, the largest body of fresh water within the district, has gently sloping banks in several places and is prone to flooding. However, the loch is part of a hydro-electric scheme which can regulate the flow of water to some extent. Most of the arable land is drained by field drains into local watercourses. The recent huge expansion in

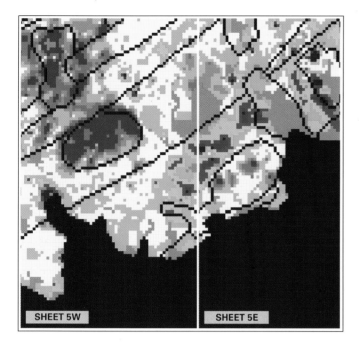

Plate 1 Acidity (pH) of surface waters in the district and environs.

Note the acidic conditions (red-brown–pH 5-6) over the granite areas, broadly neutral (yellow green – pH ~7) over the Gala Group, and mildly alkaline (blue – pH ~8) over the Hawick and Riccarton groups. (BGS, 1993a).

commercial forestry must have increased the run-off rate of rainwater and, therefore, the risk of flooding due to the extensive networks of drains and ditches dug before planting. In the past, the peaty soils in these upland areas formed a natural reservoir which stored rainwater and released it slowly, thus reducing the peak run-off during periods of high rainfall.

Mineral resources, quarrying and mining

Potentially there are very extensive hard rock resources within the district, with two major granite plutons and vast areas underlain by Silurian wackes. Two substantial hard rock aggregate quarries presently operate within the district. Craignair Quarry [81 61], near Dalbeattie, is owned by Tarmac Quarry Products and works the north-western margin of the Criffel–Dalbeattie Pluton. At Tongland, near Kirkcudbright, a quarry [69 54] operated by W & J Barr and Sons works sheet-like bodies of porphyritic microdiorite intruded into hornfelsed wackes of the Carghidown Formation.

Deposits of sand and gravel are mostly confined to the valleys of the Water of Fleet, River Dee and the Water of Urr. None have been worked on any scale. Various temporary and small-scale quarries, mostly in till or weathered bedrock, are operated from time to time by the Forestry Commission and other private forestry companies to obtain bulk material for unsurfaced roads.

Widespread disseminated copper mineralisation has been proved in the Black Stockarton Moor area (Leake and Cooper, 1983) but has yet to be fully assessed in economic terms. There is also a history of small mines or trials for copper (Wilson, 1921), hematite (Macgregor et al., 1920) and baryte (Dines, 1922) from vein-type deposits. Some unusual vein-type uranium mineralisation has also been reported in the district, associated with faulting along the southern margin of the Criffel–Dalbeattie Pluton. There are no metalliferous mining operations currently active within the district.

THREE

Concealed geology

Insights into the concealed geology of the district are provided by the results of regional gravity and aeromagnetic surveys, which can be interpreted in terms of variations in rock density and magnetisation respectively. In addition, some local information on the electrical properties of subsurface rocks is available from the results of electrical and electromagnetic surveys conducted for mineral reconnaissance.

This chapter concentrates primarily on the results of the regional surveys. After considering rock physical properties, as measured directly from samples and inferred from compositional data, variations in gravity and magnetic fields are first considered in qualitative terms and then modelled quantitatively over the Criffel–Dalbeattie Pluton.

The main gravity and magnetic anomalies in the Kirkcudbright–Dalbeattie district are associated with the major late Caledonian plutons: Criffel–Dalbeattie, Bengairn and Cairnsmore of Fleet. The low-density, more acid components of these plutons are responsible for relatively low Bouguer gravity anomalies, while conspicuous aeromagnetic anomalies occur over the more basic components. Gravity lows also occur over the low-density Upper Palaeozoic and younger sedimentary rocks within the Solway, Dumfries and Wigtown Bay basins. Elsewhere the gravity evidence suggests the possibility of variations in the thickness of the Lower Palaeozoic sedimentary rocks above relatively dense basement and/or lateral density variations within such basement. A long wavelength magnetic anomaly is due to a deep magnetic source largely underlying the major upper crustal intrusions, while high frequency magnetic lineaments are interpreted in terms of at least two phases of Tertiary dyke intrusion.

ROCK PHYSICAL PROPERTIES

Densities

Density determinations by a number of researchers indicate that the Lower Palaeozoic rocks of the Southern Uplands have an average saturated bulk density of approximately $2.72 \, Mg/m^3$ (published data reviewed by Kimbell, 1991). There is likely to be some variation between formations, with those with a greater ferromagnesian mineral content having a higher density than those rich in quartz, but currently available data are insufficient to allow reliable quantification of these contrasts.

Younger sedimentary rocks occur in the south and east of the district. There is only very limited direct information on the densities of the Lower Carboniferous rocks which crop out along the north Solway coast. Six samples

from the Kirkbean–Southerness area had a mean saturated bulk density of $2.72 \, Mg/m^3$ (i.e. similar to the underlying Lower Palaeozoic sequence), although this included an anomalously dense ($2.83 \, Mg/m^3$) sample from the Powillimount Formation (Entwisle, 1993). Equivalent strata elsewhere in the Northumberland–Solway Basin typically have densities within the range $2.5 \, Mg/m^3$ and $2.7 \, Mg/m^3$, depending on lithology (Bott and Masson Smith, 1957; Lee, 1982; Kimbell et al., 1989). Higher densities may occur in parts of the Border Group sequence that contain a significant proportion of anhydrite (density $2.90 \, Mg/m^3$), as proven by the Easton-1 Borehole [NY 44120 71705] (Chadwick et al., 1993; Chadwick et al., 1995; Ward, 1995). The density of samples of Permian sandstones from Locharbriggs Quarry in the Dumfries Basin increased from $2.25 \, Mg/m^3$ at surface to $2.33 \, Mg/m^3$ at a depth of approximately 60 m (Bott and Masson Smith, 1960). The density may increase further at greater depth due to the effects of compaction and cementation; for example, a weighted average density for Permian sandstones of $2.46 \, Mg/m^3$ was estimated by Lee (1989, fig. 4.10) from density logs in the Silloth Borehole on the south side of the Solway Firth [NY 1230 5484].

Mineralogical and geochemical variations (Stephens and Halliday, 1980; Phillips et al., 1981; Stephens et al., 1985) together with sample measurements and gravity modelling (Bott and Masson Smith, 1960) indicate that there are density variations within the Criffel–Dalbeattie Pluton. Broadly, this pluton becomes more basic and more dense towards its margins, although the pattern is somewhat asymmetrical, with the most acid 'core' being offset towards the north of its geometrical centre. The density determinations of Bott and Masson Smith (1960) are reproduced in Table 1; these can be correlated with the inferred granite composition (particularly SiO_2 content) at the sample locations (Stephens and Halliday, 1980; Stephens et al., 1985) and interpolation and extrapolation used to predict densities at other locations within the granite. This has been attempted in Table 2, in which predicted average densities have been assigned to the various zones defined by Stephens et al. (1985) for the Criffel–Dalbeattie Pluton, and Phillips (1956a) for the Bengairn Complex. The values are more tentative where the correlation is extended to the Bengairn Complex because the compositional information is limited to a few analyses by Macgregor (1937) and the qualitative descriptions of relative composition by Phillips (1956a). There is, however, a good agreement between the density predicted for the intermediate granodiorite of the Bengairn Complex ($2.67 \, Mg/m^3$) and measurements on samples from granodiorite sheets in the Black

Table 1 Published density data for intrusive rocks in the Kirkcudbright–Dalbeattie district.

Rock type	Location	Number of specimens	Saturated bulk density (Mg/m^3)	Source
'Porphyritic granodiorite' (Criffel)	Clawbelly Hill	14	2.633 ± 0.011	Bott and Masson Smith (1960)
	Glensome	13	2.654 ± 0.011	
	Craignair	12	2.662 ± 0.004	
'Main granodiorite' (Criffel)	Kippford	19	2.707 ± 0.012	Bott and Masson Smith (1960)
	NW end of Loch Kinair	15	2.697 ± 0.008	
Granodiorite	Black Stockarton	41	2.67 ± 0.01	Brown et al. (1979)

Stockarton Moor complex to the north-west (Table 1; Brown et al., 1979).

Magnetic properties

The observed magnetic field variations and magnetic susceptibility measurements on similar rocks in other districts indicate that the Lower Palaeozoic and younger sedimentary rocks in the district have low magnetic susceptibilities (generally less than 10^{-3} SI units). All the conspicuous local magnetic anomalies observed in the district are due to igneous rocks.

Published modal analyses of samples from the Criffel–Dalbeattie Pluton list magnetite contents varying between < 0.1% in the central granite and 0.5–0.7% in the outer granodiorite (Stephens and Halliday, 1980; Phillips et al., 1981). The empirical relationship of Balsley and Buddington (1958) suggests that such concentrations will correspond to magnetic susceptibilities of $< 0.6 \times 10^{-3}$ SI units and $5–8 \times 10^{-3}$ SI units respectively. The magnetic anomaly pattern indicates that magnetic rocks also occur within the Bengairn Complex and in the Black Stockarton Moor complex; susceptibility measurements on granodiorite samples from the latter area suggest a bulk average of between 6×10^{-3} and 18×10^{-3} SI units (Brown et al., 1979).

Magnetic anomalies are observed over Tertiary dykes in the region. Such bodies commonly have a remanent magnetisation component which is significantly stronger than that induced by the Earth's present field. The polarity of the remanent magnetisation, and thus of the magnetic anomaly associated with the dyke, depends on whether its was intruded during a period of normal or reversed field polarity. Reversed polarities tend to predominate in the British Tertiary Igneous Province (Musset et al., 1988).

GRAVITY DATA

Figure 5 shows contoured Bouguer gravity anomaly data for the Kirkcudbright–Dalbeattie district and surrounding area, together with the locations of the gravity stations on which the map is based. The gravity stations were established by a number of surveys spanning a period of more than twenty years (early 1960s to late 1980s); approximately two-thirds of the total were surveyed by BGS and the remainder by the universities of Durham and Newcastle. Detailed gravity surveys of the Black Stockarton Moor complex [720 550] were conducted as part of a mineral reconnaissance programme carried out by BGS on behalf of the DTI (Brown et al., 1979). The offshore data comprise sea-bottom stations in the west established by Bott (1964) and BGS surveys of 1974, which covered the intertidal zone in the east using hovercraft transport. Bouguer gravity anomalies have been calculated using a reduction density of 2.72 Mg/m^3 (the estimated mean density of the Lower Palaeozoic country rocks). Figure 6 is a contour map of the Bouguer anomaly data after the application of a filter designed to suppress

Table 2 Predicted mean saturated bulk densities for subdivisions of the Criffel–Dalbeattie Pluton and the Bengairn Complex as defined by Stephens et al. (1985) and Phillips (1956a) respectively.

Igneous body	Subdivision	Predicted density (Mg/m^3)
Criffel–Dalbeattie	Clinopyroxene hornblende biotite granodiorite (CHB)	2.71
	Hornblende biotite granodiorite (HB)	2.67
	Biotite granite (B)	2.65
	Muscovite biotite granite (MB)	2.63
	Biotite muscovite granite (BM)	2.62
Bengairn Complex	Quartz diorite (QD)	2.72
	Intermediate granodiorite (IG)	2.67
	Fine-grained granodiorite (FG)	2.65

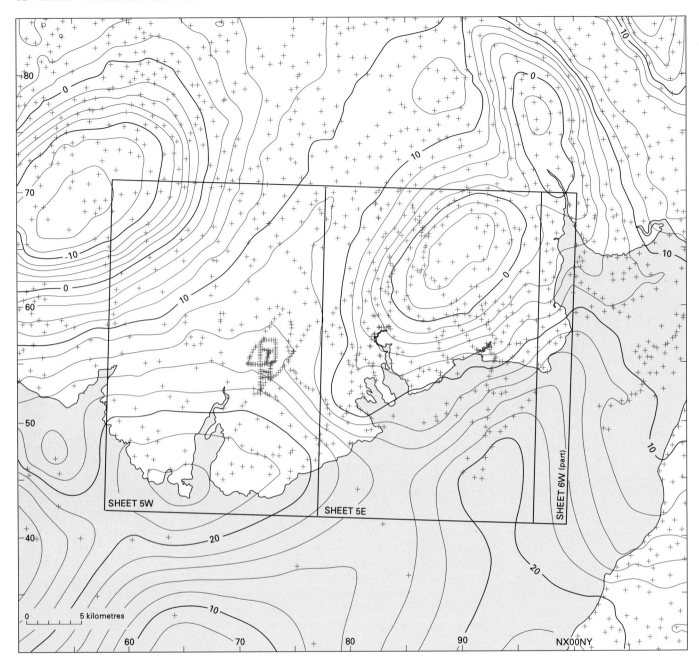

Figure 5 Bouguer gravity anomaly map of the region around Kirkcudbright and Dalbeattie. Crosses indicate gravity stations. Anomalies calculated against the Geodetic Reference System 1967 and referred to the National Gravity Reference Net 1973. Reduction density = 2.72 Mg/m^3. Contour interval = 2 mGal (1 mGal = 10 m/s^2). The locations of the boundaries of sheets 5W (Kirkcudbright), 5E (Dalbeattie) and part of 6W (Kirkbean) are shown.

wavelengths greater than 20 km; this transform accentuates components of the Bouguer anomaly field which are due to near-surface density contrasts.

Major Bouguer gravity anomaly lows occur over the low-density intrusive rocks of the Criffel–Dalbeattie [900 650] and Cairnsmore of Fleet [255 890] plutons. The latter is considered in detail in the account of the adjacent Kirkcowan–Wigtown district (Sheets 4W and 4E) by Barnes (In preparation). Both bodies are of late Caledonian age and have similar forms and inferred intrusive volumes. The amplitude of the gravity anomaly associated with the

Criffel–Dalbeattie Pluton is, however, approximately 10 mGal less than that over Cairnsmore of Fleet, because it is on average more basic in composition and thus more dense {compare the average density of the Cairnsmore of Fleet, Pluton of 2.62 Mg/m^3 (Parslow and Randall, 1973) with Table 2}.

The filtered Bouguer anomaly map (Figure 6) accentuates the elongation of the Cairnsmore of Fleet and Criffel–Dalbeattie plutons parallel to the north-east regional strike direction of the host turbidites. Images of this gravity field and its transforms reveal a linear north-east-trending

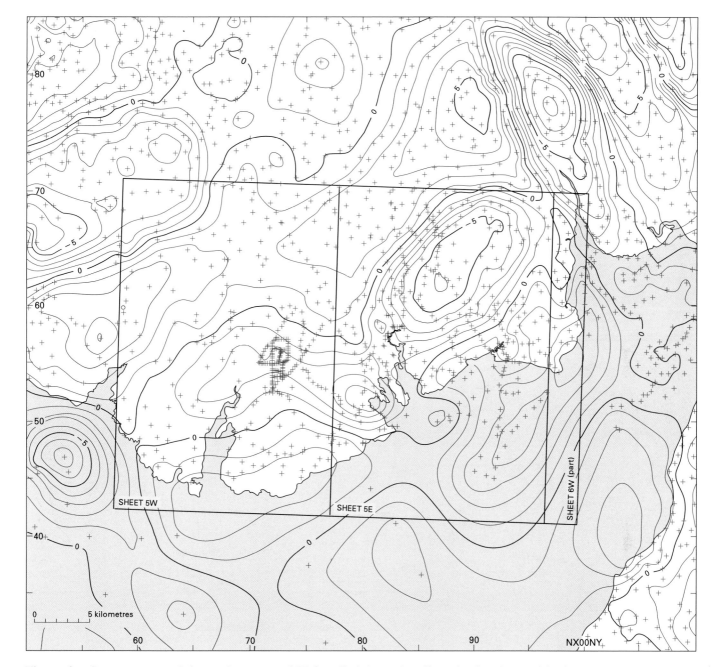

Figure 6 Contour map of the region around Kirkcudbright and Dalbeattie showing residual Bouguer gravity anomalies after application of filter to suppress wavelengths greater than 20 km. Coloured lines indicate geological boundaries (Figure 1). Contour interval = 1 mGal.

maximum along the northern margin of the Criffel–Dalbeattie Pluton (feature G1 in Figure 7), which may signify structural control over its intrusive form. To the southwest there is a secondary Bouguer anomaly minimum over the Bengairn Complex [800 520]. The filtered map (Figure 6) indicates a residual low extending north-westwards from the Bengairn Complex, which probably relates to the combined gravity effect of the granodiorite sheets and 'porphyrite' dykes associated with the Black Stockarton Moor subvolcanic complex (Brown et al., 1979; Leake and Cooper, 1983).

Bouguer anomaly lows also occur over the Permo-Triassic basins of the Southern Uplands, but these only affect the extremities of the Kirkcudbright-Dalbeattie district. The western margin of the Dumfries Basin lies at the north-eastern corner of the district, while the postulated Wigtown Bay Basin (Parslow and Randall, 1973; Barnes, In prep.) may extend into its south-western extremity. Assuming a density contrast of -0.4 Mg/m^3 with the underlying basement, Bott and Masson Smith (1960) calculated that the Dumfries Basin would contain approximately 1.1 km of Permo-Triassic rocks; they

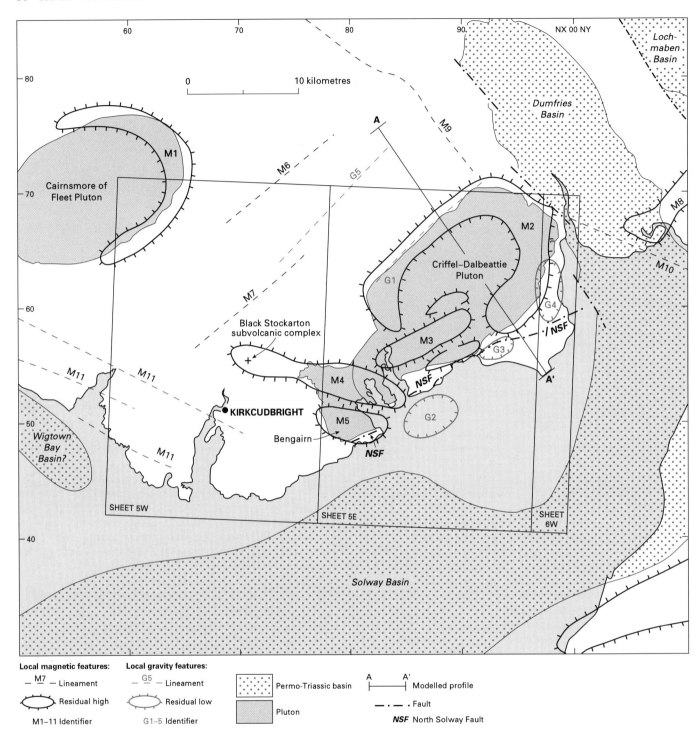

Figure 7 Summary map showing local geophysical features of the region around Kirkcudbright and Dalbeattie, as discussed in the text. Conspicuous Bouguer gravity anomaly lows occur over the major late Caledonian intrusions and Permo-Triassic basins.

inferred that its western margin was somewhat steeper than that to the east and suggested that this indicated a degree of fault control, although it is not as markedly asymmetrical as the Stranraer Basin farther west (Mansfield and Kennet, 1963; Bott, 1964; Stone, 1995). Residual and gradient plots of the gravity data reveal

lineaments along the south-western side of the Dumfries Basin (Figure 7) which also suggest fault control along this margin. An apparent offset between linear segments occurs at the projection of the linear northern margin of the Criffel–Dalbeattie Pluton, and the basin thickness appears to increase to the north of this line. It is possible, therefore, that a north-east-trending structure which influenced the form of the late Caledonian intrusion was later reactivated (as a transfer fault?) during the subsidence of the Dumfries Basin. To the south of the district, a thick Permo-Triassic sequence is developed within the Solway Basin (Chadwick et al., 1993; Beamish and Smythe, 1986). Gravity data are sparse in this area and the northern margin of the Permo-Triassic component of the Solway Basin drawn in Figure 7 is highly conjectural; relatively high Bouguer anomaly values do, however, suggest that Permo-Triassic cover is thin or absent over an area extending into the Solway Firth to the south of the Criffel–Dalbeattie Pluton.

Carboniferous rocks crop out along the north Solway coast and extend beneath Permo-Triassic cover in the Solway Basin. On the basis of seismic reflection data, Chadwick et al. (1993) estimated that the total thickness of the Carboniferous sequence exceeded 7 km in the deepest part of the Solway Basin, which lies just to the east of the district. Major variations in the thickness of the Carboniferous strata are associated with syn-depositional faulting in Lower Border Group times, with rocks of this group thickening to more than 4 km adjacent to the Maryport–Stublick–Ninety Fathom fault system (Chadwick et al., 1993). The considerable thickness of Carboniferous rocks within the Solway Basin have a small gravity effect compared with the clear signature of the overlying Permo-Triassic sequence. The probable explanation for this is the substantial proportion of anhydrite inferred to be present within the Lower Border Group in the deepest part of the basin, which will result in average densities which are similar to, or even higher than, that of the underlying Lower Palaeozoic rocks.

The limited data currently available does not provide evidence of a significant density contrast between the Lower Carboniferous sequence exposed in the Kirkcudbright–Dalbeattie district and the underlying rocks. Displays of the gravity data, nonetheless, indicate local features which can be correlated with the hanging-walls of faults which offset the Carboniferous rocks. Residual Bouguer anomaly lows G2 and G3 lie adjacent to the North Solway Fault, while G4 apparently relates to a north-trending structure which forms the western margin of the Carboniferous rocks to the east of the Criffel–Dalbeattie Pluton. These gravity features could arise because low-density parts of the Carboniferous sequence are offset at the mapped faults, although there is a strong possibility that thickening of the Quaternary sequence (perhaps indirectly related to the bedrock structures) contributes to the observed signatures (Smith et al., 1996). An alternative explanation for G2 is a south-eastward extension of low-density intrusive rocks associated with the Bengairn Complex; this is considered less likely, however, because of the lack of magnetic evidence for such an extension (see Figure 8 and following section).

Bouguer anomaly values reach a maximum in the Ross area [650 440], and this lies on an axis of higher values which extends both to the west-south-west, across the Wigtown Peninsula, and to the east-north-east. The latter extension is not easily discerned because of the presence of the Criffel–Dalbeattie Pluton but is evident in the rise (of about 8 mGal) in 'background' values from north to south across this pluton (Figure 5). The southward decrease of Bouguer anomalies away from the high axis can be explained by the effects of the Solway Basin, but an explanation is required for the decrease northward. It is considered unlikely that the gradient is due to density variations within the Lower Palaeozoic wackes, because it is very difficult to explain the observed smooth variation in terms of contrasts between the exposed, steeply inclined strata. One possibility is that the effect arises because of density contrasts within the underlying basement; these could occur because of dense rocks beneath the coastal strip and/or widespread granite at depth towards the north. An alternative explanation is that the gravity gradient indicates a northward increase in the depth to an underlying, relatively dense basement.

The only indications of near-surface density contrasts within the Lower Palaeozoic sedimentary rocks are very weak north-east-trending gravity lineaments, of which G5 (Figure 7) is the most clearly resolved, and may relate to the tract-bounding Laurieston Fault.

AEROMAGNETIC DATA

Aeromagnetic surveys were flown over the Kirkcudbright–Dalbeattie district in 1959 by Canadian Aeroservices Inc., as part of the National Aeromagnetic Survey conducted for the Geological Survey of Great Britain. Survey lines were orientated in a north-south direction at a spacing of 2 km, with east-west tie lines at 10 km intervals; the sensor elevation was nominally 305 m above terrain. The analogue results have since been digitised (Smith and Royles, 1989), and the digitisation points are shown in Figure 8, together with contours of the reduced-to-pole aeromagnetic field. Reduction to pole is a transform which improves the spatial correlation between magnetic anomalies and the bodies which cause them, provided the magnetisation is in the direction of the Earth's present field. The transform was applied to a gridded data set covering a much larger area than that shown in Figure 8, to ensure that long wavelength features were properly sampled and transformed. In addition to conventional contour maps, identification of local magnetic features (shown schematically in Figure 7) was based on the study of a set of derived images; enhancement methods such as frequency filtering and colour and shaded-relief imaging were used to accentuate subtle magnetic field variations.

Long wavelength variations

The Kirkcudbright–Dalbeattie district lies on the southern flank of a major, long-wavelength magnetic anomaly which extends in a north-east–south-west direction for about 150 km from the Moffat area to the North Channel. The south-eastern flank of the anomaly is evident in Figure 8 as a broad magnetic gradient zone defined by contours extending from the south-western to the north-eastern corner of the figure, while the north-western flank of the anomaly appears in the extreme north-western corner of the figure. There is a magnetic minimum along the Solway Firth, with the field increasing southwards from this towards the Lake District.

The lack of strong interaction between the base of the largely non-magnetic Cairnsmore of Fleet Pluton and the source of the magnetic high over the Southern Uplands suggests that the latter largely underlies the granite at mid to lower crustal depths (Powell, 1970). Kimbell and Stone (1995) noted apparent correlations between the margins of the deep magnetic source and known major structures—the Orlock Bridge Fault to the north, the Iapetus suture to the south, as inferred from seismic reflection evidence; (Brewer et al., 1983). They suggested that this configuration could indicate a relatively magnetic 'terrane' concealed beneath the Southern Uplands and bounded by these major structures, and that this terrane could relate to an underthrust volcanic arc or a fragment of (Precambrian) magnetic basement which originally rifted from the Avalonian continent. The latter hypothesis is supported by geochemical similarities between granitoids in the southern part of the

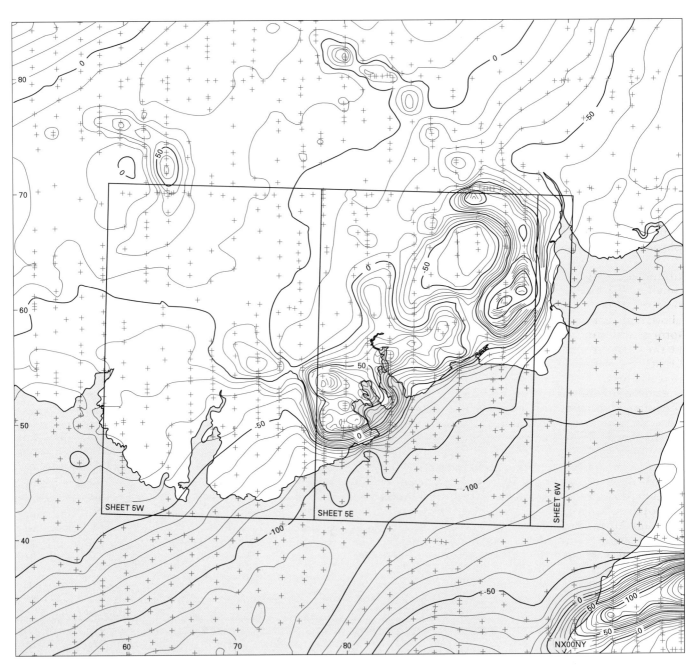

Figure 8   Reduced-to-the-pole aeromagnetic map of the region around Kirkcudbright and Dalbeattie. Crosses indicate digitised points. Magnetic field data have been referred to a linear reference field for the UK. Contour interval   10 nT.

Southern Uplands (south of the Orlock Bridge Fault) and in the Lake District (Thirlwall et al., 1989; Stone et al., 1997). Kimbell and Stone (1995) also noted a correlation between the eastern margin of the deep magnetic source and the Moffat Valley lineament (Stone et al., 1993) indicating that the latter may overlie an important basement structure. Magnetotelluric and seismic reflection surveys suggest that the Iapetus suture continues in an east-north-east direction beyond the intersection with the Moffat Valley lineament (Beamish and Smythe, 1986; Freeman et al., 1988), so it appears necessary to invoke a further (nonmagnetic) terrane at depth to the east of this lineament and north of the suture.

The location of the major late Caledonian intrusions in relation to the inferred pattern of major crustal structures is of interest. Both the Cairnsmore of Fleet and Criffel–Dalbeattie plutons lie at locations which might have provided sites of dilation, such as releasing bends or zones of fault convergence, under the sinistral shear regime prevalent in late Caledonian times (Hutton, 1987). The Cairnsmore of Fleet Pluton lies adjacent to the Orlock Bridge Fault where it swings from an east-north-east trend to a more north-easterly trend to the east, while the Criffel–Dalbeattie Pluton lies near the intersection of the east-north-east-trending Iapetus suture with the north-east-trending Moffat Valley lineament. However, a problem with attempting to relate the siting of major intrusive bodies in the Kirkcudbright–Dalbeattie district to the Iapetus suture is that the latter is inferred from geophysics to dip northward at a low angle (15–25°), lying at a depth of 15–20 km beneath the district and projecting to the basement surface well to the south (Beamish and Smythe, 1986; Soper et al., 1992). It is still possible, however, that shear movements on subsidiary structures above the main suture influenced the siting and intrusive form of the late Caledonian major intrusions. If dilation at these sites provided the 'space' for the intrusions (Hutton, 1982), the similarity in mechanism could explain the similarity in form of the two bodies. Further, the strike-slip movements which provided the sites for intrusion may themselves have played a role in magma generation (Watson, 1984; Leake, 1990).

The magnetic low beneath the Solway Basin may be due in part to subsidence-related displacement of a deep magnetic basement in Carboniferous and later times. There are difficulties, however, in applying this hypothesis to the south-west, where the low becomes broader and in apparent continuity with a feature crossing the Leinster Massif in Ireland, where such a subsidence history cannot be invoked. It appears likely, therefore, that lateral magnetisation contrasts within the basement contribute to the Solway Firth magnetic low. An explanation offered by Kimbell and Stone (1995) is that under-thrusting in the Iapetus suture zone resulted in relatively non-magnetic sedimentary material being sandwiched between magnetic basement blocks at depth.

Magnetic anomalies over late Caledonian intrusions

Conspicuous magnetic anomalies are associated with the major late Caledonian intrusions in the Kirkcudbright–Dalbeattie district. The anomaly over the margin of the Cairnsmore of Fleet Pluton (M1 in Figure 7) is discussed by Barnes (in prep.). More pronounced anomalies are evident over the Criffel–Dalbeattie Pluton and the Bengairn Complex. Modal analyses indicate that the outer granodiorite of the Criffel–Dalbeattie Pluton contains significantly more magnetite than the inner granite (see above), and this is substantiated by the observed ring of positive aeromagnetic anomalies which encircles the complex (Figure 8; M2, M3 in Figure 7). The marginal magnetic belt is narrower to the north than to the south, in agreement with the inferred compositional pattern (Stephens and Halliday, 1980; Stephens et al., 1985). There is a distinct drop in anomaly amplitude within the magnetic belt at [910 580] on the south side of the complex (shown schematically as a discontinuity between anomalies M2 and M3 in Figure 7). The reason for this is not known, but it is possible that it relates to alteration of magnetite in a zone with a particularly high density of north-west-trending fractures (Phillips, 1956a). Immediately to the west of this zone, the magnetic anomaly over the granodiorite appears to include residual maxima to the north and south of the main axis (M3); the airborne survey coverage is insufficient to resolve the geometry of these features in detail, but there does appear to be a more complicated magnetisation structure within this part of the complex.

The magnetic anomaly over the Bengairn Complex has two lobes (M4 and M5 in Figure 7), with the northern lobe extending to the WNW into the Black Stockarton Moor area. The relatively non-magnetic component of the complex, indicated by the decrease in magnetic values between the two lobes, may be a north-westward extension of the fine-grained granodiorite exposed on the west shore of Auchencairn Bay (cf. Phillips, 1956a, p.236). Although the aeromagnetic map (Figure 8) shows a single magnetic high over Black Stockarton Moor [720 550], detailed ground magnetic investigations in that area (Brown et al., 1979) revealed a complicated anomaly pattern, illustrating the relatively low resolution of the regional airborne survey. The ground magnetic traverses indicated that the magnetic rocks were not confined to a single intrusive phase, but that anomalies occurred over granodiorite sheets (with evidence of significant magnetisation variations within individual sheets) and later east-south-east-trending porphyrite dykes (Brown et al., 1979).

Other short wavelength magnetic features

Short wavelength magnetic field variations over the Lower Palaeozoic sedimentary rocks exposed in the Kirkcudbright–Dalbeattie district are generally subdued. Very weak apparent magnetic lineaments such as M6 and M7 (Figure 7) are parallel to the regional strike of the turbidites and may indicate small contrasts in their magnetic mineral content.

Magnetic high M8 (Figure 7), on the eastern margin of the study area, lies along strike from magnetic anomalies associated with the outcrop of the Lower

Carboniferous Birrenswark Volcanic Formation to the north-east, and is probably due to a continuation of these rocks beneath drift and Permo-Triassic cover. A small outcrop of the Birrenswark Volcanic Formation rocks occurs in Kirkbean Glen [971 593] in the Dalbeattie district. In this area the formation is too thin and altered to produce a discernable anomaly in the regional aeromagnetic survey data, although it is detectable by ground magnetic survey (Smith et al., 1996).

A narrow, north-west-trending magnetic low which crosses the north-eastern corner of the study area (M9 and M10 in Figure 7) is due to a Tertiary dyke (or dykes). These have not been observed at outcrop within the district, although exposures do occur to the north in the Thornhill district (Sheet 9E) at Skeogh Hill [861 785] and in the New Galloway district (Sheet 9W) near Troston Loch [710 900]. The southern segment of the anomaly is continuous with an anomaly which occurs over outcrops of the Cleveland Dyke in northern England, strongly suggesting a common origin. The dyke probably originated at the Mull volcanic centre, and the inferred emplacement mechanism is rapid lateral transport within the crust over a period of 1 to 5 days (Macdonald et al., 1988). Reversed remanent magnetisations have been observed in samples from the dyke (Dagley, 1969), and are consistent with the negative polarity of its associated anomaly. Pre-existing structures appear to have influenced the course of the dyke to some extent, as is evidenced by changes in the strike of its associated magnetic anomaly at the north-eastern corner of the Criffel–Dalbeattie Pluton (between segments M9 and M10) and near Marglolly Bridge [840 800]. The apparent gap between M9 and M10 may simply be due to the masking effect of the stronger anomaly due to the Criffel–Dalbeattie Pluton, although a change in the thickness and/or magnetic properties of the dyke in this area is possible.

There is evidence of three weak positive magnetic lineaments in the south-western corner of the study area (M11 in Figure 7). These are probably due to Tertiary dykes and appear to be associated with the Arran volcanic centre. The southernmost of these dykes is observed at outcrop near Kirkandrews [595 481]. The polarity of the associated magnetic anomaly suggests that either the dykes were intruded during a period of normal magnetic field polarity or that their remanent magnetisation is significantly weaker than that induced by the Earth's present field.

The pronounced magnetic anomaly in the south-east corner of Figure 8 is due to magnetic rocks of the Eycott Volcanic Group, which extend beneath Carboniferous cover in the Cockermouth–Workington area.

GEOPHYSICAL MODELLING

Quantitative potential field modelling has been used to investigate the form of the Criffel–Dalbeattie Pluton and the relationships between the density and magnetisation variations within this body. The density estimates used in the modelling are set out in Table 2. The various rock units were assigned magnetisations which provided the best fit with observed anomalies. Two-and-a-half dimensional (2.5-D) simultaneous modelling of the gravity and magnetic fields was conducted using the GRAVMAG program (Busby, 1987; Pedley, 1991). A 2.5-D model is one that has finite strike length and constant cross section, and is assumed to be bisected by the modelled profile; it is an approximation in the case of the bodies under consideration, but is adequate to illustrate the principal features. An initial assumption was made that magnetisation is in the direction of the Earth's present field, and the subsequent modelling results provided no evidence that would justify the inclusion of a significant remanent component in a different direction.

Model profile AA' is similar in location to one used by Bott and Masson Smith (1960) for gravity modelling, and the new model (Figure 9) generally corroborates their conclusions. The Criffel–Dalbeattie Pluton broadens downwards, and has a lateral increase in density towards its southern and, to a lesser extent, northern margins, in line with the mapping of Stephens et al. (1985). It is inferred to extend to a depth of about 9 km, although this is poorly constrained as it is dependant on the density structure assumed for the deeper parts of the intrusion and for the adjacent country rocks. The model reproduces the underlying southward rise of Bouguer anomalies by incorporating a dense basement unit to the south, as was postulated by Bott and Masson Smith (1960); such a configuration could signify either a discrete dense body or a southward decrease in the depth to a relatively dense basement. The model illustrates that if the more basic parts of the pluton (clinopyroxene hornblende biotite granodiorite, hornblende biotite granodiorite and biotite granite) are given higher magnetisations than the neighbouring rocks, an approximate fit with the observed magnetic anomalies is achieved. The magnetic susceptibilities required are of a similar magnitude to those predicted from observed magnetite content. Mismatches in the wavelength of observed and calculated magnetic anomalies on the north-west side of the pluton are principally due to poor sampling of the former, although a slight widening of the magnetic zone is likely as a result of the presence of magnetite in country rocks adjacent (within about 300 m) to the contact in this area (Kafafy and Tarling, 1985). In order to match the magnetic anomaly on the south-eastern side of the pluton, it is necessary to subdivide the clinopyroxene hornblende biotite granodiorite into inner (more magnetic) and outer zones. Some support for this is provided by the modal analyses of Phillips et al. (1981, table 3) which indicate that magnetite concentrations within this granodiorite increase to a maximum about 1 km from the south-eastern contact; the pattern is not identical, as the modelled higher susceptibility zone lies more than 1 km from the contact, but this may be the result of different sampling locations (the locations of the samples of Phillips et al. (1981) are not known).

Modelling of an orthogonal profile along the axis of the Criffel–Dalbeattie and Bengairn intrusions (not shown) confirms the general relationship between the density and magnetisation of the intrusive units discussed above, and suggests that these two bodies have similar depth extents.

LOCAL SURVEYS

Several local geophysical surveys have been conducted in the region as part of the BGS Mineral Reconnaissance Programme, funded by the Department of Trade and Industry. In addition to detailed gravity and magnetic surveys, a programme of induced polarisation (IP) and resistivity measurements were undertaken to investigate the extent and nature of conductive mineralisation associated with the Black Stockarton Moor subvolcanic complex (Brown et al., 1979; unpublished data from the Over Linkins–Ben Tudor [760 550] and Screel Burn [780 550] areas). The IP surveys at Black Stockarton Moor revealed an anomaly of about 6 km in length, which drilling showed to be due to a zone of pyrite mineralisation, possibly a segment of the pyrite 'halo' characteristic of porphyry copper deposits (Brown et al., 1979).

Unpublished data are held in the BGS archives for two local geophysical surveys elsewhere in the Kirkcudbright–Dalbeattie district. A trial IP/resistivity survey was conducted in the Barcloy–White Hills area [870 530] in 1976–1977 to investigate possible porphyry copper mineralisation; a north-east-trending zone of higher chargeability was detected which probably relates to pyrite mineralisation and/or black shales; the exploration was not pursued. Very low frequency electromagnetic

(VLF–EM) measurements in the Lotus Hill area [900 680] in 1979 located a north-west-trending fault zone within the Criffel–Dalbeattie Pluton, but geochemical sampling over this structure did not detect anomalous levels of tungsten, which was the target of the reconnaissance.

Gravity, VLF–EM and magnetic surveys have been conducted in the Kirkbean area in an attempt to delineate structures at the margin of the Solway–Northumberland basin which could provide sites for carbonate-hosted (Irish-style) mineralisation (Smith et al., 1996). The faulted margin of the Carboniferous rocks against the eastern flank of the Criffel–Dalbeattie Pluton was detected as a distinct VLF–EM and gravity feature and a local gravity high was observed over a thick baryte vein associated with this structure. Elsewhere, magnetic data showed potential for aiding in structural mapping by delimiting the Birrenswark

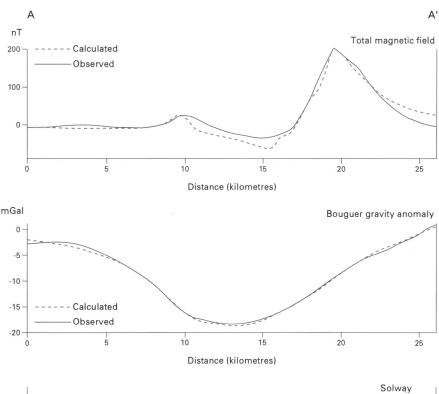

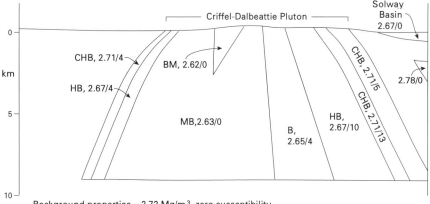

Figure 9 Gravity and magnetic model for profile AA' (Figure 7). Alphabetic codes indicate components of the igneous body (cf. Table 2). Numerical values indicate density/magnetic susceptibility where densities are in Mg/m^3 and susceptibilities in 10^{-3} SI units. Half strike length of 9 km assumed for all components of pluton except BM granite which is assumed to lie within the MB granite and have a half strike length of 2 km; other bodies are 2–D. Assumed background gravity field = 14 mGal; assumed background magnetic field decreases linearly from 30 nT at the north-west end of the profile to - 60 nT at its south-east end.

Lava Formation and weak gravity gradients could be correlated with mapped faults, although it appeared likely that the gravity response over certain structures was due, at least in part, to variations in drift thickness which were indirectly related to the bedrock structures.

BOREHOLES

A total of 118 boreholes from the district are registered with BGS (Table 3). The vast majority are very shallow (less than 9 m) and were sunk for site investigation (chiefly roads) or as wells for water (Chapter Two). A few deep bores were sunk, mostly in the Black Stockarton Moor and Screel Burn areas, for the purpose of mineral reconnaissance investigations (Brown et al., 1979).

Table 3   List of boreholes in the district with maximum depth reached and purpose of drilling.

1:10K sheet	No. of bores	Max. depth (m)	Purpose
NX 65 SW	10	25	site investigation, water
NX 65 SE	23	33	water
NX 67 SE	1	6	water
NX 74 NW	1	?	water
NX 75 NW	5	303	mineral reconnaissance (see Brown et al., 1979)
NX 75 NE	4	137	mineral reconnaissance
NX 75 SW	9	407	mineral reconnaissance (see Brown et al., 1979)
NX 75 SE	1	?	water
NX 76 NW	6	6	water
NX 76 NE	2	7	water
NX 76 SW	9	5	water
NX 76 SE	29	8	water
NX 85 NW	8	6	water
NX 86 NW	2	3	water
NX 86 SW	3	4	water
NX 95 NW	3	83	geological survey
NX 95 NE	1	4	water
NX 96 NE	1	?	water

FOUR

Ordovican and Silurian

The biostratigraphy of the Ordovician and Silurian rocks of the Kirkcudbright–Dalbeattie district is based on graptolite zonation and the resultant tectonostratigraphical framework is shown on Figure 4. In order to constrain the biostratigraphical ages vital to the construction of this framework, graptolites were collected from as many tectonostratigraphical units as possible. Where no data were available from localities within the district, correlations have been made with zones proved from adjacent districts (see Rushton et al., 1996, fig. 5 for a synthesis). In some instances graptolites were obtained from beds interbedded with the turbidite successions. Commonly, however, the main biostratigraphical evidence comes from the extensive graptolite faunas, usually spanning several zones, in the underlying Moffat Shales. The age of onset of turbidite deposition is then inferred from the youngest graptolite zone present in the Moffat Shales.

The faunal lists are summarised in Appendix 1. During the present resurvey new collections have been made at many localities and, where still available, old collections made by Macconochie for Peach and Horne (1899) have been re-examined. However, no fossils have survived for a number of the old localities and material from some faunal lists referred to by Peach and Horne could not been traced. All the fossils are housed in the BGS collections located at Murchison House, Edinburgh and/or Keyworth, Nottingham. Details of the fossil localities, specimen registration numbers and faunal lists are held as BGS biostratigraphical records, and are summarised in a series of internal reports by A W A Rushton, S P Tunnicliff and D E White.

The Ordovician and Silurian graptolite biozones are shown in Figure 4. The rationale for the choice of graptolite biozones is discussed in some detail by Rushton (*in* Stone, 1995) and the zonal scheme adopted for the Ordovician follows that outlined therein and in Rushton et al., 1996. The use of the Silurian zones essentially follows the proposals of Rickards (1976), except that the *persculptus* Biozone is now included as the highest zone of the Ordovician rather than basal Silurian.

CRAWFORD GROUP

The basal lithologies of the Ordovician succession in the Southern Uplands are basaltic lavas, many pillowed, interbedded with banded chert, mudstone and hyaloclastite, all of which are now included within the Crawford Group (Floyd, 1996). This assemblage is known to be as old as Arenig but its minimum age is generally constrained by a Caradoc (*gracilis* Biozone) graptolite fauna in the immediately overlying black shales of the Moffat Shale Group (see below). Within the Kirkcudbright–Dalbeattie district, the only beds which are probably referable to the Crawford Group are the bedded volcanic tuffs and grey cherts which appear to underlie the black shales of the Moffat Shale Group along the line of inliers (the Laurieston Line) associated with the Laurieston Fault. Due to its small outcrop, poor exposure and structural complexity, the Crawford Group is not separately distinguished on the 1:50 000 map and is included within the outcrop of the Moffat Shale Group.

MOFFAT SHALE GROUP

The Moffat Shale Group is a condensed sequence dominated by graptolitic, carbonaceous black shale (locally pyritous) and siliceous mudstone, which ranges in age from a poorly defined base in the mid-Ordovician to the late-Llandovery. There are some unfossiliferous beds of grey mudstone and siltstone as well as metabentonite horizons. This sequence has been subdivided into four named units with formation status (Lapworth, 1878; Peach and Horne, 1899; Floyd, 1996). The lowest unit is the Glenkiln Shale which is dominated by black shale, siltstone and mudstone and includes the Caradoc *gracilis* and *peltifer* biozones. This is succeeded by the Lower Hartfell Shale (*wilsoni* to *linearis* biozones) of fossiliferous black mudstone with thin chert bands, and the Upper Hartfell Shale (*complanatus* and *anceps* biozones) of massive grey silty mudstone or siltstone with few fossiliferous black mudstone beds. The Birkhill Shale, the youngest formation of the Moffat Shale Group, consists of grey to black fossiliferous mudstone with numerous thin horizons of pale metabentonite, ranging in age from the Ordovician Ashgill *persculptus* Biozone to the Silurian Llandovery *turriculatus* Biozone. In addition to the discrete metabentonite horizons, which represent original silicic vitric volcanic ash, many of the black shales also contain a significant proportion of ash (Merriman and Roberts, 1990). The Moffat Shale Group has been widely interpreted as of pelagic open-ocean origin (Leggett, 1987), although the ubiquitous presence of detrital mica from a terrigenous source (Merriman and Roberts, 1990) and the rare but significant horizons of interbedded wacke (Rushton and Stone, 1991) cast some doubt on this interpretation, particularly for the younger (Silurian) parts of the sequence.

The above description is of an idealised Moffat Shale Group succession, which unfortunately never crops out as a complete sequence and usually occurs as a tectonically disrupted unit which has acted as the basal décollement horizon during the development of the imbricate thrust stack. Because of the small size and structural complexity of the Moffat Shale Group outcrops, exacerbated by their generally poor exposure, the group has not been differentiated into separate formations on the 1:50 000 sheets which accompany this memoir.

Gillespie Burn Line

Elongate outcrops of Moffat Shale Group (the Gillespie Burn Line), located just north of the Gillespie Burn Fault, are presumed to underlie the Gala 4 tectonostratigraphical unit (Chapter 5). Recent collecting from the Gillespie Burn Line has supplemented the earlier records of graptolites from the area north-west of Parton [6950 7010], where the River Dee enters Loch Ken. Peach and Horne (1899, p.171) recorded *Dicellograptus anceps* from the banks of the River Dee near Hensol House [6780 6990], which remains the only evidence for Ordovician rocks there; the specimen cannot be traced and all other collections suggest an early Llandovery age. By way of confirmation, the *acuminatus* Biozone is proved by the zone fossil among Peach and Horne's collections from Hensol House which also indicate that there may be horizons representative of the *acinaces–cyphus* biozones present at this locality and nearby [c.670 702 and c.685 703]. In the Gillespie Burn Line further east and in a roadside lay-by near the eastern end of the Loch Ken viaduct [6850 7040], several collections from black silty mudstones with thin metabentonite horizons suggest a similar age range to that seen at Hensol House; *Climacograptus trifilis* and *Parakidograptus acuminatus* clearly indicate a mid-*acuminatus* Biozone age, while *A. atavus*, *A. gracilis* and cf. *C. cyphus praematurus* strongly suggest the presence of the *atavus* Biozone. The possible presence of *C. cyphus* s.l. in one of the collections from this locality might be taken as evidence for faunas as young as the *cyphus* Biozone, but this is by no means certain. However, confirmation of a *cyphus* Biozone age may be indicated in the equivalent tectonostratigraphical unit farther to the south- west where shales interbedded with Gala 4 turbidites at Sinniness [2154 5214], south of Glenluce, have yielded a *cyphus* Biozone fauna.

Further rocks of Moffat Shale Group affinity crop out on the Gillespie Burn Line within the district along strike to the south-west on the south slope of Bennan Hill [6470 6848] as a sequence of strongly cleaved and metamorphosed flinty black shales lying within the thermal aureole of the Cairnsmore of Fleet Pluton. Although no graptolites have been recorded here, the lithologies are typical of the Birkhill Shales. As in the section at the Loch Ken viaduct, thin metabentonite horizons are interbedded with the black shales.

Other than the thin bentonites reported above, no rocks of igneous origin have been identified from the inliers along the Gillespie Burn Line.

Garheugh Line

The Garheugh Line of Moffat Shale Group inliers underlies the Gala 5 tectonostratigraphical unit in the tract between the Garheugh and Gillespie Burn faults and is best recognised to the west in the Kirkcowan district (Sheet 4W) and the Wigtown district (Sheet 4E), where several graptolite zones have been proved at Garheugh [276 504] (BGS, 1992a). Cleaved and hornfelsed black shales cropping out immediately north of the Garheugh Fault on the east side of Doon of Culreoch [591 633] may represent Moffat Shale Group of the Garheugh Line in the district but have yielded no confirmatory faunal evidence. On the Rhins of Galloway to the south-west, the base of the Gala 5 unit is interbedded with graptolitic shale of the *magnus* Biozone (Stone, 1995).

Laurieston Line

The Laurieston Line, an elongate series of inliers of Moffat Shale Group and Crawford Group, lies along the southern margin of the Gala 7 tract and is bounded by the Laurieston Fault to the south. Extensive graptolite collections have been made from the basal Moffat Shale Group in the area of Dinnance [6740 6410] and extending north-eastwards to Tottlehams Glen [7769 6985]. Along the Laurieston Line, faunas have been recognised which range from the *gracilis* Biozone of the Caradoc to the *sedgwickii* Biozone of the mid-Llandovery, thus implying a maximum *sedgwickii* Biozone age for the base of the overlying Gala 7 turbidites.

For the most part, exposure is poor and restricted to watercourses and recently excavated drainage ditches. The best sections are: in the Urr Water and Tottlehams Glen [7766 6973–7691 6931]; in Trowdale Glen and fields to the south [7604 6878–7646 6856]; roadside exposures to the south-east of Balgerran Farm [7540 6813]; Kilnotrie [7513 6736]; near Crossmichael [7320 6691]; at Bellymack by Laurieston [6906 6456]; and in a series of tectonic slice sequences around Dinnance [6745 6431] and Gatehouse Burn [6700 6400], south-west of Laurieston. The lithological associations at each of these localities is described briefly below, from north-east to south-west.

In the Tottlehams Glen Burn section, east of the Urr Water (Figure 10), fossiliferous black shales are interbedded with fissile grey shales and range in age from the *gracilis* Biozone to the *acinaces* Biozone. In this area, the Moffat Shale Group succession is underlain to the north-west by bedded volcanic tuffs with minor chert [7772 6997], probably representing part of the Crawford Group. The lithological association and biostratigraphical ages suggest that the overall sequence youngs to the south: from the basal pelagic-volcanic sequence through the fossiliferous black mudstones of the Glenkiln Shale and the non-fossiliferous silty mudstones of the Upper Hartfell Shale to the black shales of the Birkhill Shale (Figure 1). New collections from the latter in Tottlehams Glen [7758 6964] contain *Parakidograptus acuminatus* and *Cystograptus vesiculosus* indicating the upper part of the *acuminatus* Biozone of the Llandovery, while at another locality [7766 6973], the zonal range may extend as high as the *acinaces* Biozone, based on the occurrence of '*Climacograptus*' *innotatus* and a form comparable with '*Orthograptus mutabilis*'. Although no younger ages are recorded in this north-eastern part of the Kirkcudbright–Dalbeattie district, the Laurieston Line can be traced north-

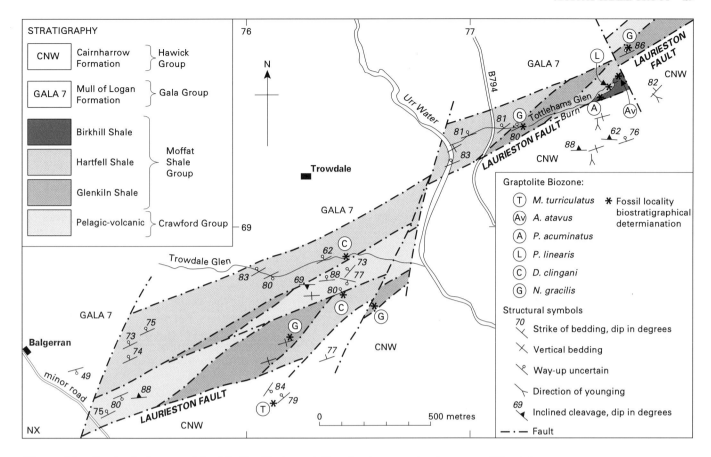

Figure 10   Geological map of the Moffat Shale and Crawford groups in the area of Tottlehams Glen, Trowdale Glen and Balgerran.

eastwards into the Thornhill district (Sheet 9E). There, in Glen Burn [837 762], recent work has confirmed the presence of the *acuminatus* to *cyphus* biozones and shown that part of the Upper Birkhill division of the Moffat Shale Group is also present with a fauna approximately of the *sedgwickii* Biozone.

On the east bank of the Urr Water, to the south of its confluence with the Tottlehams Glen Burn [7691 6930], a 50 m section of steeply dipping, laminated, unfossiliferous grey-green silty mudstone is probably referable to the Upper Hartfell Shale. Thus, in the area east of the Urr, the implication of the lithological associations allied to the biostratigraphical determinations is that both the southern and northern contacts of the Moffat Shale Group with the Gala and Hawick turbidites are faulted. The eastwards extension of the Tottlehams Burn outcrop to the area west of Kirkpatrick Durham [7800 7020] is the only occurrence of Moffat Shale Group in the Dalbeattie (Sheet 5E) part of the district.

In the Trowdale to Balgerran section (Figure 10), a more complete sequence of the basal pelagic-volcanic sequence of the Crawford Group can be seen, particularly in Trowdale Glen and in roadside exposures to the south-east of Balgerran farm. At the latter locality [7540 6813], a sequence of interbedded felsic tuff, chert, silicified black shale and grey-green siltstone occurs adjacent to the Laurieston Fault.

A similar sequence wedged between fossiliferous black shales of Glenkiln and Lower Hartfell Shale affinity occurs in Trowdale Glen and in the fields to the south. New graptolite collections from Trowdale Glen suggest a Lower Hartfell, *clingani* Biozone age, although Peach and Horne (1899, p.166) recorded a Glenkiln, *gracilis* Biozone fauna for which there is no new evidence. No Birkhill Shale faunas have been recorded from Trowdale Glen.

About 1 km further south-west, near Kilnotrie [751 674], banded cherts and felsic tuffs crop out to the north of the farmhouse while interbedded fossiliferous black shales (*peltifer*? to *linearis* biozones), cherts and metabentonites occur in a recently excavated cutting immediately west of the farmhouse. A short distance to the north, tuff interbedded with black shale occurs in small, detached outcrops to the east of Erncrogo Loch [7474 6767]. Similar lithologies are recorded in the Moffat Shale Group in the vicinity of Crossmichael, where a 20 m section of well-bedded felsic tuff and grey chert bands are interbedded with black shales in a distinct knoll to the east of the village [7320 6691].

At Bellymack, just east of Laurieston, a series of new exposures of Moffat Shale Group in a drainage ditch [6909 6456] has produced faunas ranging from the *clingani* and *linearis* biozones of the Caradoc to a possible *cyphus* Biozone age. At the northern margin of the outcrop at Bellymack [6895 6471], isolated outcrops of banded grey chert and thin felsic tuff horizons with dark grey unfossiliferous shales occur adjacent to massive coarse-grained sandstones of the Gala 7 turbidite sequence. If the pelagic-volcanic lithological association represents part of the Crawford Group, then the contact with the turbidites to the north is a fault, a similar relationship to that recognised in the Tottlehams Glen area. The relative position of the proven biozones in the Moffat Shale Group outcrops at Bellymack indicates considerable structural imbrication hereabouts.

The westernmost outcrops of the Laurieston Line in the district occur in the disrupted sequences at Dinnance [6745 6413] and Gatehouse Burn [670 640] where biostratigraphical determinations indicate an age range equivalent from Lower Hartfell Shale (*wilsoni* Biozone?) to the upper part of the Birkhill Shale (*convolutus* and *sedgwickii* biozones). Near Dinnance [6743 6422; 6744 6419] the zonal range is from a probable *wilsoni* or low *clingani* age to the *atavus* Biozone, while close by, in Gatehouse Burn [c.669 640], the range extends from a probable *cyphus* age to the *sedgwickii* Biozone. This juxtaposition of different ages suggests tectonic imbrication which is emphasised by the fact that to the north of Dinnance, at Barlue [6739 6543], an isolated sliver of Moffat Shale beneath Gala 7 has yielded a *convolutus* Biozone fauna, possibly extending down to the *gregarius* Biozone near Cullenoch [6678 6450]. At both of these localities the younger black shale beds are interbedded with turbidite sequences and occur in a series of folded and imbricated slices. To the north-east of Laurieston [6740 6532], fossiliferous variegated black, green and red-brown silty mudstones with thin metabentonites of the Birkhill Shale (up to *convolutus* Biozone) occur in an isolated tectonic sliver in the hanging wall of the Laurieston Fault. A similar tectonic sliver occurs as a sequence of intensely deformed, slickensided graphitic black shale in a roadside quarry in Laurieston Forest [6678 6450].

Moffat Shale Group inliers within the Hawick Group

At Barlay Burn [6211 5842], a small enigmatic outcrop of strongly tectonised black shale occurs adjacent to the Innerwell Fault which forms the southern boundary of the Cairnharrow Formation. Peach and Horne (1899, p.171) recorded graptolites from what they described as a small sliver of 'cleaved and corrugated' Moffat Shale Group at this locality. Many of their specimens are still available for inspection and include forms which suggest a zonal range from as low as *acuminatus* to the *convolutus* Biozone. Although some of the Barlay Burn localities described by Peach and Horne can be readily identified on the ground, outcrop is poor and recent collecting has produced only an undiagnostic fauna of poorly preserved *Normalograptus* sp. Field relationships are unclear, but this locality appears to represent a rare instance of turbidites of Hawick Group affinity directly in contact with Moffat Shales (Rushton et al., 1996).

In the Coalheugh Burn, a tributary of the Tarff Water flowing off Dullarg Hill [6797 5927], three en-echelon

lozenge-shaped outcrops of strongly deformed black shales have been mapped. The presence of a trial adit, allied with the name of the burn, suggests that early attempts were made to work the slickensided black and grey shales in the belief that they were coal. Although no graptolites were found during the resurvey, Peach and Horne (1899, p.172) recorded *Diplograptus acuminatus* and *Climacograptus normalis* from the Coalheugh sections and the lithologies are also suggestive of the Birkhill Shale Formation. A limited and poorly preserved acritarch assemblage indicates only a Silurian age (Barron, 1988).

Lithologically similar outcrops of black shale recently discovered along strike at Barstobrick [6860 6009] have yielded a sparse graptolite fauna including the form *Climacograptus trifilis* indicating a mid-*acuminatus* Biozone age. A further collection from Barstobrick contains faunal evidence of a slightly younger *atavus–acinaces* Biozone age, including doubtful examples of *Atavograptus atavus* and *Cystograptus vesiculosus*. Exposure at this locality is poor and the relationship with the overlying turbidites is unknown. Very poorly preserved chitinozoa were also recorded from this locality.

The black shales from Coalheugh Burn and Barstobrick are all adjacent to the Garlieston Fault, an intratract fault within the Kirkmaiden Formation, and, if the shales are indeed Moffat Shale Group, would show the Kirkmaiden tract to be compound.

GALA GROUP

The Gala Group comprises a sequence of wacke-dominated units overlying Moffat Shale Group strata of Llandovery age. Three tectonostratigraphical units of the Gala Group have been recognised in the Kirkcudbright–Dalbeattie district and correlated with similar rocks to the south-west in Wigtownshire: Gala 4 (equivalent to the Sinniness Formation); Gala 5 (equivalent to the Garheugh Formation); Gala 7 (equivalent to the Mull of Logan Formation).

The Gala Group crops out over an area of about 90 km^2 within the district. The succession strikes north-east with a cross-strike outcrop width of about 5 km, is dominantly northward-younging and for the most part beds are steeply dipping or even vertical. Thus, even with the probability of some repetition of strata by folding or faulting, the succession is of the order of several thousand metres thick. As with most successions in the Southern Uplands, a combination of poor exposure and inadequate stratigraphical control makes it impossible to give more than general estimates for the thickness of units.

Biostratigraphical constraints on the age of the group within the district are determined by inference from the youngest graptolites in the underlying graptolitic black shales of the Moffat Shale Group. Graptolite-bearing shale laminae interbedded with the turbidites have been recorded from the Gala Group further south-west and allow ages to be inferred via lithostratigraphical correlation.

The current definition of the Gala Group follows that of Barnes et al. (1987) as amended by White et al. (1992). Earlier descriptions by Lapworth and Wilson

(1871) and Peach and Horne (1899) referred to the equivalent rocks in Dumfriesshire as the Queensberry Grits. Other local formational and descriptive terms have been used from time to time. In Peeblesshire for example, about 50 km to the north-east of the district, Walton (1955) applied one of the first systematic petrological studies of the Southern Uplands turbidites to subdivide what is now defined as the Gala Group into Pyroxenous, Intermediate and Garnetiferous 'groups'. These subdivisions were broadly adhered to by Morris (1987) but have not been adopted in the current work since the compositional differences noted by Walton are not so readily identified in the south-western sector of the Southern Uplands.

Unlike the Ordovician succession of the Southern Uplands, formal lithostratigraphical subdivision of the Gala Group is limited because there is little systematic lithological, sedimentological or compositional variation in the turbidite sequences between the fault-defined tracts. Within the Kirkcudbright–Dalbeattie district, three tectonostratigraphical units have been mapped which become sequentially younger southwards (Figure 4). These units are numbered Gala 4, Gala 5 and Gala 7, and were first recognised and defined in the area to the south-west of the district. They have been reliably traced into the Kirkcudbright area using the tract-bounding faults which may be delineated as discrete topographical features and may or may not include discontinuous outcrops of Moffat Shale Group (the Gillespie Burn, Garheugh and Laurieston lines). The disposition of the units and the tract-bounding faults are shown in Figure 13, while Table 4 shows the correlation with local lithostratigraphical terminology previously used in the geological literature.

Subtle compositional variations within the Gala Group have been highlighted by Stone (1995) in a description of the equivalent rocks on the Rhins of Galloway. Most of the important trends noted on the Rhins of Galloway are reflected in the Gala Group of the Kirkcudbright–Dalbeattie district. Representative modal composition data for the district are included in Appendix 2 and plotted as histograms in Figure 11. The main elements of the modal composition of the Gala wackes are shown on the Q-F-L plot of Figure 12. All Gala Group wackes are quartzose, with quartz content in the range 30 to 55%. However, there is no clear trend in the data comparable to the systematic increase in quartz content with decreasing age described from the Peebles–Hawick area by Walton and Oliver (1991), using data from Casey (1983). In Figures 11 and 12, no distinction has been made between plagioclase and K-feldspar in the samples from the Kirkcudbright–Dalbeattie district but there is an overall decrease in total feldspar within the younger Gala tracts (average of 16% for Gala 4 as compared to 13% for Gala 7). As on the Rhins of Galloway (Stone, 1995), there is a southward increase in the abundance of detrital muscovite in the district, with up to 10% mica recorded in the youngest Gala tract.

The occurrence of volcaniclastic andesitic detritus is uniformly low, varying from an average of 2.5% in Gala 4 to less than 1% in Gala 7. The balance of the lithoclasts consists of varying amounts of acid igneous, altered spilitic basalt, low-grade schistose metamorphic rocks and intrabasinal sedimentary rocks. Whereas on the Rhins of Galloway the non-andesitic lithic component rarely exceeds 5%, this is not the case in the Kirkcudbright–Dalbeattie district where acid igneous clasts (including granitoids) can contribute up to 15%, and average 12.5% in Gala 4, 8% in Gala 5 and 9% in Gala 7.

Gala 4 (local stratigraphical names: Sinniness Formation, Float Bay Formation). The base of the Gala 4 tectonostratigraphical unit is defined by the Moffat Shale Group inliers of the Gillespie Burn Line which lies immediately north of the tract-bounding Gillespie Burn Fault. Faunas possibly as young as the *acinaces* or possibly *cyphus* Biozone are reported from the Gillespie Burn Line in the district, suggesting that Gala 4 is of *cyphus* Biozone age or younger.

The Gala 4 unit is poorly exposed within the district and only the basal portions crop out in the north-west part of the district, mostly within the aureole of the Cairnsmore of Fleet Pluton. First defined at the Mull of Sinniness in Wigtownshire, the turbidite sequence is characterised by thinly to thickly bedded (10–75 cm), fine- to coarse-grained wacke predominantly in graded units (T_a of Bouma, 1962) which may have a cross-laminated top (T_{ac}). Cross- and parallel-lamination is usually better developed in the more thinly bedded wackes (< 20 cm thick), occurring in combinations of T_{abc}, T_{bc} and T_c units. These more thinly bedded sequences are normally associated with laminated siltstone and silty mudstone intervals up to 1 m thick. There are also rare packets up to 10 m thick of thickly bedded (up to 1.5 m), amalgamated massive wackes.

In equivalent lithologies on the Rhins of Galloway and on the eastern shore of Luce Bay, Kelling et al. (1987) recorded a general axial (i.e. parallel to the overall trend of the depositional basin) palaeocurrent direction towards the south-west and interpreted the depositional setting of the turbidites as unconfined sheet flows with minor channelling.

Table 4 Correlation of GALA 4, 5 and 7 tectonostratigraphical units with local lithostratigraphical units previously named in the literature.

Unit	Rhins of Galloway	Whithorn peninsula	Creetown
GALA 7	Mull of Logan Formation	Corwall Formation[1]	Craignell Formation[3]
GALA 5	Stinking Bight Beds	Garheugh Formation[1]	
GALA 4	Float Bay Formation	Sinniness Formation[2]	

1 Kelling et al., 1987; 2 BGS, 1992a; 3 Cook and Weir, 1980.

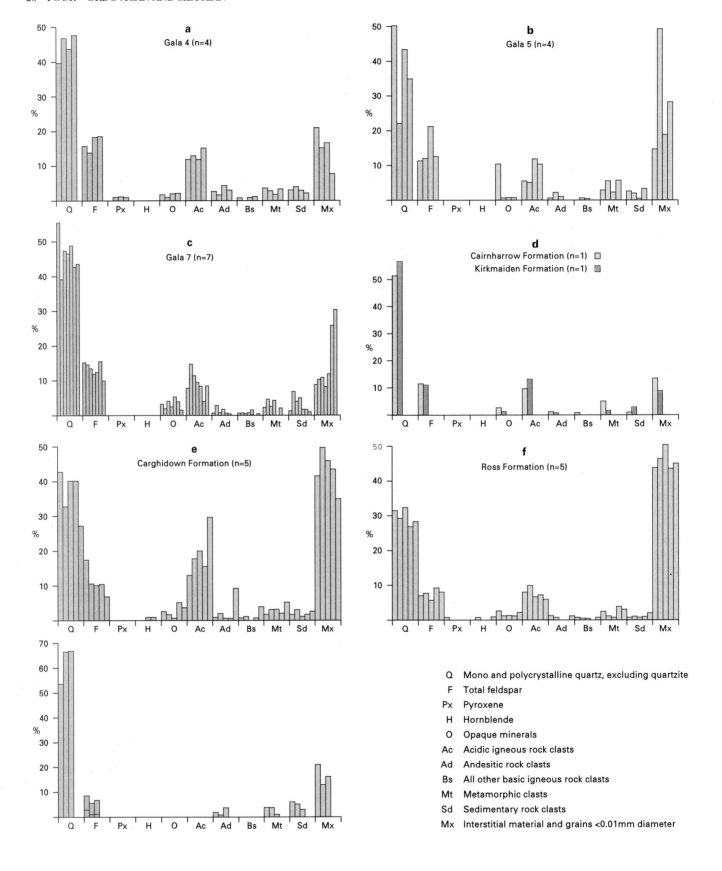

Figure 11 (*opposite*)   Summary histograms of modal composition data for representative wackes from the district. 1000 points were counted in each thin section. Samples representative of the GALA 4 unit are from the New Galloway district (Sheet 9W), immediately north.

BGS registered sample numbers (from left to right in each column):

Gala Group
a   GALA 4   S 93146, S 93151, S 93161, S 93168
b   GALA 5   S 78257, S 78259, S 78319, S 78278
c   GALA 7   S 78252, S 78260. S 78262, S 78272,
            S 78274, S 78306, S 80376

Hawick Group
d   Cairnharrow Formation   S 78284) combined
         Kirkmaiden Formation   S 78291) in one diagram
e   Carghidown Formation   S 78177, S 78181, S 78182,
                                                S 78207, S 78229
f   Ross Formation   S 78239, S 78244, S 78193,
                                                S 78202, S 78203

Riccarton Group
g   Raeberry Castle Formation S 78219, S 78216, S 78212

Note that in the Raeberry Castle Formation the total feldspar column is divided to show the plagioclase (lower part) and K-feldspar (upper part) components.

Gala 5 (local stratigraphical names: Stinking Bight Beds, Garheugh Formation).   The Gala 5 tectonostratigraphical unit is bounded to the south by the Garheugh Fault and to the north by the Gillespie Burn Fault. Although no unequivocal Moffat Shale Group outcrops of the Garheugh Line occur within the district, turbidite deposition is dated as occurring during the *magnus* Biozone by interbedded graptolitic shales in equivalent strata on the Rhins of Galloway (Stone, 1995). The youngest underlying Moffat Shale Group below Gala 5 is therefore shown as *triangulatus* Biozone in Figure 4.

Lithologically the unit is dominated by medium- to coarse-grained, thickly bedded wacke with interbedded units of laminated siltstone and thinly bedded wacke. The location of a representative measured section from the Gala 5 sequence is shown in Figure 13 and the log shown in Figure 14a. Using the turbidite facies classification of Pickering et al. (1986) the Gala 5 units can be assigned to the B2 (organised sands), C2 (organised sand-mud couplets) and D2 (organised silts and muddy silts) subfacies. Thickly bedded wackes (commonly greater than 1 m) are usually well graded, with a pebbly base containing quartz clasts up to 1 cm in diameter. Parallel-, cross- and

Figure 12   Compositional range of the Gala Group wackes in terms of quartz (Q), feldspar (F) and labile components (L). Provenance fields after Dickenson and Suczec, 1979. Note that data for GALA 4 are not from the district but from equivalent rocks to the north-east in the New Galloway district. Field of Gala Group wackes from the Peebles - Hawick area obtained by Casey as reported by Walton and Oliver, 1991; arrow indicates increase in quartz content with decrease in age. Rhins of Galloway data from Stone, 1995.

BGS registered numbers of specimens:

GALA 4	1	S 93155
	2	S 93168
	3	S 93161
	4	S 93146
GALA 5	5	S 78257
	6	S 78319
	7	S 78278
	8	S 78259
GALA 7	9	S 78306
	10	S 78252
	11	S 80376
	12	S 78274
	13	S 78262
	14	S 78272
	15	S 78260

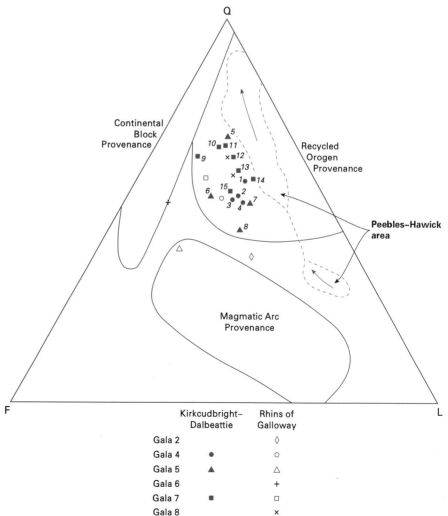

	Kirkcudbright–Dalbeattie	Rhins of Galloway
Gala 2		◊
Gala 4	●	○
Gala 5	▲	△
Gala 6		+
Gala 7	■	□
Gala 8		×

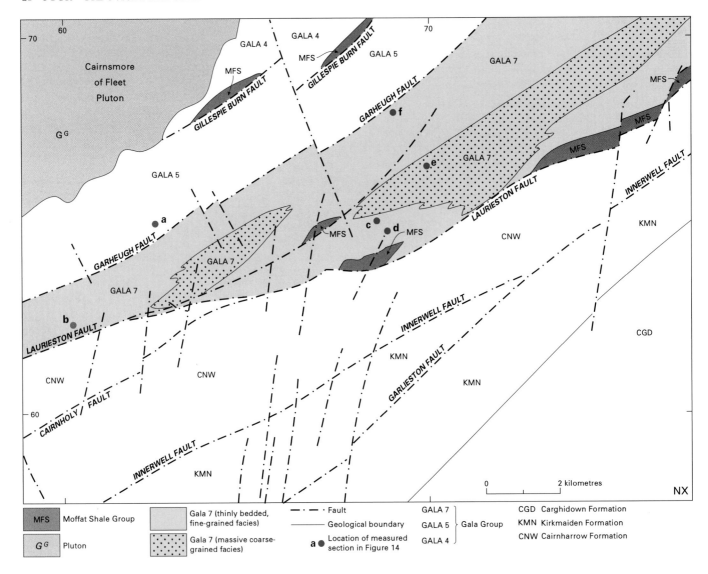

Figure 13 Tectonostratigraphical tracts within the Gala Group and tract-bounding faults in the area north-west of Castle Douglas.

convolute-laminations in combinations of T_{ab}, T_{ac} and T_{abc} are well developed in the thinner bedded units. An erosive base and lenticular geometry in the coarse-grained wacke bodies suggest deposition within channels. The equivalent rocks on the Rhins of Galloway and the east side of Luce Bay have been interpreted by Kelling et al. (1987) as channel-fill and sheet-flow deposits.

Good outcrops of Gala 5 turbidite sequences can be seen in several sections: Drumglass Hill [6800 6850] to Hensol Wood [6767 6914]; Nether Crae [6595 6798] to Crae Hill [6570 6900]; Loch Hill [6275 6500] to Clack Hill [6270 6700]; Doon of Culreoch [5870 6314] to Burnfoot Burn [5900 6485]. Although generally folded and cleaved, each of these sections shows an overall younging to the north-west, which coincides with a decrease in bed thickness and grain size in the same direction due to an increase in the laminated silty mud-stone component in the sequence. This up-sequence

decrease in grain size and bed thickness culminates, to the south-west of Hensol Wood, in a 30 m thick sequence of strongly cleaved laminated siltstone and grey to dark grey mudstone with thin interbeds of coarse-grained ('gritty'') sandstone. A similar thinly bedded sequence occurs in the metamorphic aureole of the Cairnsmore of Fleet Pluton at Clack Hill [625 669]. To the north of the representative measured section (a on Figure 13) on the

Figure 14 *(opposite)* Representative measured sections for the Gala Group. See Figure 13 for location map.

GALA 5	**a.**	Grobdale of Balmaglie	[6273 6521]
GALA 7	**b.**	Craig of Grobdale	[6068 6266]
	c.	Quintinespie Hill	[6879 6555]
	d.	Quintinespie Hill	[6899 6512]
	e.	Meikle Dornell	[7000 6685]
	f.	Ullioch	[6905 6816]

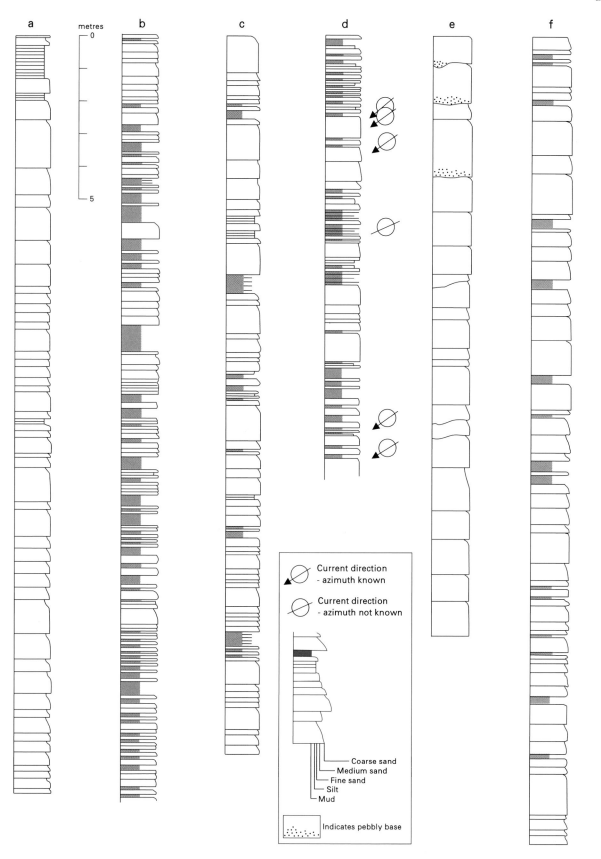

a

metres
0

5

b

c

d

e

f

Current direction
- azimuth known

Current direction
- azimuth not known

Coarse sand
Medium sand
Fine sand
Silt
Mud

Indicates pebbly base

slopes of Loch Hill, interbedded units of laminated silt-stone and silty mudstone up to 10 m thick occur within the more thickly bedded, coarser grained sequence. A thick sequence of thinly bedded, fine-grained, fissile wackes interbedded with red-green siltstone occurs in the disused slate quarries at Parton [6967 7043].

Palaeocurrent data are sparse for the Gala 5 sequence in the Kirkcudbright district (Sheet 5W). Flute and groove casts on turbidite bases from the Drumglass Hill sections indicate both transverse (to the south-east) and axial (to the north-east and south-west) current directions. From a larger dataset on similar sequences to the south-west, Stone (1995) and Kelling et al. (1987) record similar variability, with a predominant axial flow to the south-west.

Gala 7 (local stratigraphical names: Mull of Logan Formation, Corwall Formation). The Gala 7 unit is bounded on the north by the Garheugh Fault and on the south by the Laurieston Line, where thick but discontinuous sequences of Moffat Shale Group strata occur at the base of the Gala 7 unit and yield a youngest graptolite age in the *sedgwickii* Biozone. No graptolite-bearing shale interbeds from within the turbidites of the Gala 7 unit have been recorded in the district. However, in equivalent strata to the south-west, at Alticry [2846 5024, 2860 5032] in the Wigtown district (Sheet 4E; BGS, 1992b), thin black shale laminae contain *Monograptus proteus*, indicating either the *turriculatus* or *crispus* Biozone (White et al., 1992). The age of deposition of the Gala 7 turbidites has been further refined in the Thornhill district to the north-east, where collecting from a 1 m thick shale interbed near Glen Farm [8300 7622], north of Crocketford, has yielded a fauna including *Streptograptus plumosus*, indicating a *turriculatus* Biozone age.

The Gala 7 tectonostratigraphical unit is lithologically the most varied of the Gala Group turbidite sequences (representative measured sections, b–f on Figures 13 and 14). At least two distinct facies can be recognised: an older, thickly bedded, coarse-grained ('conglomeratic') sequence (e on Figure 14) and a younger, finer-grained, more thinly bedded sequence (b on Figure 14). In equivalent strata on the Rhins of Galloway and around Luce Bay this variability has resulted in the recognition of four lithologically distinct members (Kelling et al., 1987).

A map of the two facies within the Gala 7 unit is included in Figure 13, along with the location of the measured sections. The coarse-grained 'conglomeratic' facies is best exposed on the crags of Meikle Dornell [6980 6680] and Little Dornell [7020 6670]. A representative section from this area (e on Figure 14) is dominated by amalgamated, thickly bedded and coarse-grained T_a, T_{ab} and T_{ac} sandstones of A2 and B2 subfacies (after Pickering et al., 1986). Bed thickness is usually greater than 50 cm and strongly erosive bases are common with quartz and intraformational lithic clasts up to pebble grade forming pockets of conglomerate. Amalgamated wackes occur in packets up to 40 m thick interbedded with sequences of thin- to medium-bedded T_{abc} sandstones and laminated silty mudstones (C2 and D2 subfacies of Pickering et al., 1986). These

Figure 15 (*opposite*) Palaeocurrent data for the Gala, Hawick, and Riccarton groups. Data are corrected for regional dip, strike and fold plunge. Some data for Raeberry Castle Formation from Kemp, 1985. n = number of readings. Inner circle = groove casts, outer circle = flute casts.

a. Gala Group, n = 19.
b. Kirkmaiden Formation, Hawick Group, n = 30.
c. Carghidown Formation, Hawick Group, n = 52.
d. Ross Formation, Hawick Group, n = 37.
e. Raeberry Member, Raeberry Castle Formation, Riccarton Group, n = 58.
f. Mullock Bay Member, Raeberry Castle Formation, Riccarton Group, n = 50.

finer grained lithologies probably represent overbank and interchannel deposits and the 'conglomeratic' facies is a channel complex which can be traced to the north-east to Loch Roan [7390 6902], where parallel- and cross-laminated 'conglomeratic' sandstones are common. As mapped (Figure 13), the channel complex appears to cut down into the Moffat Shale Group between the two main outcrops at Crossmichael and Laurieston, possibly representing an original channel feature. Although poorly exposed at the present time because of extensive afforestation, a belt of pebbly sandstones in the Black Hill–Laurieston Forest area [6450 6450] was noted during the primary survey in the 1870s (Figure 13).

Between the two belts of coarse-grained wackes, sequences of thinner-bedded and finer-grained sandstones with silty mudstones occur. Representative lithological logs are illustrated in Figure 14 as sections b, c, d and f. Sections c and d, on and adjacent to Quintinespie Hill (Figure 13), are typical of the gradational facies changes from thickly bedded, coarse-grained sandstones to thin- to medium-bedded sandstone, siltstone and mudstone sequences (Facies C2.2, C2.3 to D2 and E2 of Pickering et al., 1986) which culminate in the thinly bedded sequence dominated by silty mudstone at the Craig of Grobdale (b on Figure 14).

Palaeocurrent data from the Gala 7 unit are variable but predominantly axial, towards the south-west (Figure 15).

HAWICK GROUP

The onset of Hawick Group sedimentation overlaps the cessation of Gala Group deposition (Table 5; White et al., 1992). Within the Kirkcudbright–Dalbeattie district, the two groups are always in tectonic contact across the tract-bounding Laurieston Fault, but in Wigtownshire a lateral sedimentary transition between the two groups has been mapped (BGS, 1992a, b). This, together with the tendency for the younger parts of the Gala Group to be dominated by finer-grained, more thinly bedded turbidite sequences which are more typical of the Hawick Group, suggests an original sedimentary gradation.

The Hawick Group is characterised by very uniform sequences of medium- to thin-bedded, fine- to medium-grained, greenish grey calcareous wacke with discrete packets of interbedded silty mudstone. Based on facies

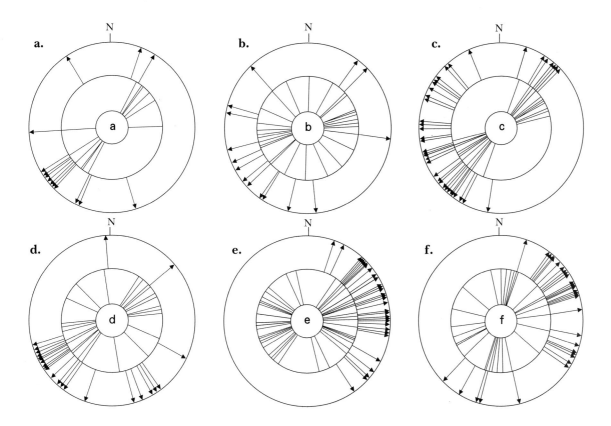

variations within the overall turbidite depositional regime, the Hawick Group has been subdivided into four lithostratigraphical units: the Cairnharrow, Kirkmaiden, Carghidown and Ross formations. The lithostratigraphical classification together with the biostratigraphical and chronostratigraphical relationships of the late Llandovery and Wenlock rocks have been studied in detail by White et al. (1992) and the results are summarised in Table 5. The work of White et al. (1992) represents a synthesis of the recent BGS resurvey of the region and is the basis for the scheme adopted for the Lower Palaeo-

zoic sequences on the accompanying 1:50 000 geological Sheets 5W (Kirkcudbright) and 5E (Dalbeattie). The Knockeans Formation of Cook and Weir (1980) is broadly equivalent to the oldest sequences of the Hawick Group (the Cairnharrow Formation and the northern part of the Kirkmaiden Formation). It should be noted that in the tectonostratigraphical scheme of Kemp (1985; 1986), the Ross Formation was regarded as the basal sequence of the Riccarton Group, but on lithological, sedimentological and structural grounds it is now considered to show greater affinities with rocks of the Hawick

Table 5 Late Llandovery and Wenlock lithostratigraphy in the south-west Southern Uplands and its relationship to biostratigraphical and chronostratigraphical classifications.

Hom.   Homerian (part) (after White et al., 1992.)

Series	Stage	Graptolite biozone		Formation	Group
Wenlock (part)	Hom.	*C. lundgreni*			
	Sheinwoodian	*C. ellesae*		Raeberry Castle	Riccarton
		C. linnarssoni			
		C. rigidus			
		C. antennularius			
		M. riccartonensis	upper	?	
			middle	Ross	Hawick
			lower		
		C. murchisoni			
		C. centrifugus		?	
Llandovery (part)	Telychian	*Mcl. crenulata*		? Carghidown	
		Mcl. griestoniensis		? Kirkmaiden	
		M. crispus		Cairnharrow	
		M. turriculatus		?	Gala (part)

Plate 2 Large flute casts on bases of wacke beds of the Carghidown Formation, Hawick Group.

Current from the south.

Point of Green, 4 km south of Borgue [6252 4443] (D 4400).

Group (Barnes et al., 1989), and is included within that group in this Memoir.

The 'Hawick Rocks' were originally defined in south-east Scotland by Lapworth and Wilson (1871). The long debate over their age has been summarised by White et al. (1992, p.299) who concluded that the Hawick Group (as defined above) ranges in age from the *turriculatus* Biozone in the Cairnharrow Formation, to the upper *riccartonensis* Biozone (early Wenlock) in the Ross Formation.

The Hawick Group was deposited by processes operative in a mid-fan environment and the constituent formations vary only in the relative thickness, frequency and proportion of the various lithologies. In terms of the facies classification scheme of Pickering et al. (1986), sequences are dominated by medium-bedded wackes (Facies C2), separated by and transitional to units of silty mudstone with thin wacke beds (Facies D2). Sparsely dispersed through the alternating Facies C and D sequences are thick- to very thick-bedded massive sandstones of Facies B2. This overall pattern is disrupted in parts of the Carghidown and Ross formations by syn-sedimentary slump deposits, showing soft sediment deformation (Facies F2). Laminated carbonaceous siltstones (hemipelagites; Facies G2) are confined to the Ross Formation and form one of its defining characteristics.

Facies C members (predominantly C2.2) are commonly made up of wacke beds of variable thickness, usually 20–60 cm but ranging from a few centimetres to 1 metre. Locally, upward-thinning sequences are recognisable and silty mudstone partings are thin (< 10 cm) or absent. Wacke beds have a parallel sharp top and base and in coherent domains are laterally continuous within the limits of outcrop (up to about 100 m along strike). The wackes are typically fine to medium grained but may include coarse-grained lithic detritus at their base. The Bouma T_a, T_b and T_c divisions are variably developed, usually alone or in T_{ab}, T_{ac} and T_{bc} combinations. Where present the T_d division is represented by the silty mudstone partings. Pelagic and hemipelagic mudstone (T_e) is only very rarely developed in the Cairnharrow, Kirkmaiden and Carghidown formations but is a characteristic component of the Ross Formation. Wacke beds commonly have groove or flute casts on their base (Plate 2) and may include mudstone rip-up clasts. Free-standing ripples, usually symmetrical and with amplitudes of 2–3 cm and wavelengths of about 20 cm, are common on bed tops (Plate 3). The ripples are usually orthogonal to flutes and other soles marks and were probably generated by reworking by non-depositional currents, although recent work from the Windermere Supergroup in the Lake District (Kneller et al.,

1991) suggests that such ripples could result from reflection of turbidity currents.

Facies D turbidites are dominated by laminated silty mudstone, with a variable proportion of very thinly bedded (1 cm) siltstone and fine-grained sandstone beds (up to 5 cm thick) typical of the D2.3 subfacies but locally transitional to C2.3. Individual sandstone beds are parallel sided and laterally continuous as cross-laminated units (T_c). The interbedded facies D members range in thickness from 10 cm to 10 m (typically 2–3 m) and locally form the upper portion of upward-thinning-and-fining sequences. Trace fossils commonly occur in this facies (e.g. Benton, 1982). Sequences of facies D silty mudstones up to 40 m thick are typical of the Cairnharrow Formation.

Facies B turbidites are composed of thick- to very thick-bedded, massive or parallel-laminated (T_b), poorly graded sandstone beds (Facies B2.1 transitional to C2.1). Individual beds range from one to several metres in thickness and normally occur in amalgamated packets up to 12 m thick. The sandstone is typically medium grained, although coarse-grained detritus commonly occurs towards the bottom of beds. Some of the thicker sandstone beds are erosive, cutting sharply down into the underlying C and D facies turbidites and are lenticular in section as if filling a shallow channel.

Facies F (F2) consists of sequences of classical turbidites (C and D facies) which have undergone soft-sediment deformation. This has normally occurred in discrete 'disrupted zones' to produce structures ranging from incipient pinch and swell to local mélange with lenses and irregular blocks of wacke in an anastomosing and flaky mudstone matrix. Slump folds are commonly asymmetric, south-east-verging fold pairs with irregular wavelengths (up to 10 m) and curvilinear hinges. Such disrupted zones have commonly acted as the focus for later deformation.

Compositionally, the wackes from each of the four formations of the Hawick Group are very similar. They are mostly fine- to medium-grained, calcareous, poorly sorted deposits consisting of angular to subrounded grains, with up to 40% clay matrix. The modal composition data for the formations of the Hawick Group are given in Appendix 2 and summarised as histograms in Figures 11d–f. The grains are predominantly of quartz, with secondary but important amounts of carbonate, feldspar, lithic fragments and mica. The quartz content varies from 30% to over 50% while feldspar (plagioclase with some K-feldspar) is usually about 10% of the sand fraction. The proportion of mica varies with grain size from approximately 3% in medium-grained wacke up to 15% in fine-grained wacke.

Carbonate usually occurs in the matrix as recrystallised grains and most is probably of detrital origin, judging from the rare fragments which are still recognisable as bioclastic. Weir (1974) suggested that the carbonate was derived from a magmatic or groundwater source but the clear evidence of bioclastic material and detrital carbonate grains points to a derivation as micritic detritus with redistribution of carbonate during diagenesis. Stone

Plate 3 Ripple marks on the tops of steeply dipping north-west-younging wackes of the Kirkmaiden Formation, Hawick Group.

Carrick Point, 6.5 km south-south-west of Gatehouse of Fleet [5743 5053] (D 4381).

Figure 16 Compositional range of wackes from the Hawick and Riccarton groups in terms of quartz (Q), feldspar (F) and labile components (L). Provenance fields after Dickenson and Suczec, 1979. Riccarton Group data (Raeberry Castle Formation–RBC) from McCaffrey, 1991. Some Carghidown Formation (CGD) data from the Rhins of Galloway (Stone, 1995) and Kirkmaiden (KMN) and Cairnharrow Formation (CNW) data from the Kirkcowan–Wigtown district (Barnes, in prep.) are given for comparison. ROSS = Ross Formation.
1 sample of coarse-grained wacke (S 78229) from the Carghidown Formation, with increased volcanic component.

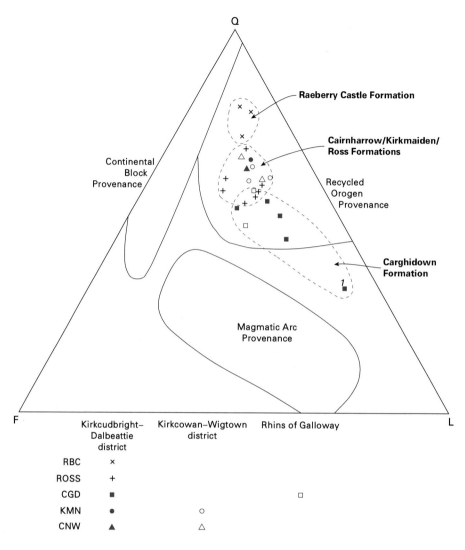

et al. (1987) suggested that the detritus was derived from a marginal carbonate facies following the model of Kemp (1985) who concluded that the bioclastic material originated from fringing reefs in a shallow-marine environment adjacent to the source area. The proportion of carbonate is particularly variable in the Cairnharrow Formation and in the northern parts of the Kirkmaiden Formation (around Fleet Bay) where it may be very low in some units within an overall calcareous-rich sequence. This interdigitation suggests an oscillatory sedimentary transition from the dominantly quartzose wackes of the Gala Group to the calcareous-rich wackes of the generally younger Hawick Group.

Lithic detritus increases from 15% in medium-grained sandstone to more than 50% in very coarse-grained sandstone (lithic arenite) and consists of volcanic rock fragments, polycrystalline quartz grains, granitic detritus and fine-grained sedimentary material. The volcanic clasts are both acidic and basic to intermediate in composition and are highly weathered. The polycrystalline quartz grains consist variously of quartz arenite, intergrown quartz crystals of vein and/or granitic origin and sporadic highly strained quartzites. Coarse-grained intergrowths of quartz and feldspar are almost certainly of granitic origin. Sedimentary rock fragments are mostly of fine-grained siltstone. Red or pink-stained cherty material can be an important constituent at some horizons in the Carghidown Formation.

Detrital 'red micas' are of particular significance in the southern outcrops of the Kirkmaiden Formation, throughout the Carghidown Formation and locally within the Ross Formation. Although only a minor constituent, these micas are visible in hand specimen as coarse-grained flakes orientated parallel to bedding.

The red colour is due to a coating of hematite on the mica flakes and, since there is no evidence for hematisation of the matrix surrounding these grains, it seems likely that they were oxidised in the source area prior to deposition. Accessory minerals include tourmaline, zircon and garnet. Scattered opaque minerals are ubiquitous and include both detrital grains and diagenetic growths.

Compositional variation in the mineralogical content of the Hawick Group wackes is illustrated on the Q–F–L plot of Figure 16, which also includes the provenance fields of Dickinson and Suczek (1979). Apart from one sample from the Carghidown Formation, the Hawick Group shows approximately the same compositional range as does the Gala Group (Figure 12). In general, the Carghidown Formation is the most lithic rich and the unusual sample (S 78229) is a coarser-grained variety which includes a greater proportion of andesitic and acid igneous clasts. The Q–F–L plot also shows data from the Riccarton Group and illustrates the marked change in composition of the Raeberry Castle Formation which is quartz rich (up to 67%) and relatively depleted in lithic clasts.

Cairnharrow Formation (CNW)*

The Cairnharrow Formation is defined in Wigtownshire by Barnes (in prep.) and is bounded by the Innerwell Fault to the south and by the Laurieston Fault to the north. The unit comprises interbedded sequences of quartzose and calcareous wackes and is both lithologically and mineralogically transitional between the Gala and Hawick groups. At least two strike-parallel within-tract faults are known, the Cairnholy and Cambret faults, which merge into the footwall of the Laurieston Fault. The formation is best exposed to the north-east of Gatehouse of Fleet in the ridges between Bengray [6295 5985] and Fell of Laghead [6139 6173], and in the section from the Tarff Water in the vicinity of Kirkconnell Linn [6735 6128] northwards to Edgarton Farm [6712 6374].

Adjacent to the Innerwell Fault in the Barlay Burn [6210 5843], the Cairnharrow Formation is in contact with a deformed sliver of possible Moffat Shale Group. Here the lithologies are dominated by Facies C turbidites in combinations of thin- to medium-bedded T_a and T_{ab} sequences, with a well-developed parallel lamination being typical of most outcrops. To the north-west, an approximately 40 m-thick sequence of Facies D turbidite occurs, consisting of thinly bedded T_c wacke, laminated siltstone, silty mudstone and grey to dark grey mudstone.

The section from the Tarff Water to Edgarton Farm is extensively folded, being dominated by reclined, north-north-east-plunging first-phase folds (F1). In the hanging wall of the Innerwell Fault a 20 m-thick south-younging sequence of thinly bedded T_{bc} wackes and laminated silty mudstone (Facies D) is succeeded to the north by a medium- to thinly bedded sequence of Facies C which includes a thin (10 cm) graptolitic mudstone interbed.

Available palaeocurrent data from flute and groove casts are limited to a few localities within the Edgarton area. However, the dominant axial (north-east) trend from this area is consistent with the south-westerly directed currents determined from directional data in equivalent sequences to the south-west (Stone, 1995).

Three occurrences of thin graptolitic shales interbedded with the turbidites of the Cairnharrow Formation have been recorded from the district: two old Geological Survey collections from Trowdale Glen [7610 6820] and Tarff Glen [6735 6130], and a recently discovered locality at Edgarton Farm [6718 6309]. The graptolite faunas from these localities were discussed in detail by White et al. (1992, pp.301, 304) who suggested a doubtful *turriculatus* Biozone age at Edgarton Farm and a *turriculatus* to *crispus* Biozone age at Trowdale and Tarff. A sample from a thin grey-to-black shale interbedded with turbidites in the Tarff Water, adjacent to the outflow from Loch Mannoch [6666 6094], has yielded an acritarch assemblage in which the forms *Ammonidium listeri* and *Domasia limaciformis* indicate an age equivalent to mid-Aeronian to Telychian (White et al., 1992).

Kirkmaiden Formation (KMN)

The Kirkmaiden Formation is bounded in the north by the Innerwell Fault, includes the within-tract Garlieston Fault, and is transitional into the Carghidown Formation in the south. It is well exposed in the coastal sections from Rough Point in Fleet Bay [5820 5390] to Castle Haven Bay [5932 4830] in Wigtown Bay. In addition to the almost continuous coastal exposure, good inland sections may be examined on the recently forested Kirkconnell Moor [6670 5900] and in the vicinity of Barstobrick Hill [6876 6067].

Representative measured sections from coastal and inland sections are illustrated in Figure 17, a–c. Lithologically the Kirkmaiden Formation is dominated by parallel-sided, thin- to medium-bedded sequences of T_a, T_{ab} and T_{abc} turbidites (Facies C.2.2/C2.3). These turbidite sequences alternate with units of thinly bedded sandstone and silty mudstone up to 8 m thick (Facies D2.1/D2.3); the thin sandstone beds are invariably dominated by cross-lamination (T_c). Additionally, packets of coarser-grained, thickly bedded T_a, T_{ab} and T_{ac} turbidites (Facies B2.1/B2.2) up to 5 m thick occur throughout the sequence. Typically these occur as amalgamated sandstones with no fine-grained interbeds and are interpreted as channel complexes within the overall sheet-flow turbidites. Paleocurrent directions are variable but with some clustering of flow from the north-east.

The boundary between the Kirkmaiden and Carghidown formations is drawn at the most northerly occurrence of interbedded red mudstone in Castle Haven Bay [5932 4830] which coincides with a late, minor north-west-directed thrust. On the Whithorn Peninsula to the west there is no evidence of a structural break and the boundary is interpreted as a conformable transition across a sequence of northward-younging strata. There, the upwards disappearance of red mudstone beds from the Hawick Group sequence shows that Kirkmaiden Formation strata locally overlie the Carghidown Formation and further complicates the stratigraphical and structural relationship (Figure 4).

Graptolites have been collected from an interbed within the Kirkmaiden Formation in a small quarry on the southern flanks of the Towers of Kirkconnell [6654 5868]. Here, a thin black mudstone lamina between turbidites has yielded a fragmented example of a form which resembles *Monograptus tullbergi*. This identification is tentative, and although the age of the specimen is uncertain, a *griestoniensis-crenulata* Biozone age is a possibility. Using better preserved material from black mudstone interbeds in the equivalent of the Kirkmaiden Formation in Wigtownshire, White et al. (1992) concluded that the turbidites belong to the *griestoniensis* Biozone, possibly the upper part. The Towers of Kirkconnell graptolite locality and a sample from the foreshore near Corseyard [5858 4869] yielded an acritarch fauna suggesting a Telychian (late-Llandovery) age.

Carghidown Formation (CGD)

The Carghidown Formation is bounded by the Ross Bay Fault in the south and is well exposed in the almost

---

* Letters in brackets refer to codes used on 1:50 000 series map.

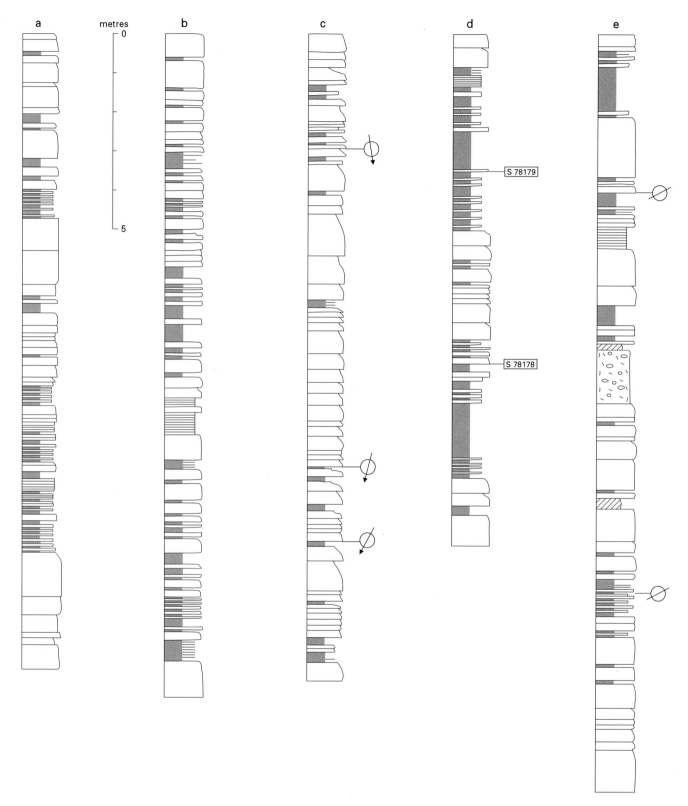

Figure 17 Representative measured sections for formations in the Hawick Group.

Kirkmaiden Formation	**a** Murray's Isles	[5629 5032]	Ross Formation	**g** Meikle Ross	[6436 4369]
	b Barlocco	[5814 4880]		**h** Meikle Ross	[6561 4395]
	c Dow Craig Hill	[6533 5964]		**i** Castlehill Point	[8526 5242]
Carghidown Formation	**d** Harrison's Bay	[6154 4493]			
	e Mull Point	[6363 4455]			
	f Boreland of Kelton	[7845 5705]			

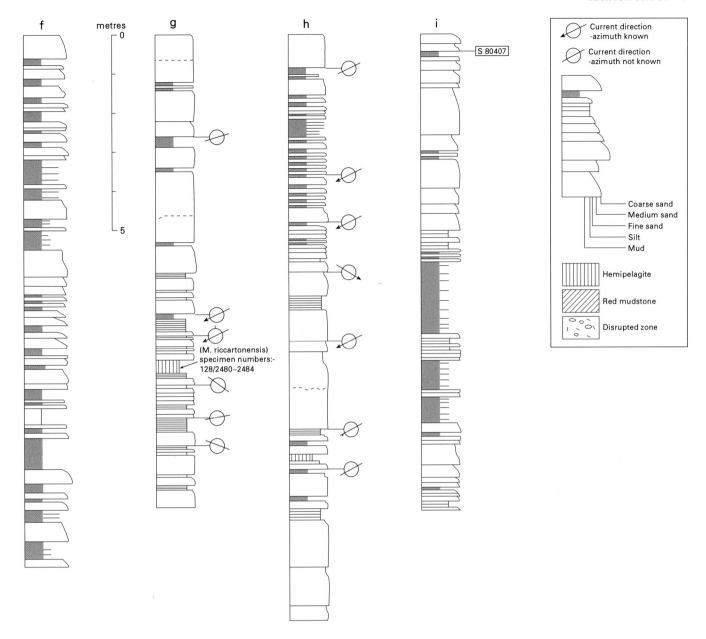

f   metres   g   h   i

Figure 17 *(continued)*.

continuous Kirkcudbrightshire shore section. Good inland exposures of the formation can be seen in the ridges formed by the metamorphic aureoles of the Bengairn Pluton on Suie Hill [7657 5083] and Screel Hill [7825 5530] and of the main Criffel–Dalbeattie Pluton in the ground between Craigton Hill [7952 5940] and Barskeoch Hill [8150 6160]. No graptolites have been recovered from the Carghidown Formation of the district, though from equivalent sequences in the Eskdalemuir area 50 km to the north-east, White et al. (1992) suggested a late Llandovery/earliest Wenlock age (*crenulata* Biozone to *centrifugus* Biozone) for the formation. Acritarch assemblages identified in specimens collected in the Eskdalemuir area and from several localities in the Carghidown Formation on the west and east

sides of Kirkcudbright Bay are also consistent with a late-Llandovery (late-Telychian) age (White et al., 1992). All the above biostratigraphical evidence is compatible with the overall tectonostratigraphical position of the formation (Figure 4).

Representative measured sections from the coastal and inland exposures are illustrated in Figure 17, d–f. In common with the Kirkmaiden Formation, the Carghidown Formation is dominated by parallel-sided beds forming thin- to medium-bedded turbidite sequences of Facies C2.2 and C2.3, with subordinate units, typically 1–2 m thick, of thinly bedded sandstone and laminated silty mudstone of Facies D.2.1/D2.3. Packets of coarse-grained, thickly bedded sandstone (Facies B2.1/B2.2) occur throughout but are less common than in the Kirkmaiden Formation. Palaeocurrent indicators are predominantly axial (towards both north-east and south-west), but with a significant component of flow to the north-west.

The red silty mudstone beds which are used to distinguish between the Carghidown and Kirkmaiden formations are thin and rare in the northern part of the outcrop. They become more common southwards and attain their maximum individual thickness of up to 6 m in the section from Mull Point [6350 4463] to Fauldbog Bay [6410 4445] where they form the local base of the sequence adjacent to the Ross Bay Fault. Here the red beds are internally structureless, laterally persistent and interbedded with sandstone and grey-green silty mudstone.

In the coastal section from Dove Cave [6040 4605] southwards, the coherent, parallel-sided turbidite sequences pass abruptly into a sequence which includes discrete zones of tectonised soft-sediment disruption features (Facies F2.1) up to 10 m thick. Coherent sequences rarely exceed 30 m thickness in this disrupted portion of the Carghidown Formation and, because biostratigraphical resolution is poor within this unit, it is impossible to estimate the total thickness of the sequence. The occurrence and significance of these disrupted zones have been highlighted by Knipe and Needham (1986), Kemp (1987a) and Knipe et al. (1988) and they are interpreted to have initially formed as zones of décollement between large masses of slumped sediment. Since the movement planes along which these early structures were generated have acted as the loci for later tectonic deformation, they are discussed in more detail in Chapter 5.

Ross Formation (ROSS)

The Ross Formation is bounded in the north by the Ross Bay Fault and in the south by the Balmae Burn Fault. Lithologically the Ross Formation is similar to the Carghidown Formation but is characterised by the appearance of thin but distinctive beds of laminated fossiliferous silty mudstone which Kemp (1985; 1987b) has interpreted as hemipelagites.

The nature of the junction between the Carghidown Formation and the Ross Formation and the relative ages of the two sequences have been controversial (e.g. Clarkson et al., 1975) but the detailed biostratigraphical work of Kemp and White (1985) and White et al. (1992) leaves no doubt that the Ross Formation is younger than the Carghidown Formation.

The crux of the debate now rests on whether:

a. the boundary is a gradational sedimentary change through a transitional facies which includes interbedded red mudstone and hemipelagite (Craig and Walton, 1959; Warren, 1964; Clarkson et al., 1975; Barnes, 1989).

or b. The contact is tectonic and the transitional zone is the result of tectonic interleaving of the two formations (Rust, 1965; Kemp, 1985; 1986).

The critical exposures in the low-lying, drift covered area of Fauldbog Bay [6450 4450] are discontinuous and the available evidence is equivocal, though Clarkson et al. (1975) clearly recognised at least some interbedding of red mudstone and hemipelagite. In this memoir the boundary is regarded as a faulted conformable contact with a transitional facies identified between Fauldbog Bay [643 443], Ross Bay [655 449] and Shaw Hole [655 455].

As defined, the Ross Formation is the equivalent of the Riccarton Beds (Craig and Walton, 1959; Rust, 1965) and the Riccarton Group (Pringle, 1948). In the Hawick area to the north-east, the Ross Formation is equivalent to the Stob's Castle Beds, the Shankend Beds and the Penchrise Burn Beds as defined by Warren (1964).

Representative lithological logs from the Ross Formation are shown in Figure 17, g–i. In common with the Kirkmaiden and Carghidown formations, the Ross Formation is dominated by thin- to medium-bedded turbidites of Facies C2.2 and C2.3, interbedded with thinly bedded sandstone and laminated silty mudstone units of Facies D2.1 and D2.3. Sporadic packets of medium- to coarse-grained, thickly bedded sandstone (Facies B2.1/B2.2) occur throughout the sequence as do slumped units (Facies F2.1) similar to the disrupted portions of the Carghidown Formation. The graptolitic, dark grey laminated siltstone (hemipelagites of Facies G2) which characterises this formation typically occur either as 0.1–1.5 m-thick interbeds alternating with sandstone/silty mudstone couplets of Facies C or as thin (0.1–10 cm) laminae in Facies D. These associations are illustrated in sections g and h of Figure 17. The siltstone laminae are locally disrupted by bioturbation and can occur as rip-up clasts in overlying sandstone.

Palaeocurrent directions are predominantly axial, from the north-east, with a small but significant component of transverse currents from the north-west. A similar distribution of palaeocurrents was noted by Scott (1967) in a detailed analysis of sole structures from the sandstone beds in the Ross Formation at Torrs Point [6727 4490]. Based on the lithological and sedimentological characteristics, Kemp (1985; 1987b) has suggested a simple sheet fan model associated with the development of channel/levee complexes.

Kemp (1985; 1987b) has highlighted the difficulties of reconstructing depositional environments of the late Llandovery/early Wenlock turbidites (Carghidown and Ross formations) because of the highly disrupted (imbricated) nature of the sequence. For the same reason and because the degree of stratigraphical repetition is not known, thickness and sedimentation rates are difficult to estimate.

The Ross Formation is the youngest unit in the Hawick Group and ranges in age from the *centrifugus* Biozone, at the base of the Wenlock Series, to the highest subdivision of the *riccartonensis* Biozone (Kemp and White, 1985). A full discussion of the graptolite faunas and palynomorphs collected from the Ross Formation of the district is given in White et al. (1992). The faunas were collected from laminated carbonaceous siltstones (hemipelagites of Kemp, 1986).

The *centrifugus* Biozone has been recognised from 12 localities around Kirkcudbright Bay, Ross Bay, Fauldbog Bay and Meikle Ross. Faunas include the zone fossil and monoclimacids of the *vomerina* group, with rare *Barrandeographtus? bornholmensis*. A variety of acritarch forms have been identified in samples from the *centrifugus* Biozone and the assemblage is typical of low Wenlock (low Sheinwoodian). Despite excellent coastal exposures, no firm evidence for the presence of the *murchisoni* Biozone has been found. This may not preclude its presence since in both the Howgill Fells and Lake District successions the biozone is only of the order of 3 m thick (Rickards, 1969).

Hemipelagite beds with graptolite faunas indicative of the *riccartonensis* Biozone have been identified from 33 localities around Kirkcudbright Bay. Detailed study of the faunal assemblages has demonstrated a three-fold subdivision of the biozone in the Ross Formation, comparable to that recognised by Rickards in the Howgill Fells (1967) and the Lake District (1969). *Monograptus riccartonensis* is characteristically abundant throughout the biozone. In the lowest subdivision it is associated with *M. priodon*, which is absent in the middle subdivision. *M. firmus sedberghensis* and *Pristiograptus* cf. *dubius* make their earliest appearance in the upper subdivision. The degree of resolution afforded by this three-fold subdivision of the *riccartonensis* Biozone provides a powerful tool for the recognition of folded and thrust sequences in the Ross Formation of the east side of Kirkcudbright Bay. The preservation, abundance and diversity of acritarch forms decreases in the *riccartonensis* Biozone and, other than an indication of a Wenlock age, no stratigraphically diagnostic assemblage has been recognised. Derived early to mid-Ordovician forms have been identified in one sample from Torrs Point [6727 4490].

RICCARTON GROUP (RCN)

The Riccarton Group is bounded to the north by the Balmae Burn Fault and is unconformably overlain by Lower Carboniferous sandstones in the south. From a detailed study of the rich graptolite faunas in the interbedded hemipelagite beds, White et al. (1992), proved a Wenlock age, ranging from the upper *riccartonensis* Biozone to the *lundgreni* Biozone

In the Kirkcudbright–Dalbeattie district, the Riccarton Group is represented by the Raeberry Castle Formation, which can be correlated with the Upper and Lower Caddroun Burn Beds of the Hawick area (Warren, 1964). The Riccarton Group of the Kirkcudbright area was the subject of a detailed study by Kemp (1985; 1986; 1987b) who calculated the thickness of the group in the district to be about 900 m.

Raeberry Castle Formation (RBC)

In marked contrast to the relatively monotonous sequences of classical turbidites and massive sandstones of the Hawick Group, the Raeberry Castle Formation is characterised by a very diverse association of turbidite facies deposited in a range of depositional environments. These facies associations range from: channelised ruditearenite (Facies A and B); fine-grained, thinly bedded silty

mudstone (Facies D and E); classical thin- to medium-bedded turbidites (Facies C and D); sequences dominated by hemipelagite sediment (Facies G) up to 25 m thick. Rare thin metabentonites have been noted towards the top of the sequence (Kemp, 1985).

The modal composition data for the Raeberry Castle Formation is given in Appendix 2 and summarised as histograms in Figure 11g. The sandstones are fine-, medium- and coarse-grained and compositionally calcareous and quartz rich (up to 67%). The carbonate content, which occurs mainly as matrix, cement and detrital grains, rarely exceeds 30% and is generally lower than in the Hawick Group. In the coarser-grained sandstones, bioclastic material includes recognisable coral, bryozoan and brachiopod fragments. The feldspar content varies from 5% to approximately 10%, with K-feldspar usually more abundant than plagioclase.

Lithic detritus is less varied than in the Hawick Group, sandstones being dominated by quartz, feldspar and matrix material. Igneous clasts are rare and consist of highly altered andesitic grains. However, in the coarser-grained pebbly sandstones, lithic clasts are a significant component and consist of chert, quartzite and both calcareous and non-calcareous wacke. The latter are probably of intra-basinal origin, with some of the clasts notably containing the red hematite-coated micas which are typical of the Hawick Group wackes. Compositional variation within the Raeberry Castle Formation is shown on the Q–F–L plot of Figure 16.

The distinctive dark grey to black, finely laminated fossiliferous siltstone beds which characterise the Raeberry Castle Formation have been studied in detail by Kemp (1985) who concluded that they represent intra-turbidite hemipelagite deposits. The lamination consists of alternating layers of organic material (probably algal), terrigenous clay and silt with minor sand. The clay component has been identified as illite and chlorite while the silt/sand-grade material consists of angular to subangular quartz grains with subordinate feldspar. Framboidal pyrite and dolomite nodules of diagenetic origin are locally abundant, particularly in the thicker hemipelagite sequences which appear to have been deposited in an anoxic/sulphidic environment of low bottom water oxicity. The lack of significant bioturbation of the silt/fine sand laminae would support such an interpretation. Organic carbon content varies from 0.53% to 0.82% (Kemp, 1985). Similar hemipelagite lithologies of Wenlock age and younger have been noted in the Windermere Supergroup (Brathay Formation) of the Lake District (Kneller et al., 1994) and in the Benarth Formation and Nantglyn Flags Group in Wales (Dimberline et al., 1990). This series of anoxic events was thus widespread in most of the major basins bordering Iapetus during this period and may have been related to sluggish oceanic circulation caused by contemporary global climatic-eustatic conditions.

In his detailed analysis of the sedimentology and structure of the Raeberry Castle Formation, Kemp (1985; 1986; 1987b) divided the sequence into three, partly

Table 6 Tectonostratigraphy of the Riccarton Group. Subdivisions of the Raeberry Castle Formation (modified from Kemp, 1987b).

GP   Gipsy Point Member;
RA   Raeberry Member;
MB   Mullock Bay Member.

Series	Graptolite Biozone		Formation	Group
Ludlow				
Wenlock	*ludensis*		Raeberry Castle	Riccarton
	lundgreni	MB		
	ellesae			
	linnarssoni			
	rigidus	GP RA		
	antennularius			
	riccartonensis			
	murchisoni			
	centrifugus			
Llandovery	*crenulata*			

Sandstone   Conglomerate   Shale

coeval tectonostratigraphical units, here named as members (Table 6).

Gipsy Point Member   The basal division of this member consists of 230 m of Facies C and D turbidites which are overlain by an upper division of about 420 m of arenites, rudites and slump sheets (Facies A and F). These form channels which cut down into overbank or levee deposits represented by thin-bedded, fine-grained sandstones with siltstones and mudstones (Facies C and D). Good outcrops of the meandering channel-levee complex with its associated slump sheets and dewatering structures, including spectacular sand volcanos up to 3 m in diameter, are exposed at Gipsy Point (Walton, 1968; Lovell, 1974; Kemp, 1985; 1987b).

Raeberry Member   Graptolite faunas from interbedded hemipelagites (Kemp and White, 1985; White et al., 1992) indicate that the Raeberry Member is coeval with the Gipsy Point Member, within the precision of the zonation. The Raeberry Member can be subdivided on the basis of turbidite facies type and palaeocurrent variation into lower, middle and upper divisions. The lower division is 256 m thick and consists of a sequence of thin- to medium-bedded turbidites (Facies C and D) with sporadic hemipelagite horizons. Isolated thick beds of medium- to fine-grained sandstones occur throughout. Palaeocurrent data reflect variable current directions but show a dominant derivation of material from the west or south-west. Kemp (1985; 1987b) interpreted this litholog-ical association as typical of depositional-lobe facies within a submarine fan. A representative lithological log is shown in Figure 18, section b.

The middle division of the Raeberry Member consists of a 44 m-thick sequence of thin-bedded, fine- to medium-grained, base-absent turbidites (T_{cde}) with hemipelagite interbeds typical of deposition on the marginal or distal parts of a submarine fan. Palaeocurrents are predominantly from the north-west.

The upper division of the Raeberry Unit consists of 418 m of thin- to medium-bedded, medium- to coarse-grained, base-absent (T_{bc}) turbidites with thin hemipelagite laminae. Large-scale cross-lamination (dune structures) are typical of sandstones near the top of the sequence. Palaeocurrent data from erosional features on the base of sandstone beds (flute casts) indicate dominant flow from the south-west, whereas depositional (or reworking) currents, as determined from ripples formed at the top of turbidite units, indicate flow from the north-west (Craig and Walton, 1962; Scott, 1967). In a single bed the erosional and depositional/reworking flows are typically orthogonal to each other. The same geometrical relationship of within-turbidite flow was noted by Kneller et al. (1991) in the Winder-mere Supergroup of the English Lake District. Because the flow directions measured by Kneller et al. (1991) showed consistent variation within the same turbidite, they rejected meandering flow as a likely cause and inter-preted the variation as resulting from oblique reflection of the turbidity currents. Such changes in flow direction could result from flow within a confined basin where turbidity currents are reflected from the basin margins.

Kemp (1987b) interpreted the upper division of the Raeberry Member as a channel-mouth facies formed by rapid deposition of sediment load from meandering flows emerging from confined channels. The channel complex at Gipsy Point could represent such a source.

Mullock Bay Member   This member consists of lower and upper divisions (Kemp, 1987b). The lower division is 228 m thick and consists of channelised arenites and rudites (Facies A and B) interbedded with fine-grained, thinly bedded sandstone, siltstone and mudstone (Facies

Figure 18 Representative measured sections for the Raeberry Castle Formation, Riccarton Group.

a Mullock Bay Member (lower division), Mullock Bay
7160 4370
b Raeberry Member (lower division), Rob's Craig
7065 4355

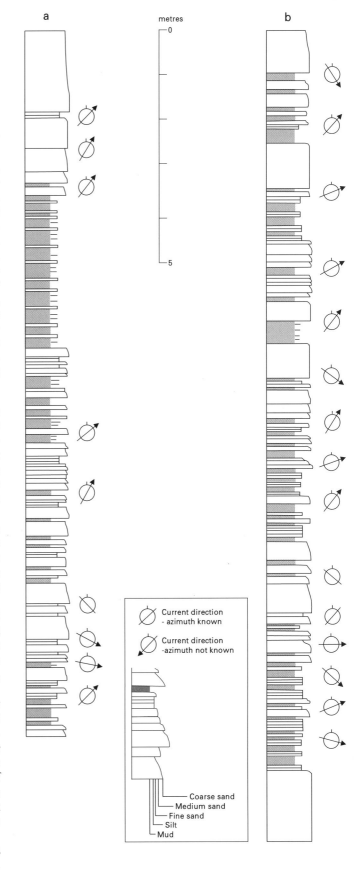

C and D). This facies association is similar to that at Gipsy Point and is compatible with deposition in a channel/levee/overbank system. Palaeocurrent data indicate a dominantly axial flow, mainly from the south-west. A representative lithological log is shown in Figure 18, section a. The upper division of the Mullock Bay Member is 346 m thick and consists of packets of thickening- and coarsening-upward cycles which commence with thin bedded mudstone and hemipelagite (Facies D, E and G). These are succeeded by thin- to medium-bedded turbidites (Facies C and D) and the cycle is completed by fine- to medium-grained, thick-bedded T_c, T_b and T_{ae} sandstones (Facies B). Kemp (1987b) interpreted this cyclicity as the transition from a basin-plain system (represented by the hemipelagite to mudstone sequence) to a prograding fan or lobe-fringe environment. Palaeocurrent data indicate transport mainly from the south-west (Kemp, 1987b).

AGE   The Raeberry Castle Formation ranges in age from the highest subdivision of the *riccartonensis* Biozone to the *lundgreni* Biozone (White et al., 1992). The *antennularius* Biozone has been identified in the Gipsy Point Member to the west of Balmae Burn [6825 4398] where the zone fossil occurs with *Pristiograptus meneghinii*. The *rigidus* Biozone occurs in the Raeberry Member between Howwell Bay and Mullock Bay [7063 4356; 7100 4390] where *Cyrtograptus* cf. *rigidus rigidus* is associated with *Monograptus flexilis* aff. *belophorus*. The *linnarssoni* Biozone has been proved in the Gipsy Point Member in hemipelagite at Balmae Burn [6835 4378]. In addition to the zone fossil, the fauna includes *Cyrtograptus* cf. *rigidus cautleyensis* and *Monograptus flexilis* aff. *flexilis*.

The *Cyrtograptus ellesae* Biozone has not been recorded from the Raeberry Castle Formation of the district but it could be represented by unfossiliferous strata. The biozone has not been found in equivalent sequences to the north-east at Langholm (Lumsden et al., 1967) nor, with certainty, in the Hawick area (Warren, 1964).

Graptolite-bearing horizons in the Mullock Bay Member in the vicinity of Netherlaw Point e.g. [7185 4340] have yielded specimens of *Pristiograptus pseudodubius*, *Monograptus flemingii* and *Monoclimacis flumendosae kingi* which White et al. (1992) regarded as indicating the *lundgreni* Biozone. According to the range charts of Verniers et al. (1995), the occurrence of the chitinozoan *Cingulochitina cingulata* in the Mullock Bay Member at Netherlaw Point [7158 4340] is consistent with the *lundgreni* Biozone age indicated by the graptolites.

Palynomorphs have been identified in all the samples examined from the Raeberry Castle Formation. Acritarchs are rare in the lower part of the formation but become more abundant and diverse from the *linnarssoni*

Biozone. The acritarch assemblages recorded from these sequences by White et al. (1992), suggests a Sheinwoodian age, consistent with the graptolite dating. In common with the Ross Formation, a specimen of an early Ordovician acritarch (*Acanthodiacrodium* sp.) has been identified from the Raeberry Member at a locality near Little Raeberry [7046 4356]. The distribution of spore material within the Raeberry Castle Formation shows a distinct increase in the number and taxonomic diversity from the *riccartonensis* to the *lundgreni* biozones. The palaeogeographical significance of this change is unclear, but White et al. (1992), while recognising that there was a world-wide diversification and rapid evolution of land plants in the late Wenlock, suggested that the variation probably reflected increased terrestrial input to the source sediments following the restriction of the basin of deposition during the late stages of closure of the Iapetus Ocean.

A calcareous sandstone from the Gipsy Point Member at Gipsy Point [6850 4360] yielded a small number of conodont elements. The presence of *Dapsilodus praecipuus* is consistent with a latest Llandovery/Wenlock age (Aldridge and Jeppsson, 1984) and the forms recorded are particularly characteristic of offshore (outer shelf and slope) facies in the Llandovery and Wenlock of the Welsh Basin (written communication, Aldridge, 1996).

FIVE

Caledonian structure and metamorphism

The Ordovician and Silurian wackes of the Southern Uplands Terrane were laid down as huge submarine fans, initially onto a floor of black shale (Moffat Shale Group), in a basin at or close to the northern margin of the Iapetus Ocean (Leggett et al., 1979; Stone et al., 1986). This ocean was actively closing during this period and biostratigraphical evidence (Chapter 4) suggests that the partly lithified sediments were deformed as numerous individual thrust-bounded slices soon after deposition and sequentially accreted against the northern continent of Laurentia (Leggett et al., 1979; Stone et al., 1987). The Iapetus Ocean finally closed in late Silurian times, when the tectonised terrane was progressively obducted onto the leading edges of Laurentia and the southern continent of Avalonia. Throughout the period of closure the tectonic regime in the Southern Uplands Terrane was driven by north-west directed subduction, initially orthogonal but with an increasing component of sinistral shear as the two continents approached final collision (Barnes et al., 1989). This ongoing compression progressively produced the steep dips, complex folding and regional tectonic/burial metamorphic signature which are such characteristic features of the terrane. The intrusive history includes several dyke swarms which were emplaced contemporaneously with deformation during the Silurian, and culminated in the late Silurian to early Devonian with emplacement of the large granitic plutons. The latter were essentially post-tectonic and superimposed a thermal metamorphic overprint on their host rocks (Figure 19).

Tectonic uplift of the Lower Palaeozoic rocks, associated with the granite plutonism, was accompanied by rapid erosion during which the coarse-grained clastic red-beds of the Devonian Lower Old Red Sandstone were deposited in many parts of Scotland, though none are known

at outcrop within the district. Beginning in the late Devonian, a thin sequence of terrestrial red beds and lavas was deposited with marked unconformity on the eroded Lower Palaeozoic rocks. The volcanic rocks were succeeded by an early Carboniferous terrestrial and shallow-marine succession laid down in the north-east-trending, fault-bounded Solway Basin, whose depocentre lay to the south of the district. These strata were in turn gently folded and/or tilted during the late Carboniferous and early Permian. Subsequent extension caused reactivation of some of the Lower Palaeozoic faults forming graben in which late Permian and Triassic rocks were deposited. Although later tilted by small amounts, the latter strata have remained essentially undeformed.

SOUTHERN UPLANDS TERRANE

During the primary geological survey of the Southern Uplands in the 1870s, difficulties were experienced in interpreting the complex folding apparent in the coastal sections, whilst the absence of a clear stratigraphical framework gave little appreciation of the overall structure of the region. Interpretations made in the early survey work were quickly superseded by Lapworth's regional biostratigraphical correlation based on graptolite faunas (Lapworth, 1889). In this model, the succession was thought to be relatively thin but repeated by complex isoclinal folding, with the overall structure interpreted as an anticlinorium/synclinorium pair. This basic structural model became widely accepted and was

Figure 19 Geochronological framework of tectonomagmatic events in the Southern Uplands thrust belt (cf. Barnes et al., 1989).

Age of post-tectonic plutons:
Carsphairn: 410 ± 4 Ma, Rb–Sr, Thirlwall (1988)
Loch Doon: 408 ± 2 Ma, Rb–Sr, Halliday et al. (1980)
Fleet: 392 ±2 Ma, Rb–Sr, Halliday et al. (1980)
Criffel: 397 ± 2 Ma, Rb–Sr, Halliday et al. (1980)
Dyke ages (range): 425–395 Ma, Rb–Sr and K–Ar, Barnes et al. (1986)

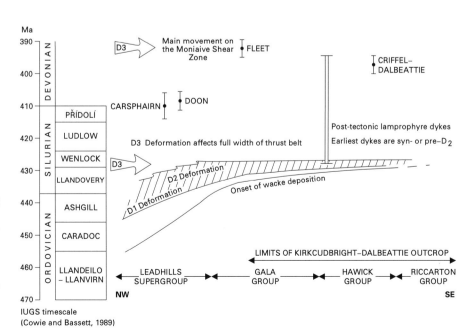

adopted with only minor modifications by Peach and Horne (1899).

Little reinterpretation of the structure of the region was attempted until Craig and Walton (1959), using sedimentary way-up evidence, were able to demonstrate that the anticlinorium–synclinorium model was inconsistent with the predominantly northward-younging strata of the Hawick Group in the Kirkcudbright area. To account for this, Craig and Walton interpreted the major structure as a series of fault-bounded, northward-facing monoclines consisting of alternating flat and steep belts. This model was accepted and embellished by Rust (1965), Weir (1968) and Cook and Weir (1979) in adjacent areas, suggesting up to five phases of folding. Subsequently, Stringer and Treagus (1980; 1981) suggested that the structure was actually relatively simple, with only two main phases of deformation. This view has been supported by more recent work (Knipe and Needham, 1986; Kemp, 1987a; Barnes, 1989; Barnes et al., 1989; Needham 1993).

Analysis of the stratigraphy and structure of the Southern Uplands over the last two decades has broadly been in agreement as to the nature of the regional structure, although a limited range of possible tectono-stratigraphical models have evolved. Following an early attempt by Dewey (1971) to place the Southern Uplands into a plate tectonic setting, the first integrated tectono-stratigraphical model (McKerrow et al., 1977; Leggett et al., 1979; 1982) interpreted the evolution of the terrane in terms of an accretionary complex developed at the northern margin of the Iapetus Ocean. This model has proved very robust (Stringer and Treagus, 1980; 1981; Kemp, 1985; 1986; Knipe and Needham, 1986; Needham and Knipe, 1986) and is still favoured by many authors (Needham, 1993). However, it apparently cannot account for all the observed features in the Southern Uplands Terrane, particularly palaeocurrent and provenance data (Chapter 4). Alternative models (Murphy and Hutton, 1986; Stone et al., 1986; 1987; Morris, 1987) concur with the previous model in regarding the overall structure as a south-west-vergent imbricate thrust stack but they offer different interpretations of the tectonic setting and, to a limited extent, timing of deformation. Deformation of a Silurian successor basin to an Ordovician accretionary prism was proposed by Murphy and Hutton (1986), whereas Stone et al. (1986; 1987) suggested closure of a back-arc basin and the generation of a southerly prograding foreland basin. However, the geometry of the finite structure is compatible with each of these possible models and cannot, given the present level of understanding of the structural processes operating at active convergent margins, be used to satisfactorily constrain, let alone prove, the efficacy of any one particular model.

Regional structural pattern

The Ordovician and Silurian turbidite sequences of the Southern Uplands are typically steeply dipping to vertical, north-east- to east-north-east-striking, and generally young northwards in a series of fault-bounded tectonostratigraphical tracts (Figure 4). In northern and central parts of the Southern Uplands, including the north-western part of the Kirkcudbright–Dalbeattie district, the bounding fault-traces are marked by discontinuous slivers of the thin, but usually fossiliferous Moffat Shale Group (Chapter 4) preserved beneath the turbidite sequence. In some tracts the minimum biostratigraphical age of the Moffat Shale is the only indication of the maximum age of the turbidite sequence. Where faunas are available from within a turbidite sequence, they usually represent a single biozone, either equivalent to the youngest fauna within the underlying Moffat Shale Group or one zone younger. Such biostratigraphical evidence defines a sequential decrease in the age of the turbidite sequence from north to south across the Southern Uplands (Figure 4). The change at the base of the sequence from tract to tract may simply be a result of progradation and thus may have no particular tectonic significance. However, the parallel temporal curtailment of the sequence in each tract suggests a tectonic mechanism, most probably the effective southwards propagation of the thrust front into progressively younger strata contemporaneously with continuing deposition to the south (Leggett et al., 1979; Stone et al., 1987). This progressive accretion of new material may have been responsible for much of the rotation of the system into its present, near-vertical orientation, subsequently completed by collisional processes as the Iapetus Ocean finally closed.

REGIONAL (D$_1$) DEFORMATION

Early movement on thrusts propagated at a low angle to stratigraphy, some of which eventually became the present tract-bounding faults, was probably associated with the only phase of ductile deformation (D$_1$) to have affected many of the rocks in the Southern Uplands. From the biostratigraphical arguments above, it is likely that this was diachronous, becoming younger southwards. D$_1$ is most commonly expressed as a penetrative cleavage (S$_1$) in fine-grained rocks, although this can be locally quite weak. Folds, typically gently plunging, tight to isoclinal structures, were variably developed with long homoclinal sections across-strike, usually of steeply inclined north-younging strata, interspersed with highly folded zones. This variation in structural style is, at least in part, related to the nature of the strata, with thickly bedded, massive wacke less likely to have been folded than more thinly bedded strata. Slickensides or slickenfibres in thin veins along bedding surfaces, perpendicular to the fold axial orientation, demonstrate flexural slip.

S$_1$ is widely developed as a slaty cleavage in the fine-grained, muddy lithologies congruous with the folds but commonly varying either in dip or strike from being truly axial planar. Cleavage is rarely apparent macroscopically in sandstone, except in parts of the Hawick Group where it is relatively pervasive and may be strongly refracted through graded beds. A pervasive foliation is also present in the Moniaive Shear Zone, although its association with S$_1$ is unclear (see below). Significant variation in the dip of the cleavage from that of the fold axial surface may cause bedding to be downward facing, other than in the immediate vicinity of fold hinge zones. This is particularly apparent in overturned, south-dipping beds where cleavage commonly dips more steeply than bedding. As a consequence of this effect, the assessment of way-up or vergence from bedding-cleavage relationships is generally unreliable in the Southern Uplands. S_1 typically contains the fold axial orientation in the northern part of the Southern Uplands but begins to transect the fold axis by up to $10°$ clockwise in central parts. This effect becomes commonplace throughout the Hawick Group due to systematic divergence between the strike of the cleavage and that of the fold axial surface (cf. Anderson, 1987). The development of the transecting cleavage within the D_1 stress system has been the subject of a variety of studies and explanations (Stringer and Treagus, 1980; Gray, 1981; Sanderson et al., 1985).

Individual tectonostratigraphical tracts are usually characterised by subtle variations in the style, orientation and intensity of D_1 folding (Barnes et al., 1989; Stone 1995; and below). D_1 deformation was particularly intense in the generally finer-grained, more calcareous rocks of the Hawick Group in the southern part of the Southern Uplands, where it is associated with the highest grades of regional metamorphism (see below).

POST-D_1 DEFORMATION

The extent and character of post-D_1 deformation varies widely across the Southern Uplands. In the south, post-D_1 folding and development of crenulation cleavage is most widespread in parts of the Hawick Group. Here, minor to mesoscale, inclined and recumbent D_2 folds, commonly seen to refold D_1 structures, are associated with a more widely developed, flat-lying crenulation cleavage. D_1 and D_2 structures are coaxial and apparently formed as parts of the same tectonic event.

Steeply plunging sinistral folds are developed locally, usually in narrow zones of shearing adjacent to tract bounding faults and therefore probably associated with reactivation of these structures (Barnes et al., 1989). The relationships of these folds to D_2 are ambiguous (Barnes et al., 1989; Stone, 1995) and suggest various episodes of sinistral shear. Such folds are the only post-D_1 deformation usually apparent in northern and central parts of the Southern Uplands.

The Moniaive Shear Zone (Barnes et al., 1995; Phillips et al., 1995) is a zone of high strain kinematically similar to, but much more extensive than, the narrow shear zones associated with tract-bounding faults. The zone is up to 5 km wide and affects mainly the older parts of the Gala Group for about 100 km parallel to the regional strike through the central part of the Southern Uplands. It is characterised by the intermittent development of a pervasive foliation near-parallel to bedding, locally with a strong linear component and commonly transposing all original structure. Strain within the shear zone is very variable (Phillips, 1992; Phillips et al., 1995) but a variety of kinematic indicators consistently show a sinistral sense of shear. Because the shear-zone fabric is subparallel to the relatively weak S_1 cleavage outwith the shear zone, the two can only rarely be differentiated and unequivocal relative age relationships are difficult to establish. Cordierite porphyroblasts, widely distributed throughout the thermal metamorphic aureole of the early Devonian (about 390 Ma — Chapter 6) Cairnsmore of Fleet Pluton, are

deformed by the shear-zone foliation but the latter is generally overprinted by the biotite hornfelsing and later stages of the thermal metamorphism, closely constraining the timing of the final part of its development. Relatively high grades of regional metamorphism in the zone (see below) indicate that it formed at depth. Barnes et al. (1995) suggested that the Moniaive Shear Zone is a composite feature, representing progressive but intermittent sinistral deformation over a long time period from its initiation during D_1 until the early Devonian.

CROSS-STRIKE FAULTS

North-west- and north-trending faults, usually with an original dextral and sinistral component of movement respectively, are common throughout the Southern Uplands and are well displayed in the district. Their conjugate orientations and movement directions indicate that they formed as a brittle response to north-north-west compression and/or east-north-east (along strike) tension. They were probably initiated during the late Silurian because they were utilised by post-D_1 dyke swarms (see above) and are usually cut by the c.400 Ma granitic intrusions. Locally, some faults affect the hornfels aureoles around the granite intrusions which may be a result of reactivation during later tectonic episodes.

Such reactivation is shown, for example, by the important set of north-west-trending faults, the principal members of which define a system of 20–30 km-broad horst/graben structures across the Southern Uplands (Stone et al., 1995, fig. 4) and control many of the extensional basins containing Permo-Carboniferous outliers in the Southern Uplands. These faults, in conjunction with segments of the northeast-trending tract-bounding faults, allowed differential uplift of blocks, as shown by the juxtaposition of rocks of quite different metamorphic grades.

Structure of the district

Resurvey of the district concentrated on coastal sections in the west and south and in the better-exposed inland areas in the north-west and around the fringes of the Criffel–Dalbeattie Pluton. Description of the structure given below is based on the study of these areas. However, it is apparent from previous work and through along-strike correlation to the west (Barnes et al., 1987) that the structure of the resurveyed areas is probably representative of the district as a whole. Recent studies of the southern parts of the district by Kemp (1987a) and Needham (1993) give more local detail on the structure.

The structure is described in five structural domains (Figure 20), defined primarily on differences in the style, frequency and plunge of the first fold structures, although these also reflect variation in the nature of post-D_1 deformation.

DOMAIN 1 GALA GROUP

This domain encompasses the turbidites of the Gala Group in the north-western part of the district. It extends across several tracts separated by strike-parallel faults which are marked by discontinuous inliers of Moffat Shale Group. Bedding is consistently NNE striking, very

Figure 20
Structural
domains in the
district, areas
mapped in detail
and illustrated
by stereograms
in Figure 21, and
location of
structural
sections on
Figure 22.

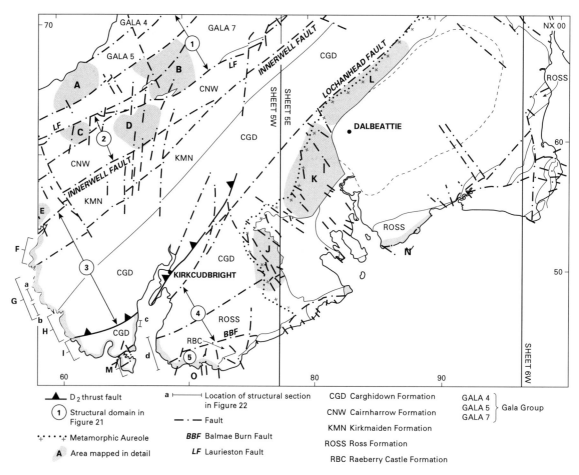

▲—▲ D_2 thrust fault

① Structural domain in
    Figure 21

+⁺·⁺·⁺ Metamorphic Aureole

A Area mapped in detail

a ⊢————⊣ Location of structural section
            in Figure 22

—·—·— Fault

BBF Balmae Burn Fault

LF Laurieston Fault

CGD Carghidown Formation

CNW Cairnharrow Formation

KMN Kirkmaiden Formation

ROSS Ross Formation

RBC Raeberry Castle Formation

GALA 4 ⎫
GALA 5 ⎬ Gala Group
GALA 7 ⎭

steep north or south dipping to vertical (Figure 21A, B), and dominantly youngs northwards. D_1 folds are few, upright and shallow to moderately plunging and generally are very tight to isoclinal in form. Cleavage, close to axial planar, is variably developed and typically only present in mudstone and the finer-grained parts of sandstone beds.

Cleavage increases in intensity towards the north-west, becoming pervasive in rocks close to the margin of the Cairnsmore of Fleet Pluton. However, this is a consequence of the gradational passage into the superimposed high-strain regime of the Moniaive Shear Zone (see above), the development of the shear-zone fabric being the only significant post-D_1 structural feature in this domain.

DOMAIN 2 CAIRNHARROW FORMATION TRACT

A single tract towards the northern edge of the Hawick Group outcrop is characterised by variable bedding attitude with a distinctive rotation from the regional north-east strike (Figure 21C–E). This is due to a combination of D_1 and post-D_1 effects. D_1 folds vary from moderate to gently north-east plunging and are reclined (Plate 4; Figure 21D) in zones with well-developed D_2 folds and a flat-lying crenulation cleavage. There is also evidence of a component of sinistral shear parallel to the bounding faults, particularly along the southern margin of the tract where steeply plunging folds are locally

developed, associated with steeply dipping, pervasive, easterly striking cleavage. In the Kirkcudbright–Dalbeattie district, the steeply plunging folds deform the S_1 cleavage, although the relative timing with respect to D_2 structures cannot be demonstrated. However, similar steeply plunging folds occurring at the southern margin of the same tract in Wigtownshire do refold the flat-lying S_2 cleavage, and were therefore assigned to a D_3 event (Barnes et al., 1989).

DOMAIN 3 KIRKMAIDEN FORMATION TRACTS AND COHERENT CARGHIDOWN FORMATION

This domain comprises the Kirkmaiden Formation tracts and the northern part of the Carghidown Formation outcrop and is well exposed in the coastal sections extending north from Dove Cave [605 465] into Fleet Bay (Figure 20). It is equivalent to Zone 2 of the Hawick Group in the adjacent Wigtown district (Barnes, 1989). The domain is characterised by abundant gentle north-east- or south-west-plunging, predominantly rectilinear, upright and steeply inclined folds at a variety of scales. Folds show an overall similar style, although slickensides on bedding planes and mineral lineations in fine, bedding-parallel veins are perpendicular to fold axes and testify to bedding-plane slip in fold development. Locally, at Meggerland Point [597 473], these lineations are deformed by S_1 cleavage indicating that at least the early stages of folding was initiated prior to its development.

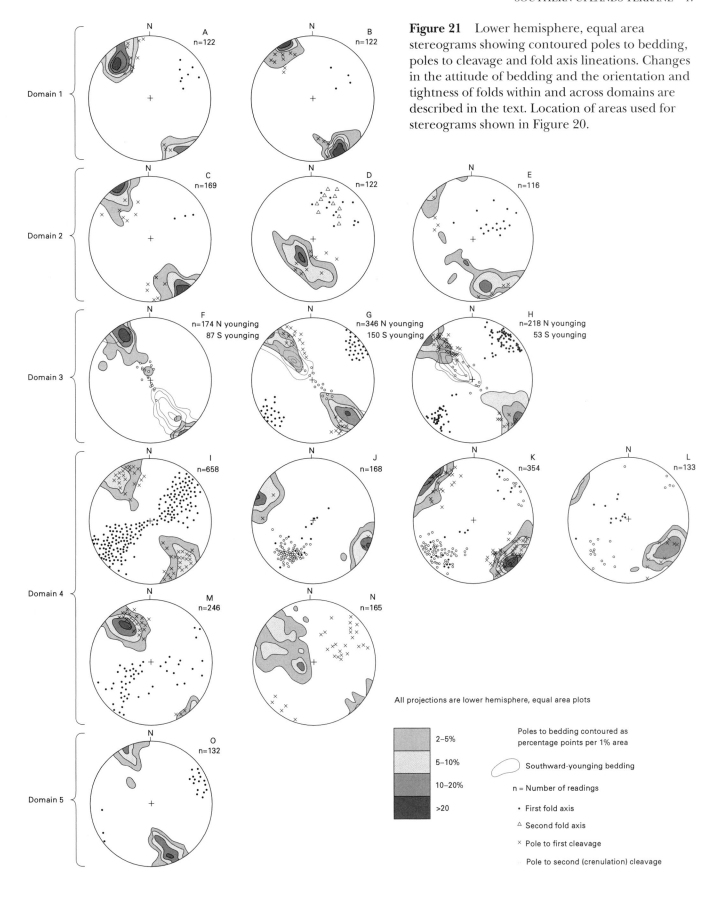

Figure 21   Lower hemisphere, equal area stereograms showing contoured poles to bedding, poles to cleavage and fold axis lineations. Changes in the attitude of bedding and the orientation and tightness of folds within and across domains are described in the text. Location of areas used for stereograms shown in Figure 20.

All projections are lower hemisphere, equal area plots

2–5%	Poles to bedding contoured as percentage points per 1% area
5–10%	Southward-younging bedding
10–20%	n = Number of readings
>20	• First fold axis
	△ Second fold axis
	× Pole to first cleavage
	Pole to second (crenulation) cleavage

Plate 4

Reclined F_1 fold in Cairnharrow Formation (Domain 2).

Upper Lairdman-noch, 3 km south-west of Laurieston [6614 6235] (D 4410).

Subsequent flattening of the folds, seen in deformed concretions and sand volcanoes parallel to cleavage, have tightened the interlimb angle. S_1 is well developed in muddy units but is also variably developed in sandstone. It is usually axial planar to the folds but locally becomes up to 20° clockwise transecting.

The majority of folds are close to tight, although they vary to isoclinal, and of constant attitude producing different dip in north- and south-younging strata over wide areas (Figure 21F–H). Within this overall pattern, systematic changes may result from variation in the dip of the fold axial planes and the interlimb angle. Fold vergence varies between common south-east-verging folds in dominantly north-younging strata and intensely folded zones of essentially neutral vergence (Figure 22a, b). Variation in the sheet dip between these zones suggests an overall structure resembling a series of large south-verging monoclines. However, a number of significant thrust faults are probably present and contribute to the large-scale structure, particularly in the unusually broad Carghidown Formation tract, although in the absence of detailed biostratigraphical control in the Hawick Group these faults cannot be located.

In the west of the district, post-S_1 structures are spatially related to the main strike-parallel, tract-bounding faults. The frequency and intensity of D_2 gradually increases northwards in the domain and they are particularly well developed adjacent to the fault which forms the junction between the Cairnharrow and Kirkmaiden formations. In the Fleet Bay area, two sets of conjugate, gently north-east-plunging structures are grouped as D_2. The first set comprises widespread, steeply inclined, south-east-verging structures with gently dipping short limbs up to 100 m long and a weakly developed crenulation cleavage. The second fold set consists of relatively small-scale (short limbs < 5 m), recumbent or gently inclined, open to close folds (Plate 5; Figure 22a). These are associated with an intense, sub-horizontal S_2 crenulation cleavage which is much more widely developed than the folds. Both sets of D_2 folds are well developed to the west in Wigtownshire where they fold bed-parallel lamprophyre dykes (Barnes et al., 1986).

To the north of the Criffell–Dalbeattie Pluton, a zone of pervasive, steeply dipping, east-striking, post-S_1 cleavage is locally present in the Carghidown Formation on both sides of the Lochanhead Fault (McMillan, in press). This fabric is interpreted as a result of late

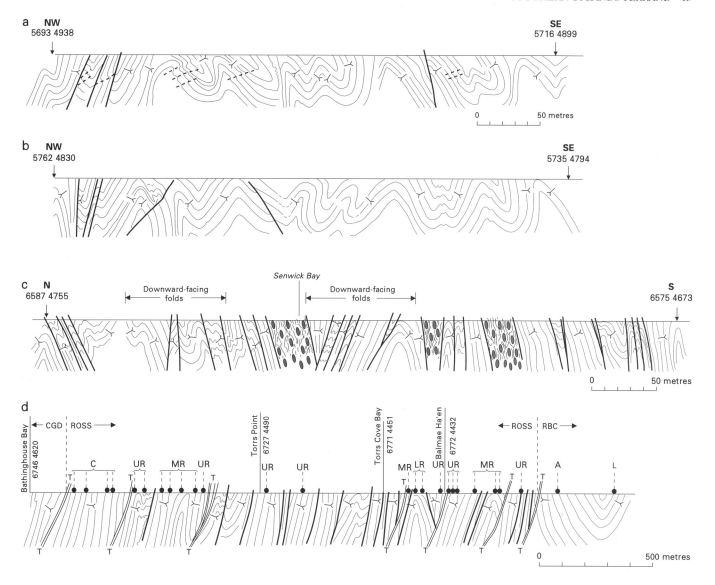

Figure 22   Structural cross-sections illustrating the style of D$_1$ and D$_2$ folding in Domains 3 and 4 as described in the text. Locations of sections shown on Figure 20.

a.   Ardwall (Domain 3)
b.   Barlocco (Domain 3)
c.   Senwick Bay (Domain 4)
d.   Kirkcudbright Bay (Domain 4)

Graptolite Biozones: L   *linnarssoni* Biozone
A   *antennularis* Biozone
UR   upper)
MR   middle) *riccartonensis* Biozone
LR   lower   )
C   *centrifugus* Biozone

sinistral movement along the fault, comparable to the late cleavage locally developed at the southern margin of Domain 2.

DOMAIN 4 DISRUPTED CARGHIDOWN FORMATION AND ROSS FORMATION

This domain, equivalent to Zone 1 of the Hawick Group in Wigtownshire (Barnes, 1987), includes the southern, disrupted portion of the Carghidown Formation and the lower Wenlock Ross Formation. It is well exposed in the coastal sections extending south from Dove Cave [605 465] to Little Ross Island [660 433] and on the east side

of Kirkcudbright Bay to Balmae Burn [681 440] (Figure 20). Although intensely folded as in Domain 3 (Plate 6), Domain 4 is characterised by coherent bedded units separated by anastomosing disrupted zones and by strongly curved fold hinges (Plate 7) and steeply plunging folds.

North-younging strata with asymmetric south-east-verging folds predominate. The range in fold interlimb angle is less than in Domain 3, the style being more consistently tight to isoclinal. The folds are upright with near-vertical bedding in the Carghidown Formation (Figure 21I–L) and steeply inclined to the south in the

Plate 5 D$_1$ and D$_2$ folds, Kirkmaiden Formation (Domain 3).

Craigmore Point, 5.5 km south-west of Gatehouse of Fleet [5729 5178] (D 4380).

Ross Formation (Figure 21M–N). Curvilinear fold hinges range from gentle to steeply plunging. Cleavage is variably developed but may be intense in finer-grained lithologies (Plate 8); it ranges from axial planar to 20° clockwise transecting. Steeply plunging sinistral folds, with short limbs up to 100 m, occur locally throughout the domain. The association of the folds with the S$_1$ cleavage implies that they are part of the main phase of D$_1$, although perhaps initiated at a relatively late stage as they are locally seen to refold earlier structures (Barnes, 1989; Kemp, 1987a).

Disrupted zones ('sheared zones' of Kemp 1987a) up to 30 m wide, separating packets of more coherently bedded strata, are common in the Carghidown Formation and occur locally in the Ross Formation. Sandstone lenses of varying size and density occur in a silty mudstone matrix. Folds are common with widely variable axial orientations on steeply dipping axial planes. Boundaries with coherent strata may be gradational but many have been replaced by anastomosing sheared zones. Internal disruption has commonly been accentuated by boudinage and intense veining, the veins themselves frequently being folded and sheared. Commonly, the lower limbs of folds at the base of a coherent unit are truncated by the underlying disrupted zone, indicating that folding was initiated prior to at least some of the deformation represented by the disrupted zones, although these may have acted as a locus for ductile deformation over a long period of time (Knipe and Needham, 1986).

The steeply plunging, locally downward-facing folds present in this domain have been variously interpreted as due to local variation in strain, rotation of packets of folds in zones of strong deformation or due to thrust morphology and differential movement in thrust sheets (Stringer and Treagus, 1980; 1981; Knipe and Needham, 1986). Such models could be invoked to explain local development of steeply plunging folds, for example, in the disrupted zones where there is evidence of rotation of fold hinges. However, they cannot easily explain broad zones of consistently downward-facing, gentle to moderately plunging folds. Such a zone is exposed around Senwick Bay [657 472] (Figure 22c), the downward facing folds occurring in packets of relatively coherent strata cut by disrupted zones. This complex is interpreted as two main slump sheets (together about 220 m thick) separated by disrupted zones marking the décollement zones. Steeply plunging

Plate 6 Tight south-east-verging D_1 folds, Carghidown Formation (Domain 4).

Hare Glen, 4 km South of Borgue [6227 4455] (D 4396).

folds only occur within the disrupted zones and adjacent to the base of the slump-sheet where there is evidence for refolding of a slump fold closure.

In the Ross Formation tract, the close biostratigraphical control afforded by the interbedded graptolite-bearing siltstone beds and the finely divided biozones of the lower Wenlock gives a particularly clear insight into the level of structural imbrication. A 2.5 km section in the eastern side of Kirkcudbright Bay (Figure 22d) shows at least six thrust slices from as little as 200 m thick. Whilst it is possible that this intensely imbricated section is an isolated occurrence, it seems likely that it is representative of the structure in other zones within the outcrop of the Hawick Group, if not the entire Southern Uplands Terrane at varying scales.

Post-S_1 structures are rare in Domain 4 compared with Domain 3, although minor folds and minor, gentle to moderate south-dipping, north-west-directed thrusts which occur locally may be a manifestation of D_2.

DOMAIN 5 RICCARTON GROUP

The southern structural domain stretches from Balmae Burn [681 440] to the end of the Lower Palaeozoic outcrop at White Port [723 434] and includes three internally coherent thrust slices, 0.8 to 1.2 km thick, in the Wenlock Riccarton Group (Kemp, 1987a; b). Significant deformation is confined to narrow (< 50 m) zones of shearing, adjacent to the thrust faults, including steeply plunging sinistral folds. Otherwise, steeply dipping, northward-younging beds predominate with sparse folds gently north-east-plunging (Figure 22O) and tending to chevron geometry; cleavage is absent or only very weakly developed. The scale and intensity of deformation within this domain is much less than further north and suggests that the Balmae Burn Fault represents a major structural break.

METAMORPHISM

Studies of regional low-grade metamorphism in the Lower Palaeozoic rocks of the Southern Uplands of Scotland by Oliver and Leggett (1980) have shown that the prehnite-pumpellyite facies is widely developed in volcaniclastic turbidites and associated metabasites. A single cross-strike sampling traverse through the Kirkcudbright area was employed by Kemp et al. (1985) to record white mica (illite) crystallinity, K–white mica b lattice parameters (b_0) and graptolite reflectance data; these indicated that mostly anchizonal and late diagenetic grades are developed in pelitic lithologies. Based

Plate 7
Curvilinear D$_1$
fold axis,
Carghidown
Formation
(Domain 4).

Manxman's Rock,
4 km south-south-
west of Borgue
[6121 4496]
(D 4393).

on the improved tectonostratigraphical scheme (Chapter 4; Figure 4), a collaborative study with Birkbeck College, University of London, systematically examined variations in white mica crystallinity in the Kirkcudbright district (Sheet 5W) using a sampling density of approximately 1 pelite per 2.5 km^2. A lower sampling density was used in the Dalbeattie district (Sheet 5E) where the ground is dominated by the outcrop of the Criffel–Dalbeattie Pluton and an extensive thermal aureole has overprinted the regional pattern of metamorphism in the Lower Palaeozoic country rocks.

The white mica crystallinity survey sampled pelitic lithologies, including mudstone, shale and slate, which together typically constitute 5–10% of the stratigraphical succession. Mudstone and shale are the dominant lithologies in the Moffat Shale Group and also form interbeds of variable thickness within all of the greywacke-dominated formations. With advancing deformation and metapelitic grade, mudstone and shale transform to slate which, in the Southern Uplands Terrane, commonly develops a cleavage subparallel to bedding lamination (Merriman et al., 1995). The slate has occasionally been quarried locally for roofing material, as at Parton Quarry [697 702], but is generally of poor quality and is no longer worked.

The textures of some typical pelite samples were characterised by optical and scanning electron microscopy (SEM). Mudstones and shales which are representative of the late diagenetic zone, with white mica crystallinity Kubler indices (KI) > 0.42 $\Delta°$ 2θ, typically show silt-size grains of quartz, albite, K–feldspar and micas and a few TiO$_2$ grains in a clay matrix which lacks an obvious fabric (Plate 9A). Muscovite and chloritised biotite are commonly present as detrital flakes and both may show evidence of compactional deformation. In calcareous mudstones, particularly those in the Raeberry Castle Formation, early diagenetic calcite partially cements the clay matrix. In shales and slates of the anchizone (KI 0.25–0.42 $\Delta°$ 2θ), flakes of detrital muscovite and chloritised biotite, and some elongated quartz grains, define the bedding lamination; alkali feldspar and minor TiO$_2$ grains are also present. The clay matrix forms a microfabric of anastomosing white mica and chlorite intergrowths orientated approximately parallel to the lamination (Plate 9B). As cleavage development intensifies, slates of epizonal grade (KI < 0.24$\Delta°$ 2θ) show a coarser microfabric of orientated matrix phyllosilicates which, together with detrital micas, encloses grains of quartz, alkali feldspar and sporadic TiO$_2$ grains (Plate 9C). Within the aureole of the Black Stockarton Moor subvolcanic complex, metapelites typically show randomly orientated white mica and chlorite aggregates growing across the bedding lamination (Plate 9D). These pelitic hornfelses have also developed discrete epidote and sphene in the matrix and carry thin veins of quartz + epidote + acti-nolite ± sphene ± calcite.

The less than 2 μm mineralogy of 189 pelite samples from the Kircudbright–Dalbeattie district was analysed by X-ray diffraction (XRD) techniques at Birkbeck College, University of London, and at BGS, Keyworth, Nottingham. Mudstone and shale of the late diagenetic zone consist of chlorite and illite with minor amounts of kaolinite, mixed-layer illite/smectite, albite, quartz, calcite, dolomite and haematite. Illite shows broad, generally symmetrical 10 Å peaks with KIs in the range 0.42–0.73 Δ° 2θ. Shale and slate of anchizonal grade are typically composed of chlorite and $2M_1$ K–mica, with minor albite and quartz; neither corrensite nor parago-nite is detectable in the less than 2 μm fractions. Epizonal slates contain $2M_1$ K–mica and chlorite, with minor albite, quartz and rutile.

White mica crystallinity data (KI) from the 189 samples were used to generate a contoured metamorphic map (Figure 23). The techniques used to obtain the data and the basis for selecting the isocryst intervals used are detailed in Roberts et al. (1991), and the measuring con-ditions used are those recommended by Kisch (1991). The map shows two distinct patterns of metamorphism in Lower Palaeozoic strata. The regional pattern shows isocrysts delineating areas of anchizonal or late diage-netic grade that are commonly subparallel or at a low angle to the tract-bounding faults, suggesting a relation-ship between the imbrication of the succession and meta-morphism. A different pattern is found adjacent to late Silurian/early Devonian granitoid intrusions and dyke complexes, where isocrysts trend at a high angle to the tract-bounding faults as a result of contact overprinting of the pattern of regional metamorphism. Contact

Plate 8 S_1 cleavage, Carghidown Formation (Domain 4). Brighouse Bay, 3 km south of Borgue [6325 4531] (D 4402).

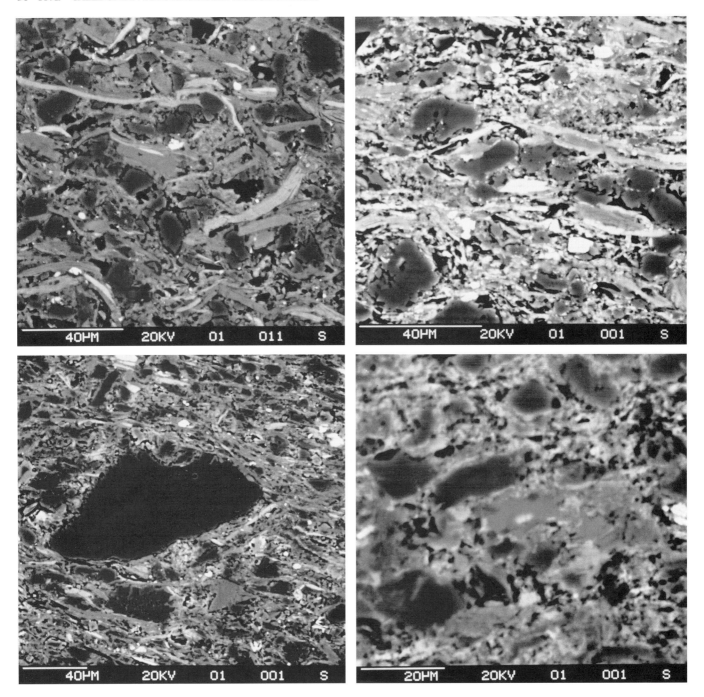

Plate 9   Scanning electron microscope photomicrographs of low-grade metamorphic fabrics from the district. Scale (white bar) is in microns.

metamorphism typically reaches high-anchizonal to epizonal grade, but within approximately 300 m of some intrusive contacts higher-grade hornblende hornfels facies metasediments are developed. Despite these relatively high grades, some spotted slates show anomalously high KIs, indicative of the late diagenetic zone. Initial results of transmission electron microscope (TEM) studies suggest that this is caused by retrogressive growth of very fine-grained white mica in cordiorite spots and thin veins. Contact metamorphism develops a pattern of isocrysts broadly concentric with igneous outcrop, as seen around the Cairnsmore of Fleet and Criffel–Dalbeattie plutons and the Black Stockarton Moor subvolcanic complex. Concentric isocryst patterns are generally wider than aureoles delineated by recognisable hornfelsing. Both the regional and contact metamorphic patterns have been affected by a conjugate set of late Caledonian north-west- and north-east-trending faults, and faulting associated with Permo-Carboniferous basin development.

The pattern of regional metamorphism shows no evidence of a systematic variation in grade in relation to the younging direction of strata within fault-bounded tracts. However, the distribution of crystallinity data in relation to the tectonostratigraphy shows distinctive trends of grade rising and then falling through sequentially younger tracts of strata. Ranges and mean KI values for the major tectonostratigraphical units are shown in Figure 24, plotted on a biostratigraphical chart simplified from Figure 4. Because of poor exposure, no crystallinity data were obtained from the Gala 4 tract. Through sequentially younger tracts southwards from Gala 5 and Gala 7 to the Cairnharrow Formation, the grade, as indicated by the mean KI, generally increases, despite the contact overprinting of some older strata in the aureole of the Cairnsmore of Fleet Pluton. A similar pattern is found on the Whithorn peninsula where the Cairnharrow Formation consistently shows relatively high epizonal grades of regional metamorphism in an area free of contact overprinting (Barnes, in preparation). Grade then falls across sequentially younger tracts of the Hawick Group, from the Cairnharrow

Formation through to the Carghidown Formation (Figure 24). A further fall in grade occurs across the Balmae Burn Fault, reflecting the late diagenetic grade shown by 53% of samples from the Raeberry Castle Formation. An exception to the general trend of grade falling through sequentially younger strata of the Hawick Group is found in the Ross Formation which shows a marked difference in grade on either side of Kirkcudbright Bay. On the west side, outcrops on Meikle Ross are within the high anchizone (mean KI 0.27 $\Delta°$ 2θ), a grade consistent with the well-developed slaty cleavage found in pelites and thinly bedded sandstones. East of Kirkcudbright Bay, the grade of the Ross Formation ranges from the lower anchizone to the diagenetic zone, with a mean KI (0.43 $\Delta°$ 2θ) only slightly higher than that of the Raeberry Castle Formation (0.47 $\Delta°$ 2θ). The contrast in grade is thought to be the result of post-metamorphic faulting juxtaposing strata which have experienced different levels of burial and implies that a depth-related pattern of metamorphism was acquired by burial of already steeply inclined strata (Merriman and Roberts, 1993; Stone, 1995). The regional pattern of metamorphism

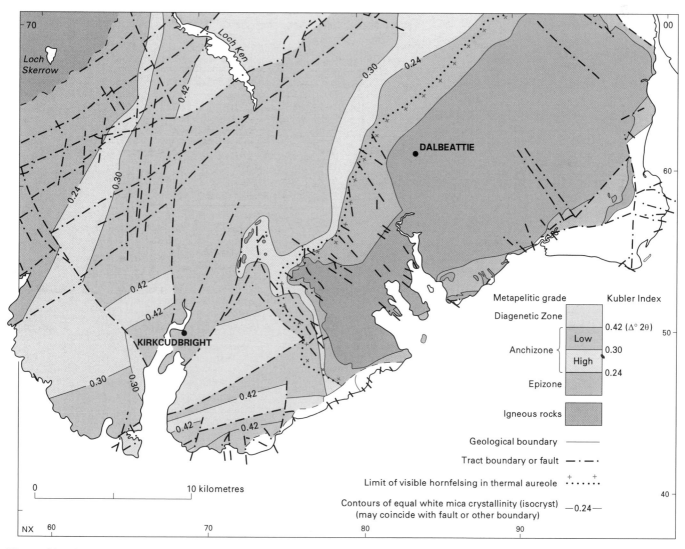

Figure 23 Contoured metamorphic map of white mica crystallinity (Kubler Indices).

appears to reflect a continuum of events as components of the tectonostratigraphical succession were assembled into a thrust stack. This involved initial imbrication and rotation of strata followed by burial and metamorphism with further imbrication. The juxtaposition of tracts showing markedly different grades is a common feature of the regional metamorphism across south-west Scotland. On the Rhins of Galloway this has been interpreted as representing two distinct levels of burial brought together by faulting, with the more deeply buried strata representing the underthrust or underplated components of an accretionary complex (Merriman and Roberts, 1993; Stone, 1995). The composition of fabric-forming phyllosilicates developed in these rocks indicate burial depths of 8 to 13 km in the thrust stack (Merriman et al., 1995). In the Kirkcudbright district a similar underplated origin is inferred for the Gala Group and the Cairnharrow Formation.

The pattern of grade falling through sequentially younger tracts from the Kirkmaiden Formation to the Raeberry Castle Formation and the predominantly late diagenetic grade of the Ross and Raeberry Castle formations suggest that the latter strata were less deeply buried than those further north (Figure 24). The Ross and Raeberry Castle formations may have formed the upper units of the thrust stack, in a similar position to that inferred for rocks of late diagenetic grade on the Rhins of Galloway, where burial depths of 6–8 km have been suggested (Merriman et al., 1995).

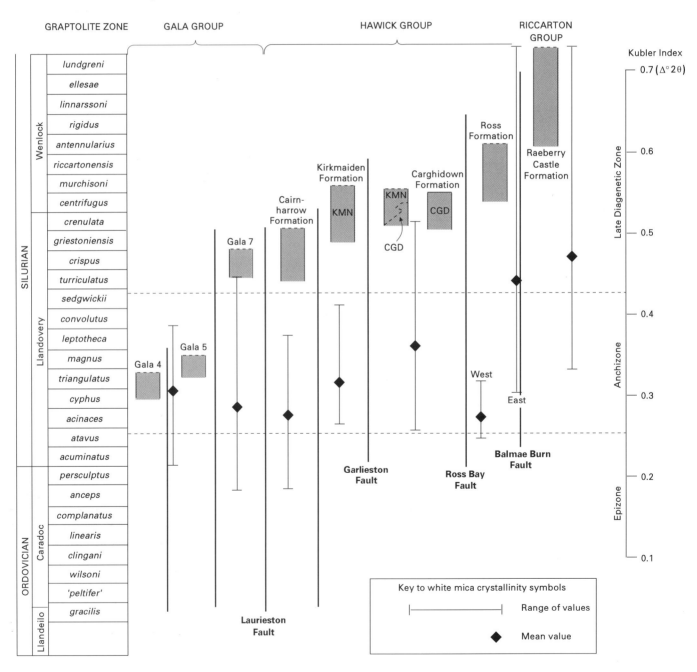

Figure 24   White mica Kubler Indices plotted on a biostratigraphical diagram for the district.

SIX

Caledonian intrusive rocks

Several suites of igneous rocks intrude the Lower Palaeozoic sedimentary rocks of the Kirkcudbright–Dalbeattie district. Recent work on the geochemical and isotopic characteristics of the igneous suites together with field relationships constrained by isotopic age dating have provided a geochronological framework for establishing the tectonomagmatic evolution of the district (Figure 19). Intrusive activity resulted in the development of an extensive swarm of syn- to post-tectonic, calc-alkaline dykes (Barnes et al., 1986; Rock et al., 1986b), culminating in the emplacement of a series of calc-alkaline plutons during the Lower Devonian (Halliday et al., 1980). Most workers, for example Leake and Cooper (1983), Rock et al. (1986b) and Henney (1991), have concluded that emplacement of these igneous suites took place between about 430 and 390 Ma; a time span of some 40 Ma. These intrusive rocks form part of a continuum, resulting from related but evolving magmatic processes.

In the Kirkcudbright–Dalbeattie district the largest concentration of Caledonian minor intrusions occurs to the west of the Bengairn and Criffel–Dalbeattie granitoid plutons, where it forms the Black Stockarton Moor subvolcanic complex (Leake and Brown, 1979; Leake and Cooper, 1983). This complex comprises a mass of intersecting lamprophyre and microdiorite dykes, granodiorite sheets, small granodiorite stocks and breccia pipes (Table 7). The greater part of the complex was intruded in the first phase of activity which included the main granodiorite sheets and stocks. This phase was followed by, and possibly culminated in, the emplacement of the dioritic to granodioritic Bengairn Complex (Leake and Cooper, 1983). The Bengairn Complex is interpreted to have been intruded by the Criffel–Dalbeattie Pluton (Phillips, 1956a), although, no unequivocal intrusive relationships have been recognised in the field. Emplacement of the plutonic bodies was closely followed by a regional suite of north-west-trending lamprophyric and porphyritic dykes which locally form the later phases of the Black Stockarton Moor complex (Leake and Cooper, 1983). This prolonged phase of igneous activity was completed by the emplacement of the Cairnsmore of Fleet Pluton.

PLUTONIC ROCKS

Bengairn Complex

The Bengairn Complex is a north-west–south-east-orientated composite pluton lying between the Black Stockarton Moor subvolcanic complex to the north-west and the Criffel–Dalbeattie Pluton to the north-east. Its emplacement postdates the first phase of activity within the Black

Stockarton Moor complex (Table 7; Leake and Cooper, 1983) but it is intruded by a suite of north-west-trending lamprophyre and porphyritic microdiorite dykes which form part of the later phase of the subvolcanic complex (see below). Although no intrusive contacts between the Bengairn Complex and the Criffel–Dalbeattie Pluton have been recorded in the field, Phillips (1956a) concluded that the Bengairn Complex was emplaced prior to, and is intruded by the Criffel–Dalbeattie Pluton; this conclusion has been widely accepted by subsequent workers (e.g. Stephens and Halliday, 1980). Evidence for this intrusive relationship is provided by the angular discordance between the primary igneous foliations (defined by aligned mafic minerals and xenoliths) developed within granodiorites of the two plutons and the apparent cross-cutting nature of the margin of the Criffel–Dalbeattie pluton (Phillips, 1956a). Despite its important position within the tectonomagmatic evolution of the area, the Bengairn Complex has received very little attention since the early work of Macgregor (1937). The complex was re-mapped by Phillips (1956a; b) but most of his work was concentrated on the Criffel–Dalbeattie Pluton. No recent geochemical or isotopic data are available for the complex.

The Bengairn Complex is a zoned pluton with an incomplete outer rim of quartz-diorite which is intruded by a granodiorite core. The quartz-diorite contains xenoliths of partially assimilated, hornfelsed country rock and clots of basic igneous material (?diorite). At its maximum width in the vicinity of Bengairn Hill [771 545] the quartz-diorite rim is up to 3 km across. The quartz-diorite is typically grey in colour, but varies from pink to brown particularly adjacent to the north-west–south-east-oriented faults. The rock is medium- to coarse-grained and consists of plagioclase (An_{37}–An_{20}), hornblende, biotite, quartz and K–feldspar (orthoclase - microperthite) with accessory sphene, apatite and, particularly at the margins, pyroxene. A weak foliation defined by the orientation of the ferromagnesian minerals and xenoliths has been recognised (Phillips 1956a; A A McMillan, personal communication, 1992), although the geometry of this fabric is still poorly understood.

The granodiorite ('intermediate granodiorite' of Phillips, 1956a), is a medium- to fine-grained rock composed of oscillatory zoned plagioclase (An_{30}–An_{15}), quartz, K–feldspar (microperthite), biotite and hornblende. A finer-grained, typically lighter coloured variety of the granodiorite is exposed on the western side of Auchencairn Bay [819 501]. Xenoliths are not common within the granodiorite, but where present are aligned (N–S orientation) parallel to a more widely developed primary igneous fabric defined by aligned mafic minerals.

Table 7
Igneous sequence in the Black Stockarton Moor subvolcanic complex (after Brown et al., 1979; Leake and Cooper, 1983).

Related igneous events	Phase of activity	Lithology	Mineralogy
CRIFFEL–DALBEATTIE PLUTON BENGAIRN COMPLEX	3	'PORPHYRITE' DYKE SWARM: (minor): E–W-trending porphyritic microgranodiorite	**Phenocrysts**: oligoclase/andesine, green hornblende, chlorite, biotite, ± quartz **Matrix**: feldspar, quartz, hornblende, opaque minerals, apatite
	2	BASIC DYKE SWARM: (minor): spessartite, ophitic dolerite	Brown hornblende, plagioclase, ± biotite, ± olivine, opaque minerals
		'PORPHYRITE' DYKE SWARM: sigmoidal, NW–SE-trending porphyritic microgranodiorite	**Phenocrysts**: oligoclase/andesine, green hornblende, chlorite, biotite, ± quartz **Matrix**: feldspar, quartz, hornblende, opaque minerals, apatite
VOLCANIC VENTS	1	INTERMEDIATE STOCKS: elliptical granodiorite bodies	60–70% oligoclase/andesine, 10–15% quartz, 10–15% hornblende + biotite, 5% opaque minerals minor myrmekite, apatite
		INTERMEDIATE SHEET COMPLEXES: NE–SW-trending granodiorite laccoliths (minor diorite)	60–70% plagioclase, 15–25% hornblende, quartz, biotite, opaque minerals, ± graphic quartz-feldspar intergrowth
		BASIC DYKE SWARM: (minor component): spessartite, ophitic dolerite	Brown hornblende, plagioclase, ± biotite, ± olivine, opaque minerals
		'PORPHYRITE' DYKE SWARM: sigmoidal, NE–SW-trending porphyritic microgranodiorite	**Phenocrysts**: oligoclase/andesine, green hornblende, ± chlorite, ± quartz **Matrix**: feldspar, quartz, ± chlorite, ± biotite, opaque minerlas, apatite

Criffel–Dalbeattie Pluton

The Criffel–Dalbeattie Pluton is a composite, approximately concentrically zoned granitic body (Figure 25). It has a distinctive ovoid shape measuring 23 km × 11 km with its long axis trending north-east, parallel to the regional strike. In the south-west the long axis coincides with the line of the tract-bounding Ross Bay Fault, while in the north-east it is slightly north of the presumed extension of this structure. The pluton intrudes Hawick Group (Silurian) sedimentary rocks of the Carghidown and Ross formations, and is interpreted as having also intruded the Bengairn Complex (Phillips, 1956a). It was probably emplaced at quite a high level in the crust as boulders of the granodiorite are found in feldspathic sandstones of Lower Carboniferous age a few kilometres to the south, [e.g. 8610 5250]. Thermal metamorphism associated with the emplacement of the Criffel–Dalbeattie Pluton resulted in the development of a 2–3 km wide zone of biotite-hornfels and hornblende-diopside-hornfels (Figure 23).

The first description of the Criffel–Dalbeattie Pluton was given by Horne et al. (1896). The petrography, structure and intrusive relationships have subsequently been studied and reported on by Macgregor (1937; 1938) and Phillips (1955; 1956a), who also produced the first detailed geological map of the pluton and its associated minor igneous intrusions. Recently, more detailed petrographical as well as extensive geochemical and isotopic studies have been carried out by Stephens and others (Stephens, 1972; Stephens and Halliday, 1980; Halliday et al., 1980; Stephens et al., 1985; Stephens, 1992). These geochemical studies together with structural investigations of Phillips et al. (1981) and Courrioux (1987) have led to sophisticated petrogenetic modelling. The three-dimensional geometry of the pluton with steeply dipping contacts has been modelled from Bouguer gravity data by Bott and

Figure 25 Petrographical facies of the Criffel–Dalbeattie pluton and associated dyke swarm. Foliated granodiorite (outer)/granite (central) boundary after Phillips, 1956a. Granodiorite/granite boundary as chemically defined by Stephens and Halliday (1980). Petrographical facies and boundaries after Stephens et al., 1985.

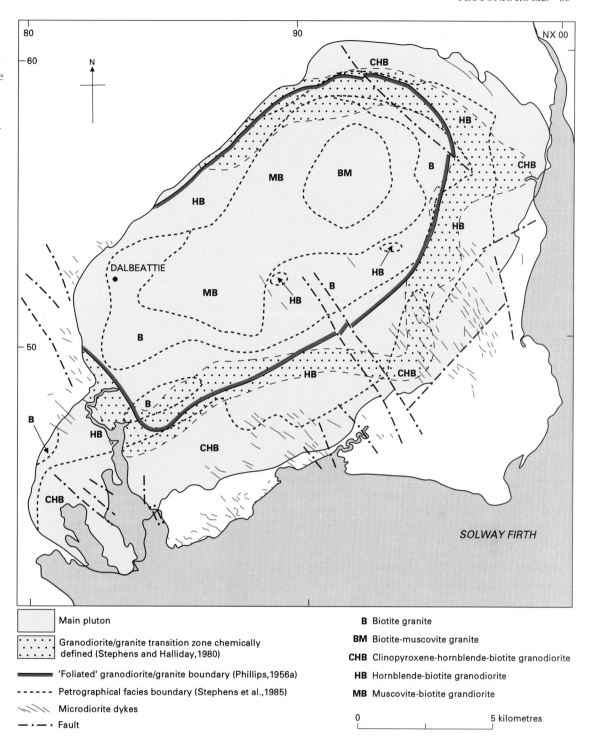

Main pluton

Granodiorite/granite transition zone chemically defined (Stephens and Halliday, 1980)

'Foliated' granodiorite/granite boundary (Phillips, 1956a)

Petrographical facies boundary (Stephens et al., 1985)

Microdiorite dykes

Fault

B Biotite granite

BM Biotite-muscovite granite

CHB Clinopyroxene-hornblende-biotite granodiorite

HB Hornblende-biotite granodiorite

MB Muscovite-biotite grandiorite

0   5 kilometres

Masson Smith (1960). More recent models based on the regional gravity and magnetic data are discussed in Chapter 3.

The pluton has been dated at 397 ± 2 Ma (Rb–Sr whole-rock, Halliday et al., 1980), 406 ± 15 Ma (U–Pb in zircon, Pidgeon and Aftalion, 1978), and 397 ± 8 Ma and 391 ± 8 Ma (K–Ar mineral ages, Brown et al., 1968). The 397 Ma age has been assumed to date emplacement of the granite in the Emsian, very late within the overall Caledonian orogenic cycle (Figure 19).

Apart from a limited amount of re-mapping within the marginal facies of the granite, very little additional work has been undertaken during the resurvey and the following account is based on a review of the literature outlined above.

PETROLOGY AND GEOCHEMISTRY

The Criffel–Dalbeattie Pluton is a composite body of zoned and unzoned components (Figure 25). Phillips (1956a) and Phillips et al. (1981) identified an outer shell of foliated granodiorite containing xenoliths of diorite surrounding a core of unfoliated porphyritic granite. The granodiorite consists of an inequigranular assemblage of plagioclase (An_{15}–An_{35}, 48 modal %), quartz (20%), K–feldspar (15%), biotite (10%) and hornblende (6%) with minor to accessory clinopyroxene (diopside), sphene, apatite and opaque oxides. Subhedral K–feldspar megacrysts are a prominent feature of the granite which comprises the assemblage plagioclase (40%), K–feldspar (30%) and quartz (24%), with primary muscovite only occurring near the centre of the pluton. Both the granodiorite and granite are cut by thin (< 2.5 cm) aplite veins which consist of quartz, K–feldspar and plagioclase in varying proportions.

On the basis of variable mafic mineral content, Stephens et al. (1985) subdivided these two main facies into five petrographical types (Figure 25). The incomplete marginal phase of the pluton is a clinopyroxene-bearing hornblende-biotite-granodiorite (CHB of Figure 25) which passes into a hornblende-biotite-granodiorite (HB). These two phases approximately coincide with the boundary between an inner core of porphyritic granite and the marginal shell of variably foliated granodiorite with diorite xenoliths of Phillips (1956a) and Phillips et al. (1981). The outer granodioritic phases are succeeded by a biotite-granite (B) which is locally porphyritic and includes small enclaves of HB. The remaining two petrographical types occupy the core of the pluton and consist of a muscovite-biotite-granite (MB) and biotite-muscovite-granite (BM). No intrusive contacts between the various petrographical types have been noted in the field; the most distinct mappable boundary is that between the outer foliated granodiorite and the unfoliated granitic core.

The pluton has a typical calc-alkaline chemistry with a range in SiO_2 values from 58% (weight % oxide) in the granodiorite to 75% in the inner granitic core. Detailed geochemical studies have shown that the pluton comprises two geochemically distinct components, which correspond in part with the main petrographical variations (Stephens and Halliday, 1980; Halliday et al., 1980; Stephens et al., 1985; Holden et al., 1987). This takes the form of a discontinuous, unzoned outer margin of metaluminous hornblende-granodiorite and an inner core of increasingly peraluminous granite which shows normal continuous zoning. The boundary between these two components is represented by, on average, a 2 km-wide zone of rocks of intermediate bulk and isotopic compositions, characterised by steep geochemical gradients. Stephens and Halliday (1980) have interpreted this feature as an interaction zone between two geochemically distinct magmas. The marginal granodiorite facies have a lower $^{87}Sr/^{86}Sr$ initial ratio (0.7052 compared with 0.7069 for the granitic core) and more radiogenic εNd values (- 0.4 to - 3.1 for the granitic core, Halliday, 1984). Values for $\delta^{18}O$ range from 8.54 to 11.84‰. The sequence from clinopyroxene-bearing granodiorite through to muscovite-bearing granite is one of total rare earth depletion, with the clinopyroxene-bearing granodiorites being the least evolved having the highest total REE, moderate La/Yb and no Eu anomaly (Stephens et al., 1985).

DEVELOPMENT AND EMPLACEMENT

Various petrogenetic models have been proposed for the development of the zonation within the pluton. These vary from the convective in situ crystal-liquid processes of Phillips et al. (1981) to the open-system models of Stephens et al. (1985) and Holden et al. (1987). The latter model is based on the discontinuity trend of the chemical and isotopic data which suggests that the zonation is not the product of simple fractionation of a mafic precursor (I-type granites of Chappell and White, 1974) or the progressive assimilation of country rock (S-type granites of Chappell and White, 1974); either of these processes would produce continuous isotopic and elemental trends. These authors suggest a two-stage model in which the granodiorites and granites represent separate pulses of magma; the outer granodiorites were derived from a mantle or lower crustal source (I-type granite) while the more evolved granitic core of the pluton was generated by partial melting of middle and upper crustal immature metasedimentary rocks (S-type granite) either by an assimilation-fractional crystallisation (AFC) process or by the incorporation of anatectic melts. Isotopic systematics (Nd and Sr) of the diorite xenoliths present in the marginal granodiorite led Holden et al. (1987) to conclude that they represent synplutonic injections of mantle-derived mafic magma within the host granitoid magma.

The emplacement mechanism for the pluton and the origin of the foliation within the marginal granodiorite phase has been discussed in detail by Phillips (1956a), Phillips et al. (1981) and Courrioux (1987). Courrioux recognised a well-developed deformation fabric defined by the preferred orientation and cataclasis of feldspar, hornblende, biotite and the elongation of quartz. In general, the fabric has a strong planar component with a weak lineation defined by hornblende. The deformation fabric is also defined by the preferred orientation of dioritic xenoliths within the marginal phase. By contrast the inner granite shows a very weak anisotropy defined by the orientation of K-feldspar and biotite. The most intense fabric within the granodiorite phase is developed at the south-east margin, on the flanks of Airdrie Hill [9460 5855]. Here, the moderately dipping cataclastic fabric is defined by elongate diorite xenoliths parallel to the foliation and a well-developed sub-horizontal lineation. Cross-cutting aplite veins are also foliated. The contact of the granite is faulted at this locality. Courrioux (1987) has mapped the foliation trajectories within the pluton and they display a general concentric pattern that broadly conforms to the elliptical shape of the pluton. The lineation is predominantly subhorizontal. Courrioux's (1987) detailed analysis of xenolith axial ratios and quartz c-axes suggests both sinistral and dextral shear components were operative during formation of the fabric elements. This data was interpreted by Courrioux (1987) in terms of a model involving oblique north-east-directed diapirism by which the inner granite was forcefully emplaced into an envelope of crystallised granodiorite to form the deformation fabric within the outer shell.

In contrast Phillips (1956a) and Phillips et al. (1981) recognised two fabrics: the first resulting from laminar flow and a later deformation fabric formed during emplacement of the pluton by stoping processes. In the Phillips et al. (1981) model the preferred orientation of the dioritic (cumulate) xenoliths results from the operation of convection circulation in the magma chamber during consolidation of the granodiorite envelope, subsequently modified by deformation during intrusion of aplite veins and porphyry dykes.

Cairnsmore of Fleet Pluton

The Cairnsmore of Fleet Pluton is the youngest and most acidic of the major plutons in the Southern Uplands. The granite was reported on by several early authors but was first described in detail by Gardiner and Reynolds (1937). More recently it has been extensively studied and described by Parslow (1964; 1968; 1971), Parslow and Randall (1973) and Cook (1976). Although a limited amount of additional work was undertaken during the current re-survey (Fettes and Timmerman, 1993), the following descriptive account is largely based on the work of Parslow and Cook.

The outcrop of the pluton is ovoid measuring 18 × 11 km, the long axis lying north-east–south-west parallel to the regional strike. The granite is bounded to the north by the Orlock Bridge Fault zone and to the south by the Gillespie Burn Fault, and lies wholly within the Moniaive Shear Zone (Phillips, 1992). The granite cross-cuts intermediate tract boundaries but also partly distorts the regional strike. Although it lacks the dioritic and granodioritic phases of Criffel, the Fleet pluton is similarly compositionally zoned with a marginal coarse-grained, commonly feldsparphyric facies and a central fine- to medium-grained aphyric facies; both phases plot as true granites in Le Maitre's (1989) classification. The boundary between the two phases is irregular but generally sharp and blocks of the coarse-grained granite within the medium-grained variety suggests that the latter was a later intrusive phase.

Geophysical studies of the pluton (Parslow, 1968; Parslow and Randall, 1973) suggest that it is part of a larger batholith. The pluton has a steep contact to the south and east but more shallow to the north and west.

FIELD RELATIONSHIPS

Only the south-east quadrant of the mass crops out in the north-west corner of the Kirkcudbright–Dalbeattie district, where it forms a series of low craggy hills. Exposure is relatively good and the contact with the sedimentary rocks can be closely constrained at a number of localities, particularly round Rig of Burnfoot [59 65] and Laughenghie Hill [60 66]. Here, the contact appears steep and is roughly parallel to the strike of the country rocks and, although generally sharp, small veins and apophyses at the granite margin demonstrably cut the regional cleavage. There are very few xenoliths present.

The contact between the coarse- and medium-grained granites has been shown by Parlsow (1968) as lying just east of Wellees Rig [585 695] and swinging round to the

west. Localised exposures of medium-grained granite along the forestry road between [586 683] and [592 691] may suggest that Parslow's boundary should be drawn a further 0.5 km to the south and west. Alternatively, as suggested by Cook (1976), the contact of the two granite types may be an irregular surface variably intercepted by the topography to give a more complex outcrop pattern. The granite is cut by numerous aplite and quartz veins.

The granite exhibits a weak foliation defined by the parallel arrangement of the tabular feldspar and mica grains. Within the district, Parslow (1968, fig. 1) showed the foliation striking between 355° and 015° subparallel to the granite margin, the dips increasing from subhorizontal near the centre to over 60° eastwards at the contact. The geometry of the fabric over the mass as a whole (Parslow, 1968) that is steepening outwards from the centre, and the general increase in the intensity of the fabric towards the contacts, are both factors which are consistent with fabric development as a result of forceful intrusion of an expanding mass (see below).

PETROLOGY AND GEOCHEMISTRY

Parslow (1968) divided the coarse-grained granite into a marginal biotite-granite and an inner biotite-muscovite-granite. Contact between the two types is transitional reflecting an overall decrease of modal biotite from the granite contact towards the centre and a corresponding increase in the modal quantities of primary muscovite. In parallel with these changes, the microcline phenocrysts, which are up to 30 mm long in the marginal facies, decrease in size and content towards the centre and the oligoclase becomes marginally more albitic. Microperthite and myrmekite, which are common in the coarse-grained granite, are virtually absent from the finer-grained varieties, whereas micrographic intergrowths increase towards the centre of the mass. Alteration of minerals also increases towards the centre with the development of chlorite from biotite, the sericitisation of feldspar, and the growth of secondary muscovite, zoisite and epidote. Cook (1976) suggested this alteration is related to a late stage metasomatic/hydrothermal event.

The granites show varying degrees of deformation associated with the fabric development. This is evidenced by undulose extinction, sutured growth of quartz, and the development of secondary mica across fractures in feldspar crystals. These textures indicate that the main phase of hydrothermal alteration was later than the fabric development.

The bulk rock chemistry characterises the Cairnsmore of Fleet Pluton as a highly evolved granite, the Thorton–Tuttle differentiation index varying from 85 in the coarse-grained biotite granite to 95 in the central facies. Variation plots show that the coarse-grained granite has an increasing fractionation trend inwards from the margin. This general trend is continued with a slight overlap across the finer-grained granite.

In a study of plots in the $Ab–An–Or–SiO_2–H_2O$ system, Cook (1976) deduced that the Fleet pluton was a typical subsolvus granite. High water pressures allowed the production of large quantities of mica and the crystallisation of two primary feldspars, subsequent exsolution of albite leading to the development of the microperthite. The plots also indicated that the magmas were largely products of the melting of Lower Palaeozoic or earlier sedimentary material.

Isotopic systematics also support an S-type model with $^{87}Sr/^{86}Sr$ ratios of 0.706 to 0.707 and $\delta^{18}O$ values of 11.17–11.33% (Halliday et al., 1980). ϵNd values of - 2.4 to - 3.1 are also indicative of a close association with Southern Uplands acidic clastic material (ϵNd = +1.1 to - 6.6; Halliday, 1984).

The $^{87}Sr/^{86}Sr$ and $^{87}Rb/^{86}Sr$ isotopic ratios indicate that the Cairnsmore of Fleet Pluton is the most evolved member of the group of three major Southern Uplands plutons (Halliday et al., 1980). In addition, measurements within the Fleet mass are broadly consistent with increasing fractionation towards the centre.

Radiometric ages of 392 ± 2 Ma (Rb/Sr whole rock, Halliday et al., 1980), 390 ± 6 Ma (U/Pb zircon, Pidgeon and Aftalion, 1978) and 390 ± 6 Ma (K/Ar biotite, Brown et al., 1968) constrain the age of crystallisation and define Cairnsmore of Fleet as the youngest of the three Galloway plutons.

DEVELOPMENT AND EMPLACEMENT

The Cairnsmore of Fleet Pluton represents a late phase in the evolution of the Southern Uplands plutons. The coarse-grained granite was initially intruded and began to fractionate before the finer grained granite was emplaced. A late hydrothermal/metasomatic episode caused alteration of the primary minerals and the growth of secondary phases. This late event was probably associated with the intrusion of aplite and quartz veins.

Although there is considerable evidence of sedimentary parentage in the magma, it is still probable that the initial melts were formed from a deep-seated, low $^{87}Sr/^{86}Sr$ source. The magmas differentiated and became progressively contaminated with sedimentary material during ascent (Halliday et al., 1980).

However, the markedly cross-cutting nature of the eastern and western contacts and the absence of country rock fabrics parallel to the margin argue against this mechanism as the dominant means of intrusion. The absence of veining and xenoliths, particularly in the roof zone, argues against significant stoping. It is therefore probable that the intrusion was facilitated by a transtensional regime (Hutton et al., 1990) related to the known movements on the tract-bounding faults.

MINOR INTRUSIONS

The most extensive suite of minor intrusions in the Kirkcudbright–Dalbeattie district is associated with the Criffel–Dalbeattie Pluton. It is dominated by members of the 'porphyrite-porphyry' series, a term introduced by the Geological Survey to describe a varied group of generally porphyritic microdiorites, microgranodiorites and microgranites (Greig, 1971). Less abundant are representatives of the calc-alkaline lamprophyres (CAL):

Table 8 Essential petrological characteristics of the lamprophyre varieties present in the district.

Lamprophyre variety	Ferromagnesian mineral	Feldspar
Kersantite	biotite	plagioclase
Minette	biotite	K-feldspar
Spessartite	hornblende	plagioclase
Vogesite	hornblende	K-feldspar

hornblende-bearing spessartites and vogesites and mica-bearing minettes and kersantites (Table 8; Rock, 1984). The petrography and field relations of the minor intrusions have been described in some detail by King (1937), Macgregor (1937) and Phillips (1956b), whilst the recent study of the Black Stockarton Moor complex provides perhaps the best synthesis of their evolution and age relations (Leake and Cooper, 1983). This summary is largely based upon the work of Henney (1991).

Lamprophyres

FIELD AND AGE RELATIONS

Lamprophyres and large numbers of less mafic dykes (the 'porphyrite-porphyry' series) are emplaced as part of the same dyke swarms. All the lamprophyre dykes are narrow bodies (< 3 m) and are distinguished, in porphyritic and coarse-grained varieties, by their abundant large euhedral crystals of hornblende or mica set in a variably coloured groundmass (Table 8). The feldspar matrix of the hornblende lamprophyres is most commonly pale pink-orange but in the mica lamprophyres it tends to be a dull grey or brown. Mica lamprophyres have a lustrous glint on fresh fracture surfaces. The fine-grained types are massive, grey-green in colour and are difficult to identify unambiguously in the field—they are likely to be misidentified as dolerites. Both mica and hornblende lamprophyres contain felsic globular structures and more diffuse segregations set in a darker matrix (Rock, 1984). In some places these structures are abundant, comprising up to 10% of an exposed surface, and are up to 5 cm across. They are commonly pale pink to white and are composed of varying proportions of carbonates, feldspar, quartz, epidote and chlorite. A few have a core of sulphides, most commonly pyrite. The globules may have originated as immiscible sulphide and carbonate phases.

Contacts with the country rocks (wackes) are sharp with some dykes showing chilled margins. There is little evidence of hornfelsing in the country rocks or fluid exchange (veining, etc.) with the wall rocks; (an exception to this is the Newmains lamprophyre [885 761] in the Thornhill district (Sheet 9E) to the north (Macdonald et al., 1986). Some lamprophyres are associated with igneous breccias: Bombie Glen, Gribdae [707 506] (Rock et al., 1986a); one lamprophyre is associated with volcanic vent activity: Shoulder o' Craig [662 491], Kirkcudbright (Rock et al., 1986b). In the Wigtown district (Sheet 4E) to the west, some lamprophyres are reportedly folded by the late stages of the regional deformation of the local country rocks (Barnes et al., 1986). However, no comparable deformed dykes occur in the Kirkcudbright–Dalbeattie district, although a few thin lamprophyre dykes in the Sandyhills Bay area are foliated and thermally metamorphosed, probably the result of the forceful emplacement of the Criffel–Dalbeattie Pluton.

Petrology and mineralogy

Hornblende lamprophyres

These rocks are dominantly composed of hornblende, which by definition should form more than 20% of the mode (Rock, 1984), and feldspar, with minor (< 10%) clinopyroxene. The typical texture displayed is that of randomly orientated, subhedral–euhedral needles and prisms of brown-green amphibole set in a panidiomorphic groundmass of interlocking plagioclase laths with minor amounts of interstitial K–feldspar and quartz. Spessartites are the most abundant variety around the Criffel–Dalbeattie Pluton with vogesites occurring only as a minor facies of the Newmains dyke (Table 8; Macdonald et al., 1986). Accessory phases in the hornblende lamprophyres include apatite, chlorite, carbonates, epidote, sericite and minor opaques disseminated through the groundmass and in minor patches of alteration associated with the breakdown of the major phases.

The habit of hornblende is generally dependent on the grain size of the rock. Coarse-grained varieties have subhedral-euhedral prisms and laths of brown-green amphibole, whereas a needle-like, acicular habit is usual for fine-grained rocks. Twinning is common, particularly in hornblendes from the fine-grained rocks. Colour zoning is uncommon and occurs only in the more coarsely grained varieties where it is generally discontinuous, with a clearly defined dark brown core and a light green margin. In fine-grained rocks, hornblendes are unzoned except for the rare, very narrow, actinolitic rim, and are either totally green or brown. This variation in colour is believed to be controlled by the oxidation state of the iron and the titanium content of the amphibole (Deer et al., 1963). In many of the more coarsely grained rocks the hornblendes appear to have been strained and disrupted, with fracturing along and across the cleavage direction. In several hornblende lamprophyres, in which there is a distinctly brown hornblende, a pale green-colourless diopsidic clinopyroxene occurs as fresh anhedral phenocrysts (Macdonald et al., 1986). Although in some rocks these pyroxenes have a corona of brown-green hornblende in a reaction relationship, in most cases both hornblende and clinopyroxene co-exist as discrete crystals without any reaction between the two phases.

Feldspars are restricted to the groundmass of hornblende lamprophyres and, as the amount of plagioclase is greater than alkali feldspar, these are therefore classified as spessartites. Plagioclase occurs as interlocking laths and forms a distinctive panidiomorphic decussate groundmass. Alteration makes accurate optical determi-

nations of plagioclase composition difficult but, where determined, composition is An_{10}–An_{40}. In most hornblende lamprophyres the plagioclase laths show albite twinning and may have a clear albite rim, particularly in the more coarsely grained rocks. Some plagioclase cores have inclusions of acicular pale brown amphibole which supports the suggestion that hornblende is an early crystallising phase.

Alkali-feldspar most commonly occurs as anhedral crystals, intimately associated with quartz in interstitial segregations between the plagioclase and amphibole and is best developed in the more coarsely grained rocks. Apatite is the most distinctive accessory and most commonly occurs as acicular needles dispersed throughout the groundmass. In more coarsely grained rocks it occurs both as discrete euhedral microphenocrysts in the feldspathic matrix and as subhedral inclusions within the amphibole phenocrysts. Chlorite occurs mainly as an alteration product of amphibole and as the filling to subspherical 'globular structures'. It is associated with quartz, epidote and minor carbonate. The two most common opaque phases are Fe–Ti oxides and pyrite. The Fe–Ti oxides occur closely associated with alteration patches and zones in the mafic phases and as disseminated grains throughout the rock. Pyrite occurs with felsic segregations, veinlets and 'globular structures', in minor veinlets and as disseminated grains in combination with carbonate, alkali-feldspar, chlorite and quartz. It appears that at least some of this pyrite is late magmatic because it forms cores to or veinlets within early felsic material and appears unrelated to post-intrusion hydrothermal alteration and mineralisation processes. However, in some rocks, pyrite and chalcopyrite accompany alteration of the host rock and quartz-carbonate veining, and their presence is clearly the result of a post-magmatic phase of mineralisation. Carbonate and epidote are most commonly associated with the alteration and breakdown of the mafic phases and are intimately associated with chlorite.

Xenoliths and inclusions are uncommon. They are restricted to a few small quartzitic bodies (< 1 cm) of unknown affinity and xenoliths of the sedimentary country rock occurring at the dyke margins. Pelitic xenoliths commonly have well-developed reaction rims, marked by the development of a fine-grained mixture of chlorite, sericite and epidote at their contact with the lamprophyric magma. Rare igneous xenoliths (< 5 cm) are porphyritic, with sparse quartz and feldspar phenocrysts, set in a fine-grained reddish groundmass.

Felsic segregations are more common than the xenoliths and are found in both fine- and coarse-grained rocks. The segregations are either diffuse, irregular patches of quartz, carbonate, epidote, chlorite, pyrite and feldspar, or sub-spherical 'globular structures' containing essentially the same minerals but sharply defined by grain size and colour from the surrounding rock. Irregular, cross-cutting veinlets of felsic material also occur but are less common and are similar to those described from the Newmains dyke (Macdonald et al., 1986) where the felsic structures are restricted to the dyke and do not cut the contact or invade the country rocks. They are present in both fresh and altered dykes in the district suggesting that they are related to a late-stage magmatic differentiation or fluid separation process rather than some post-magmatic alteration event.

Mica lamprophyres

Mica lamprophyres are not common around the Criffel–Dalbeattie Pluton, perhaps less than 20 per cent of the total lamprophyres, but are concentrated in the area around Borgue and Gatehouse of Fleet. They are most commonly porphyritic with large (5–10 mm) flakes of light to dark brown mica set in a variably coloured (grey–reddish brown), essentially feldspathic matrix. This groundmass is typically more finely grained than that of the hornblende lamprophyres and a strong flow alignment of the phenocrysts is common. Both minettes and kersantites are present, with the latter the most abundant (Table 8), though alteration of the groundmass feldspar makes identification difficult in many instances. Clinopyroxene occurs in some mica lamprophyres as colourless to pale green, anhedral phenocrysts (< 10%), and some also have a few pseudomorphs after olivine, composed of carbonate, opaque and clay minerals. Apatite is a common accessory along with chlorite, epidote and opaque minerals. Carbonate is more abundant than in the hornblende lamprophyres.

Mica occurs both as phenocrysts and as small flakes in the groundmass with typical CAL features such as undulose extinction, castellated section, pale core with a darker rim and a core crowded with inclusions, particularly of apatite (Rock, 1984; 1987). The occurrence of undulose extinction together with evidence of deformed cleavage is thought to indicate that the micas crystallised early and were deformed during the ascent and final emplacement of the magma. The light to reddish brown colour is thought to indicate a high Ti, content and the pale to dark zoning in basal sections may result from increased substitution of Fe for Mg (Deer et al., 1963).

Both plagioclase and alkali feldspars are present, but restricted to the groundmass, where they most commonly occur as subhedral, interlocking laths, generally pervasively altered. Apatite is the most abundant accessory, occurring as acicular needles in the micas, parallel to the cleavage. It also occurs disseminated throughout the groundmass and as stubby prisms in the cores of the mica phenocrysts. Fe–Ti oxides, chlorite and epidote are commonly associated with the alteration and breakdown of mica and groundmass feldspar. Secondary carbonate is associated with the breakdown of feldspar and olivine and also occurs as discrete patches both disseminated throughout the rock and within felsic 'globular structures'.

Xenoliths and inclusions are more common in the mica lamprophyres than in the hornblendic varieties and include fragments of local sedimentary country rocks and porphyritic felsic igneous material. The most distinctive inclusions are milky white to colourless, subspherical, quartzitic xenoliths, of unknown origin, which are commonly polygranular and display strain-related undulose extinction. Felsic segregations and 'globular structures' are abundant in mica lamprophyres and are very similar to those described from the hornblende lamprophyres. However, one type of 'globular structure' is unique to mica lamprophyres and consists of sub-spherical 'vugs' filled with a varied combination of carbonate, alkali feldspar, chlorite, epidote and quartz. These 'vugs' are commonly concentrically zoned with a quartz + alkali-feldspar core speckled with granules of epidote and surrounded by a rim of chlorite with the whole 'globular structure' rimmed by tangentially oriented flakes of mica. Mauger (1988) modelled the evolution of similar 'globular structures' in the Concorde minette, USA; he suggested that feldspar + chlorite + quartz-rich structures were formed by the separation of an aqueous vapour phase during the rapid ascent of the lamprophyric melt, whereas carbonate-rich segregations formed by the separation of an immiscible CO_2 liquid.

GEOCHEMISTRY

Hornblende lamprophyres

Hornblende lamprophyres range from basic to intermediate in composition with silica contents from 47.17 to 61.55% and Al_2O_3 from 12.29 to 17.87%. Silica shows negative correlations with MgO, Fe_2O_3, CaO, P_2O_5, TiO_2 and K_2O/Na_2O and positive correlations with Al_2O_3, Differentiation Index (DX), Na_2O and $Na_2O + K_2O$. K_2O shows no significant correlation with silica or most major elements but has a tentative negative correlation with Na_2O. Several of the hornblende lamprophyres are quartz normative and a few are also corundum normative but the majority have high normative diopside and olivine compositions reflecting their generally primitive nature. One rock has a small amount of nepheline in the norm and all rocks have high normative apatite. Table 9 gives some representative analyses, ranges of major oxides and CIPW Norms for hornblende and mica lamprophyres. The full data set are available in Henney (1991).

There is a wide range in trace element content characterised by high transition (Ni, Cr, V) and large ion lithophile element (LILE) (Ba, Rb, Sr) abundances compared to most other basic calc-alkaline magmas (Rock 1984; 1987; 1991). High field strength (HFS) element abundances (Nb, Zr, Y) are more typical of primitive arc magmas, though U and Th are higher (Gill, 1981). Zn, Cu and Pb abundances are variable but generally less than 150 ppm. Significantly, many of the trace elements show little correlation with silica, suggesting that the distribution of the trace elements is not strongly controlled by fractionation processes. The hornblende lamprophyres are enriched in light rare earth elements (LREE) with high La, Ce and Nd abundances which are also reflected in steep chondrite-normalised REE profiles (Nakamura, 1974) with high Ce_n/Yb_n (25.6) and low Sm/Nd (0.150) ratios.

Mica lamprophyres

The mica lamprophyres have major element compositions similar to those of the hornblende lamprophyres

Table 9 Representative analyses, CIPW norms and some ranges for hornblende (HL) and mica (ML) lamprophyres.

Sample	BP11	PFT02B	1305.00	Range	1371	BP22	PFT03	Range
Type	HL	HL	HL	HL	ML	ML	ML	ML
NGR	828 493	793 557	880 734		603 812	814 485	792 558	
SiO_2	47.47	48.05	56.47	47.17–61.55	50.06	56.08	55.78	50.06–55.78
TiO_2	1.36	1.47	1.25	2.11–0.78	0.92	1.25	1.12	1.87–0.87
Al_2O_3	12.29	14.34	15.47	12.29–17.87	12.33	15.29	14.06	16.02–12.33
Fe_2O_3	9.30	10.12	7.36	10.37–5.26	9.27	6.70	6.44	9.94–6.44
MgO	13.43	11.45	8.02	13.43–4.72	14.01	6.99	7.50	14.01–6.99
CaO	10.33	8.62	4.71	10.33–2.43	9.16	5.68	5.97	9.16–3.46
Na_2O	1.77	1.57	3.44	6.28–1.57	1.72	2.83	2.33	3.70–0.82
K_2O	2.63	3.42	2.70	4.74–1.62	1.74	4.48	5.88	5.88–1.74
P_2O_5	1.26	0.80	0.46	1.73–0.23	0.64	0.59	0.81	0.81–0.53
MnO	0.15	0.15	0.11		0.15	0.10	0.10	
LOI	3.16	2.01	3.60		10.91	1.79	1.95	
DX	30.44	33.69	48.78		24.98	52.07	54.61	
Mg#	80.33	76.19	75.50		81.04	74.69	76.71	
Ni	328	264	216		381	197	209	
V	209	221	152		866	320	289	
Cr	525	306	398		209	230	205	
Rb	71	148	56		38	111	148	
Sr	1738	1445	762		665	1245	1230	
Ba	2114	1641	786		2578	2021	2638	
U	4	5	2		3	4	7	
Th	27	20	14		11	13	21	
Zn	133	131	77		70	70	91	
Cu	111	67	16		177	114	158	
Pb	45	12	15		13	12	17	
Zr	192	200	213		294	214	288	
Nb	16	18	14		13	14	14	
Y	25	26	20		21	18	16	
La	142	105	49		34	43	84	
Ce	313	230	123		86	98	187	
Nd	143	98	59		49	49	92	
CIPW Norms								
Quartz	0.00	0.00	3.49		0.00	1.45	0.00	
Albite	14.53	13.34	29.26		14.63	24.03	19.75	
Orthoclase	15.63	20.35	16.03		10.35	26.59	34.86	
Anorthite	17.96	22.16	18.88		20.93	15.88	10.63	
Diopside	20.08	12.42	1.24		16.33	6.79	10.97	
Hypersthene	0.00	4.08	24.37		19.95	18.51	14.63	
Olivine	21.87	18.47	0.00		10.45	0.00	2.24	
Magnetite	4.07	4.43	3.22		4.06	2.93	2.81	
Ilmenite	2.60	2.82	2.38		1.76	2.38	2.14	
Apatite	2.94	1.87	1.08		1.48	1.38	1.88	
Corundum	0.00	0.00	0.00		0.00	0.00	0.00	
Nepheline	0.28	0.00	0.00		0.00	0.00	0.00	

Major oxides in %, trace elements in ppm.
LOI Loss on ignition; DX Differentiation Index; Mg# Magnesium Number (Fe normalised to Fe^3/Fe_t cation ratio of 0.3 in calculation). Analysed by XRF at University of Aston. Sample numbers from Henney (1991).

but with less variation (Table 9). Silica shows some negative correlations with MgO, CaO and Fe_2O_3 and irregular positive correlations with K_2O, Na_2O, $Na_2O + K_2O$ and DX. TiO_2, Al_2O_3 and P_2O_5 have less significant positive correlations with silica. Several mica lamprophyres are quartz normative and some have normative corundum. The majority are either olivine or diopside normative and none have any normative nepheline.

Abundances of transition elements (Ni, Cr, V) and LILE (Ba, Rb, Sr) in the mica lamprophyres are high but variable. Values for HFS elements (Zr, Nb, Y) are similar to those of the hornblende lamprophyres as are Th and U. Zn, Cu and Pb values are also low. As with the

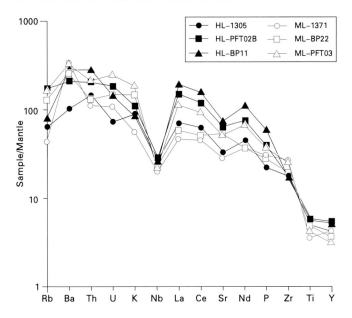

Figure 26 Primordial mantle normalised element abundance plot (spidergram) of hornblende and mica lamprophyres. Sample numbers from Henney (1991).

hornblende lamprophyres, many of the trace elements show poor or scattered correlations against silica. LREE (La, Ce, Nd) contents are generally high but variable; chondrite normalised REE profiles are steep with high Ce_n/Yb_n (47.0) and low Sm/Nd (0.154) ratios.

On a primordial mantle normalised spider diagram (Wood et al., 1979) hornblende and mica lamprophyres from the Criffel dyke swarm show very similar patterns, with a general increase in element abundance with increasing element incompatibility (from right to left, Figure 26) except for Nb and Sr. Both groups have very similar Nb, Ti, Zr, P and Y content (Table 9) but the mica lamprophyres attain higher maxima for Nd, U, Ba and Rb. Chondrite normalised REE plots (Nakamura, 1974) show that both mica and hornblende lamprophyres are strongly enriched in LREE. Neither group has an Eu anomaly but high volatile (particularly H_2O) contents recorded in lamprophyric magmas (Esperanca and Holloway, 1987) suggest oxidising conditions which may restrict the development of Eu^{2+} in such magmas (Fowler, 1988). The mica lamprophyres are generally more potassic, with higher K_2O and K_2O/Na_2O, and are more enriched in LILE, with higher Ba/Nb and Rb/Sr, than the hornblende lamprophyres. The high LILE/Nb and LREE/Nb ratios, low Ti abundance and prominent Nb anomaly displayed by both groups are characteristic of magmas associated with active or recently terminated subduction (Pearce, 1983).

ISOTOPE GEOCHEMISTRY

$^{87}Sr/^{86}Sr$ initial ratios of hornblende lamprophyres, calculated at 400 Ma, show a wide variation ranging from 0.7046 to 0.7069 (ϵSr c. + 8 to + 42). Model ages relative to bulk earth range from 1042.1 to 686.6 Ma. Two mica

lamprophyres have $^{87}Sr/^{86}Sr$ initial ratios of 0.7054 and 0.7059 (ϵSr c. + 19.0, + 27). These overlap with the field for hornblende lamprophyres as do their bulk earth model ages (988.1, 913.9). $^{143}Nd/^{144}Nd$ initial ratios for hornblende lamprophyres vary from 0.51213 to 0.5120 (ϵNd c. + 4 to - 2) with the majority close to the bulk earth value at 400 Ma. Model ages relative to depleted mantle and to CHUR range from 1069.1 to 850 Ma and from 516.5 to 240.2 Ma respectively. $^{143}Nd/^{144}Nd$ initial ratios for the two mica lamprophyres of 0.51207 to 0.51204 (ϵNd c. - 1 and - 2) are slightly less radiogenic than the hornblende lamprophyres, and the mica lamprophyres also have slightly lower Sm/Nd. Depleted mantle and CHUR model ages range from 896 to 907.1 Ma and 515 to 473 Ma respectively, overlapping with the values for hornblende lamprophyres.

PETROGENESIS

The LILE and LREE enrichments which characterise lamprophyres from the Criffel dyke swarm may indicate derivation from an enriched mantle source, or low degrees of partial melting, or they may be the result of variable degrees of fractionation and contamination of mantle-derived melts during their ascent through the crust. Quantitative modelling indicates that variations in LILE and LREE in both mica- and hornblende-lamprophyres cannot be explained by progressive fractional crystallisation of a 'parental' lamprophyre melt. Contamination during melt transport in dykes is also thought to have been insignificant in the Criffel lamprophyres. Similarly, assimilation—fractional crystallisation (AFC) models involving contamination by local crustal rocks combined with the effects of crystal fractionation in the upper crust fail to explain satisfactorily the observed incompatible element and isotope variations. The elevated LILE and LREE abundances and isotopic composition of lamprophyres appear to have been little modified by fractionation or contamination during intrusion. The Nd and Sr isotopic composition of the lamprophyres suggests a source produced by the incorporation of subducted Lower Palaeozoic sediments into a mantle which was characterised by ϵNd values close to bulk earth. However, it is not possible to resolve the relative contribution of source heterogeneity and low degrees of partial melting with the observed LILE and LREE abundances of the Criffel lamprophyres. Differences in mineralogy and composition between the mica and hornblende lamprophyres may reflect variations in the depth of melting as well as possible variation in CO_2/H_2O.

The Criffel lamprophyres are thought to have been generated by a low degree of partial melting from a mantle source, possibly subduction-modified 'Lake District' lithosphere thrust under the southern margin of the Southern Uplands during the final stages of closure of the Iapetus Ocean.

REGIONAL AND TECTONIC SETTING

The Criffel lamprophyres are thought to be part of a widespread phase of lamprophyre intrusion in southern

Scotland, Northern Ireland and northern England during the final stages of the Caledonian orogeny. Recent structural mapping and radiometric age dating of lamprophyres from southern Scotland suggested that intrusion occurred between 420 Ma and 395 Ma (Rock et al., 1986b; Macdonald et al., 1986), broadly contemporaneous with final closure of Iapetus (Leggett et al., 1979). Structural and geochemical studies by Barnes et al. (1986) and Rock et al. (1986b) indicated that the lamprophyres cannot readily be reconciled with models which propose that the Southern Uplands represent the remnants of a lower Palaeozoic accretionary prism. It has been proposed (Stone et al., 1987) that the lamprophyres were emplaced in a post-tectonic 'transpressional, strike-slip, regime', and intruded into the uplifted remnants of a foreland basin/thrust belt rather than an accretionary prism. However, the debate about the origins and nature of the Southern Uplands is far from resolved and it is difficult to reconcile the lamprophyre magmatism within any single palaeotectonic model.

It is clear that intrusion of the lamprophyres was one of the final magmatic events in the late Caledonian evolution of the Southern Uplands and that many of their geochemical characteristics are the result of petrogenetic processes associated with subduction. However, it seems unlikely that they could be related to the same north-west-directed subduction zone thought to be responsible for the late Silurian lavas in the Midland Valley because the Criffel lamprophyres are found much too close (20–30 km) to the trace of the Iapetus suture, the so-called 'Solway Line', to have been generated above this zone.

Recent Rb–Sr data (Thirlwall, 1988) indicated that the majority of the late Caledonian magmatism in the southern part of the Southern Uplands occurred at around 395 Ma and is characterised by high LILE and LREE abundances together with radiogenic $^{207}Pb/^{204}Pb$ isotope ratios compared to magmas from further north (Thirlwall et al., 1989). The 395 Ma granitoid magmas from the southern part of the Southern Uplands are considered by Thirlwall (1988) and Thirlwall et al. (1989) to be derived from old, enriched 'Lake District' lithosphere thrust under the southern margin of the Southern Uplands during the final stages of collision. Lithosphere such as this would be an ideal source for the Criffel lamprophyres, particularly if it had recently been metasomatised by a lower Palaeozoic subduction event, such as that postulated for the Ordovician Borrowdale and Eycott volcanics of the Lake District (Fitton and Hughes, 1970). It is also suggested that the close spatial and temporal association between the lamprophyres and the Criffel–Dalbeattie Pluton is not fortuitous but is the result of a direct petrogenetic link with the lamprophyres acting both as a heat source promoting crustal melting and contributing directly to the composition of the granitoid magmas (Henney et al., 1989; Henney, 1991).

'Porphyrite–porphyry' series

The majority of the minor intrusions associated with the late Caledonian Criffel–Dalbeattie Pluton are intermediate to acid microdiorites, microgranodiorites and microgranites. They are commonly porphyritic, with phenocrysts of plagioclase, amphibole, biotite and quartz, set in a feldspathic groundmass, and are known collectively as the 'porphyrite-porphyry' series (Hatch et al., 1972; King, 1937; Macgregor, 1937; Phillips, 1956b). The compositions represented by the 'porphyrite-porphyry' series have most commonly been interpreted as the hypabyssal equivalents of the granitoid magmas of the Criffel–Dalbeattie Pluton (Phillips, 1956b; Phillips et al., 1981).

FIELD AND AGE RELATIONS

The field relations and petrography of the dykes of the 'porphyrite-porphyry' series associated with the Criffel–Dalbeattie Pluton have been described in detail by previous workers (King, 1937; Macgregor, 1937; Phillips, 1956b; Leeder, 1971). These studies highlight some of the difficulties in classifying the members of the 'porphyrite-porphyry' series because of hydrothermal alteration, weathering, heteromorphism and their dominantly porphyritic texture. A three-fold classification of the 'porphyrite-porphyry' series, based on mineralogy and geochemistry, has been described from the late Caledonian dyke swarm present in the Wigtown peninsula (Barnes et al., 1986).

These petrographical types are:

'porphyrite' microdiorite with phenocryst of plagioclase ± clinopyroxene ± amphibole ± biotite set in a feldspathic matrix with minor K-feldspar and quartz

'acid porphyrite' microdiorite with a similar mineralogy but with little or no amphibole and more K–feldspar and quartz in the matrix

'porphyry' microdiorite characterised by phenocrysts of quartz and K–feldspar and with biotite as the principal mafic phase.

This classification has been slightly modified for the present study by 'merging' the 'acid porphyrite' and 'porphyrite' groups. This was done because the use of the relative proportions of quartz and K–feldspar present in the groundmass to differentiate the 'porphyrites' has not been found to be a robust discriminator where the effects of alteration and weathering can obscure the texture and mineralogy of the groundmass.

The 'porphyrite-porphyry' series rocks most commonly occur as dykes, 1–3 m wide, characterised by a pink-red colouration. Abundant pale phenocrysts of feldspar are commonly flow-aligned parallel to the dyke margins. When traversing Lower Palaeozoic strata, the dykes generally strike north-eastwards, parallel to the bedding, though some of the second phase dykes in the Black Stockarton Moor complex trend north-west across the strike (Table 7, Leake and Cooper, 1983). Dykes intruding the granodiorites and granites of the Criffel–Dalbeattie Pluton most commonly strike north-west. In the southern part of the district, dykes which cut the wacke sequence close to the southern margin of the pluton are associated with breccia pipes and localised vein-type and disseminated pyrite and chalcopyrite mineralisation. Emplacement of the 'porphyrite-porphyry' series of dykes overlapped with the intrusion of the Criffel–Dalbeattie Pluton. The early 'porphyrites' of the Black Stockarton Moor complex are cut by the outer Criffel granodiorite whereas the 'porphyrites' and 'porphyries' of the later phases intrude both the granodiorite and granite (Table 7, Leake and Cooper, 1983).

MINERALOGY AND PETROLOGY

Porphyritic microdiorite ('porphyrite')

These are the most abundant and widespread components of the 'porphyrite-porphyry' series associated with the Criffel–Dalbeattie Pluton. They make up approximately 70% of the minor intrusions (Henney, 1991). They intrude both the Lower Palaeozoic sedimentary rocks and the granodiorite and granite of the pluton. In thin section the dyke rocks range from clinopyroxene-phyric (± amphibole) composition, with sparse plagioclase, through plagioclase-phyric (± amphibole, ± biotite) types, with up to 70% feldspar phenocrysts, to varieties with abundant interstitial quartz and K–feldspar segregations. Many show the effects of hydrothermal alteration with sericitisation of the feldspars, chloritisation of the mafic phases (both the phenocrysts and groundmass) and silicification of the groundmass. No subdivision of this group has been possible on the basis of petrography.

Clinopyroxene is present in a few of the more melanocratic, second phase 'porphyrites' of the Black Stockarton Moor complex (Table 7). It occurs most commonly as colourless, anhedral phenocrysts which are commonly corroded and, in some rocks, as small grains in the groundmass. Hornblende is a more common phase, occurring as subhedral to euhedral phenocrysts, and as prismatic grains and acicular needles in the groundmass. It is commonly zoned with a dark green core and paler rim. The phenocrysts are commonly altered with actinolite and chlorite, together with Ti–Fe oxides and minor amounts of sphene, rimming and replacing the primary hornblende. Biotite is more abundant in the leucocratic varieties and occurs both as sparse phenocrysts and, more commonly, as small flakes in the groundmass. Alteration is common with the development of chlorite and Fe–Ti oxides along cleavages and many phenocrysts are bleached and partially replaced by chlorite.

Plagioclase is the most abundant feldspar in the 'porphyrites' and occurs both as euhedral phenocrysts and as interlocking laths in the groundmass. Both phenocrysts and groundmass crystals are commonly zoned, some showing complex patterns, particularly at the edges of the crystals. Many of the phenocrysts have a later thin rim of unzoned, clear feldspar, thought to be albite. In most rocks the plagioclases are altered with some being completely replaced by clays minerals, sericite, epidote and carbonate, whilst others have an altered core but relatively fresh margins. K–feldspar and quartz occur together and are restricted to the groundmass in 'porphyrites' in interstitial segregations or graphic intergrowths. Accessory phases include apatite in the more mafic rocks, and epidote, chlorite, carbonate and Fe–Ti oxides associated with alteration. A few grains of subhedral to euhedral zircon, associated with biotite, also occur in the more felsic varieties.

'Porphyries'

The 'porphyries' are distinguished from the 'porphyrites' by the presence of phenocrysts of quartz and, less commonly, K–feldspar. They range from biotite-bearing microgranodiorite to quartz- and K–feldspar-rich microgranite and aplite. Some 'porphyries' intrude the Lower Palaeozoic country rocks but they are more commonly seen intruding the granodiorite and granite phases of the Criffel–Dalbeattie Pluton. Hydrothermal alteration occurs mainly in those bodies which are intruded into the sedimentary rocks rather than those which cut the plutons. Dark brown biotite is the most abundant mafic mineral and occurs both as euhedral phenocrysts and as flakes in the groundmass. In some instances it is accompanied by minor quantities of green hornblende.

Biotite phenocrysts exhibit 'bleaching' with the development of chlorite and Fe–Ti oxides along the cleavage while groundmass biotite is replaced by fibrous 'mats' of chlorite. Biotite is least altered in the 'porphyries' intruded into the inner granite of the pluton. Plagioclase has a similar habit to that exhibited in the 'porphyrites' and, although phenocrysts are generally less abundant in the 'porphyries', they have a similar pattern of complex zoning and development of albitic rims. K–feldspar is most common in the groundmass, as anhedral 'plates' and in graphic intergrowths with quartz, and in sparse, euhedral, phenocrysts in the more leucocratic rocks. Quartz forms anhedral, interstitial segregations and subhedral to euhedral phenocrysts set in a quartzo-feldspathic matrix. Accessory minerals include apatite and sphene both of which occur associated with biotite, epidote and carbonate from the alteration of plagioclase. Small round grains of zircon are present in biotites surrounded by well-developed pleochroic halos. In some of the more felsic rocks, small, colourless flakes of muscovite occur associated with K–feldspar and quartz.

GEOCHEMISTRY

Table 10 lists some representative analyses of 'porphyrite' and quartz-porphyry dykes. As described from the Wigtown peninsula, the 'porphyrites' are the least evolved of the 'porphyrite-porphyry' series rocks, with SiO_2 content $\leqslant 60\%$ whereas the more evolved acid dykes form a continuous series with SiO_2 64–71% (Barnes et al., 1986). The existence of the silica gap between the two groups led Barnes et al. to argue that they could not be directly related and must have been derived from two separate parent magmas. Phillips (1956b) and Leeder (1971) presented some analyses of the Criffel 'porphyrite-porphyry' series dykes and observed that the 'porphyries' were more evolved than the 'porphyrites' with lower MgO, CaO, TiO_2 and P_2O_5 but greater K_2O, Na_2O and SiO_2 contents. Both authors noted the compositional similarity of the 'porphyrite-porphyry' series and the granitoids of the Criffel–Dalbeattie Pluton. In the following account (and Table 10) all major element data has been recalculated on a volatile-free basis, with total iron quoted as Fe_2O_3 (Henney, 1991).

The 'porphyrites' have a wide range of SiO_2 content (56.4–71.6%), which correlates negatively with MgO, CaO, TiO_2 and P_2O_5 and positively with K_2O and Na_2O.

Table 10 Representative analyses, CIPW norms and some ranges for the 'porphyrite (Porph)- quartz porphyry (Qtz Por)' series dykes from the Criffel dyke swarm.

Sample Type NGR	TQ04 Porph 699 544	BHD01 Porph 895 565	1357 Porph 799 883	Range Porph	1342 Qtz Por 911 746	CF02 Qtz Por 965 603	1344 Qtz Por 877 728	Range Qtz Por
SiO_2	62.37	65.94	70.34	56.4–71.6	70.43	71.71	73.04	68.5–73.1
TiO_2	0.77	0.61	0.45	0.3–1.6	0.38	0.32	0.25	0.25–0.5
Al_2O_3	16.19	16.23	16.11		15.94	15.19	15.65	
Fe_2O_3	4.77	3.64	2.56		2.38	1.99	1.77	
MgO	5.66	2.29	1.36	0.5–5	1	0.82	0.58	0.5–2.1
CaO	3.02	3.66	1.06	0.4–5.5	1.58	1.74	0.59	0.6–2.9
Na_2O	4.3	4.02	4.46	2.3–5.9	4.35	3.85	4.05	3.0–5.6
K_2O	2.57	3.36	3.43	1.3–7.2	3.68	4.21	3.86	1.8–5.7
P_2O_5	0.29	0.21	0.18	0.12–0.6	0.2	0.14	0.18	0.11–0.25
MnO	0.07	0.05	0.05		0.04	0.04	0.03	
LOI	3.16	0.58	2.81		2.87	0.62	1.69	
DX	63.71	72.01	84.81		84.63	85.54	89.63	
Mg#	77.05	63.97	60.16		54.37	53.77	48.1	
Ni	117	47	32		39	30	17	
V	110	73	41		41	33	28	
Cr	193	58	14		15	22	11	
Rb	56	121	88		139	205	189	
Sr	1109	601	290		371	320	212	
Ba	1563	718	646		723	618	620	
U	2	3	4		6	6	5	
Th	11	14	13		12	14	13	
Zn	63	48	55		48	34	41	
Cu	40	20	1		10	9	11	
Pb	12	25	9		25	34	11	
Zr	183	165	224		182	142	142	
Nb	11	11	9		11	10	10	
Y	13	12	11		11	7	8	
La	35	33	42		34	35	28	
Ce	70	65	88		66	68	57	
Nd	32	25	33		24	28	25	
CIPW Norms								
Quartz	12.02	18.11	26.76		26.02	28.11	32.56	
Albite	36.47	34.03	37.76		36.84	32.55	34.27	
Orthoclase	15.22	19.87	20.29		21.77	24.88	22.8	
Anorthite	13.09	16.39	4.06		6.53	7.69	1.76	
Diopside	0	0.33	0		0	0	0	
Hypersthene	17.35	7.96	5.08		4.13	3.39	2.71	
Olivine	0	0	0		0	0	0	
Magnetite	2.08	1.59	1.11		1.04	0.87	0.77	
Ilmenite	1.46	1.16	0.85		0.71	0.61	0.48	
Apatite	0.67	0.49	0.42		0.47	0.33	0.42	
Corundum	1.56	0	3.59		2.43	1.5	4.18	
Nepheline	0	0	0		0	0	0	

Major oxides in %, trace elements in ppm.
LOI Loss on ignition. DX Differentiation Index; Mg# Magnesium Number (Fe normalised to Fe^3/Fe_t cation ratio of 0.3 in calculation). Analysed by XRF at University of Aston. Sample numbers from Henney (1991).

They all have high Ba and Sr abundances, typical of many late Caledonian granitoids, with moderate Ni and Cr contents. All are quartz and corundum normative and also have normative hypersthene and diopside.

The 'porphyries' extend to slightly higher SiO_2 (68.5–73.1%) than the 'porphyrites' but there is a considerable overlap. MgO, CaO, TiO_2 and P_2O_5 all have negative correlations with SiO_2 while K_2O and Na_2O have positive correlations. Ba and Sr abundances are not as great as those in the 'porphyrites' and those of Ni and Cr are considerably lower. The 'porphyries' have high normative quartz and corundum contents with

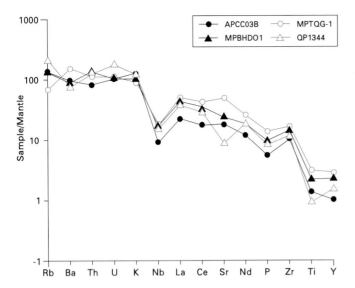

Figure 27 Primordial mantle normalised element abundance plot (spidergram) of porphyritic microdiorites ('porphyrites'). Sample numbers from Henney (1991).

correspondingly low normative hypersthene and no normative diopside (Table 10).

In both groups La and Ba show a slight decrease with increasing silica, although the trend for La is not as pronounced as that for Ba. The Rb/Sr ratio of the 'porphyrites' rises slightly with increasing silica, with a marked increase generally in the 'porphyries', whereas the K/Rb ratio has a general steady decrease. Mantle-normalised 'spidergram' patterns show both groups to have pronounced negative Nb anomalies, low Ti abundances and high abundances of LILE and LREE (Figure 27), patterns which are characteristic of arc-related magmas (Pearce, 1983). Patterns for the two groups are very similar for Rb, Th, U and K and generally have a large overlap, though the 'porphyrites' extend to higher levels for La, Ce, Sr, Nd, P, Zr, Ti and Y. Both groups have a slight negative Sr anomaly relative to the LREE and the 'porphyries' exhibit a slight depletion in Ba relative to Rb and Th. These depletions may reflect the progressive removal of Sr in plagioclase and Ba in biotite, both of which are important phenocryst phases in the majority of rocks. The more restricted range of LREE-abundances in the 'porphyries' most probably reflects removal of LREE-bearing accessory phases, such as apatite, and this is supported by the lower P content of this group.

PETROGENESIS

The Criffel dykes form a chemical continuum from 'porphyrite' to 'porphyry' which is similar to that for the granodiorite–granite of the Criffel–Dalbeattie Pluton. Mantle normalised spidergram patterns have considerable compositional overlap between the dykes and the various phases of the pluton. Some differences in trace element abundance may result from a number of different processes including varying degrees of crystal-liquid separation during transport and emplacement of the 'porphyrites'

and 'porphyries'. The compositional similarity between the dykes and pluton indicates that the two are petrogenetically linked and this is supported by AFC modelling of the evolution of the 'porphyrite-porphyry' series (Henney, 1991). It is suggested that the 'porphyrite-porphyry' dykes represent magmas periodically tapped from the granitoid magma chamber as it evolved.

REGIONAL AND TECTONIC SETTING

The evolution of the 'porphyrite-porphyry' series of dykes in the district is inextricably linked to the evolution and petrogenesis of the Criffel–Dalbeattie Pluton. The dyke rocks are most probably the hypabyssal expression of magmas tapped from the evolving plutonic magma chamber and are thus part of the post-collisional, early Devonian phase of granitoid magmatism which occurred in the southern part of the Southern Uplands between 400 and 395 Ma, and which included the Cairnsmore of Fleet and Cheviot granites.

Black Stockarton Moor subvolcanic complex

The greatest concentration of late Caledonian minor intrusions in the district occurs to the west of the Bengairn and Criffel–Dalbeattie granitoid plutons in an area between the River Dee, Kirkcudbright Bay and Screel Hill [779 553]; this is the Black Stockarton Moor subvolcanic complex (Leake and Brown, 1979; Leake and Cooper, 1983). It comprises a composite mass of intersecting lamprophyre and microdiorite dyke swarms, granodiorite sheet intrusions, small granodiorite stocks and breccia pipes (vents) which cut wackes of the Carghidown Formation and overlap in age with the Criffel–Dalbeattie Pluton. Three main phases of dyke emplacement (Table 7) have been recognised on structural and field relations (Leake and Cooper, 1983). The most common lithologies are dykes of the 'porphyrite-porphyry' series, which are present in all three dyke phases, together with granodioritic stocks, sheets and laccoliths and hornblende and mica lamprophyres all found as components of the first and second phases. Drilling carried out as part of a Mineral Reconnaissance Programme (MRP) survey for metalliferous mineralisation (Brown et al., 1979) delineated a sheeted 'cedar tree' laccolith complex which, together with rare breccia pipes, forms part of the first phase of activity. Low-grade disseminated Cu mineralisation (Chapter 10) is associated with this sheet complex.

The lamprophyres are particularly associated with a series of small subvolcanic and volcanic vents, plugs and breccia pipes which occur both on Black Stockarton Moor and on the shore of Kirkcudbright Bay (Rock at al. 1986a). Rare, highly altered, basaltic rocks are also associated with some of these structures, particularly the well-developed Shoulder o' Craig Vent described below.

Intrusive activity at Black Stockarton Moor (Table 7) began with a first phase of strike-parallel dykes and a granodiorite sheet complex; this was followed by the second phase which comprised a series of granodiorite stocks. This second phase culminated in the emplacement of the Bengairn quartz-diorite pluton, and was closely followed by a suite of dominantly north-west-trending dykes, including lamprophyres and members of the 'porphyrite-porphyry' series. These dykes show a pronounced deflection of strike around High Arkland [730 574] and Tongland [690 545], with trends swinging from north-west–south-east to almost north–south. This is interpreted as due to dyke injection into an actively opening en-echelon extensional shear system (Leake and Cooper, 1983). Some of these second phase dykes cut the nearby Bengairn quartz-diorite intrusion and thus post-date its emplacement. The third and final phase of activity was the emplacement of a suite of 'porphyrite' dykes into a series of east–west wrench faults.

PETROGENESIS AND TECTONIC SETTING

The igneous sequence within the Black Stockarton Moor subvolcanic complex is shown in Table 7. The overall similarity in chemistry and mineralogy between the Black Stockarton Moor and other Criffel–Dalbeattie dykes, together with their overlapping field relations, suggest that they all share a similar petrogenetic history. It is thought that the Black Stockarton Moor complex is the subvolcanic expression of the same magmas represented by the Criffel–Dalbeattie Pluton, and that the compositions preserved at the former, as with those of other dykes from around the pluton, represent melts periodically tapped from the same evolving plutonic magma chamber (Leake and Cooper, 1983; Henney, 1991).

Although the general petrology and mineralogy of the dykes is similar to others in the district, nearly all the rocks from Black Stockarton Moor show petrographical evidence for significant alteration (Henney, 1991). However, despite variation in absolute abundance of some of the LIL elements, the primordial mantle normalised spider diagrams (Wood et al., 1979) show that the element distribution patterns of samples from Black Stockarton Moor (Figure 27) are very similar to those described from other members of the 'porphyrite-porphyry' series around the Criffel–Dalbeattie Pluton. There is also no significant difference in the patterns of samples from the first and second phases of intrusion, suggesting that the structural evolution of the complex was not mirrored by a simple chemical evolution of the magmas.

Volcanic vents

Ten volcanic vents and related structures such as breccia pipes and sheets with contemporaneous lamprophyre dykes have recently been described by Rock et al. (1986a, b) in Table 11.

The largest and best exposed of the volcanic vents crops out at the coast on the west side of Kirkcudbright Bay, at Shoulder o' Craig [662 491]. This body is composite and intrudes folded wackes of the Carghidown Formation. In order of emplacement, the body comprises:

i   A carbonated vent agglomerate of wacke clasts in a fine-grained comminuted igneous matrix. Locally, the agglomerate contains vuggy quartz and carbonate veins, and grades into a tuff.

ii   An approximately 30 × 15 m irregular-shaped fractured and altered biotite-bearing olivine basaltic intrusion. This unit is pervasively altered, but, in one rare fresh sample, it contains olivine phenocrysts in a basaltic matrix of colourless augite, magnetite, biotite and highly sericitised plagioclase. Despite the effects of alteration, Rock et al. (1986b) suggested that geochemically this rock is a calc-alkaline basalt.

iii   Kersantite intrusions. These distinctive mica-lamprophyres occur as irregular dyke-like bodies intruding the basaltic vent and the surrounding country rock and have been dated at 410 Ma. Many of these dykes exhibit bizarre shapes, the most spectacular being the so-called 'Loch Ness Monster' dyke just to the north of the main vent outcrop (Rock et al., 1986b, fig. 4). Altered dykes of similar form and composition occur immediately to the south-west in Nun Mill Bay and 0.7 km to the south-east on St Mary's Isle [6690 4881]. Petrographically and chemically, these intrusions resemble calc-alkaline lamprophyres (Rock, 1984) and are similar to, and most probably part of, the regional dyke-swarm as defined by Rock et al. (1986a).

Table 11
Location of subvolcanic vents and related structures (after Rock et al., 1986b).

Locality	NGR	Maximum size (m)
Subvolcanic explosion-breccia pipes with little or no igneous component		
Pennan Hill	733 565	75 × 50
Weather Hill, near Pennan Hill	7365 5652	30 × 10
Subvolcanic breccia dykes/sheets with variable igneous component		
St Michael's Glen	732 515	160 × < 10
Gribdae	7246 4978	a few metres
Rockcliffe	8531 5299	a few metres
Nun Mill Bay	659 488	3 zones, 5–15 m long, in 200 m section
Subvolcanic vents with major igneous component		
Shoulder o'Craig	662 491	250 × 100
Knockorr–Bombie Glen	707 506	250 × 100 overall; 100 × 40 main body
Ingleston	662 553	?50 × 50
Knockskelly	724 545	50 × 10

iv   Late intrusive basaltic sheets and dykes which resemble ii above but are emplaced in fault zones and are associated with highly altered explosion-breccias and tuffisite veins.

v   Ramifying carbonate, chrysotile and quartz veins, probably related to late-stage metasomatic processes.

The other vent and breccia pipes are poorly exposed and their internal structures and contacts are difficult to define. Apart from the Ingleston Vent, the remaining bodies are associated with the lamprophyre and microdiorite ('porphyrite') dyke-swarm of the Black Stockarton Moor subvolcanic complex (Leake and Cooper, 1983). Most outcrops consist of highly altered vuggy wacke/siltstone agglomerate with a nonigneous matrix of comminuted sedimentary rock, carbonate, epidote and quartz with diffuse, isolated patches of carbonated tuffisite.

SEVEN

Upper Palaeozoic

Rocks of late Devonian and Dinantian (Tournaisian to Viséan) age crop out in a series of outliers on the Kirkcudbrightshire coast along the northern margin of the Solway Basin (Tables 12–14, Figure 28). Early accounts of the geology of the district include Jameson (1814), Jolly (1869), Horne et al. (1896) and Smith (1910). More recently Craig (1956), Deegan (1970; 1973), Frölicher (1977; 1984) and Ord et al. (1988) have re-examined the coastal sections. Regional interpretations of the coastal sequences in the context of the Northumberland–Solway Basin include those by Leeder (1974), Barrett (1988), Chadwick et al. (1995), Jackson et al. (1995) and Maguire et al. (1996).

The most extensive outlier, that at Kirkbean (Craig, 1956), reveals a discontinuous sequence, some 900 m thick, of shallow marine Border Group strata of Viséan age between Southerness [976 543] and Hogus Point [997 587]. Scattered inland exposures, notably in Kirkbean Glen [975 591], reveal the underlying and oldest (Tournaisian) Carboniferous sedimentary rocks of the district; these overlie a thin development of basaltic lavas and Upper Old Red Sandstone strata. East of Southerness, the Carboniferous strata are hidden under the coastal drift deposits of Preston Merse. At Southwick Merse [920 560], scattered outcrops of arkosic conglomerate and sandstone represent the easternmost extension of several isolated outcrops of the Colvend and Rerrick Outliers (Figure 28; Craig and Nairn, 1956; Deegan, 1970; 1973). These rocks, which are bounded to the north by the North Solway Fault, comprise dominantly coarse-grained, 'red bed' sequences but locally they contain marine mudstones and limestones which enable tentative correlation to be made with the Kirkbean Outlier (Table 12).

The generalised vertical section for Sheet 5E (Dalbeattie) and Table 12 show the relationship between the lithostratigraphical formations recognised on the Solway coast and the divisions (Lower, Middle and Upper) of the Border Group of the Langholm (Lumsden et al., 1967) and Bewcastle (Day, 1970) districts. The lithostratigraphical formations of the north Solway coast have been placed within a single unit, the Border Group (Table 12) as used by Hughes (1995) for BGS Sheet 6W (Kirkbean) (BGS, 1996) and by Smith and McMillan (1996). The tripartite division of the Langholm and Bewcastle areas, although reflecting lithological differences, was primarily distinguished on biostratigraphical grounds with the top and base of each unit defined by marker horizons. Modern lithostratigraphical practice could, however, consider these tripartite divisions as component formations within the Border Group. The following account describes, where appropriate, biostratigraphical equivalence between the two areas.

The lowermost rocks of the Border Group in the region comprise basalts of the Birrenswark Volcanic Formation and these define the base of the Carboniferous system along the northern margin of the Northumberland–Solway Basin. These rocks, together with the succeeding Kirkbean Cementstone Formation and part of the Southerness Limestone Formation, are of approximately the same biostratigraphical age as the Lower Border Group (Lumsden et al, 1967; Day, 1970; Brand, 1996). The upper part of the Southerness Limestone Formation, the succeeding sandstone-dominated strata of the Gillfoot Sandstone Formation and the overlying Powillimount Sandstone Formation are generally equivalent in age to the Middle Border Group (Brand, 1996). Craig (1956) correlated the Gillfoot Sandstone Formation and the Powillimount Sandstone Formation with the Fell Sandstone of the Scottish Borders and Northern England (Peach and Horne, 1903). The youngest strata of the Kirkbean Outlier, the Arbigland Limestone Formation, have some faunal similarities with the upper part of the Middle Border Group, but the closest comparison of the fauna lies with strata between the Scott Beds and Burns Beds of the Upper Border Group of the Langholm area (Brand, 1996).

North of Kirkbean, a small part of the Permian Dumfries Basin lies within the district. In his revised lithostratigraphy for the basin, Brookfield (1978) recognised two interdigitating formations, the Locharbriggs (formerly Dumfries) Sandstone Formation and the Doweel Breccia Formation, laid down under desert conditions. The latter is best observed west of Dumfries and occupies much of the western part of the basin. The western margin of the basin is probably faulted, as Bott and Masson Smith (1960) indicated from geophysical evidence, although the contact between the breccias and Silurian turbidites is not exposed west of the Nith estuary. East of the River Nith, conglomeratic breccias of the Doweel Breccia Formation are present on the coast at Glencaple [994 685].

UPPER DEVONIAN

UPPER OLD RED SANDSTONE

A thin sequence of sedimentary 'red beds' assigned to the Upper Old Red Sandstone (Horne et al., 1896; Craig, 1956) is exposed in Kirkbean Glen [9715 5920] and Ladyland Burn [9645 5795], north of Prestonmill. The strata rest with marked angular unconformity on steeply inclined Ross Formation turbidites of Wenlock age and underlie basaltic lavas of the Birrenswark Volcanic Formation (Tables 12–13). In Kirkbean Glen, 8.4 m of

Table 12   Lower Carboniferous stratigraphy, northern margin of the Solway Basin.

Series	Stage	Kirkbean Outlier Lithostratigraphy: Kirkbean and Southerness–Borron Point–Hogus Point		Colvend and Rerrick outliers lithostratigraphy	Langholm biostratigraphy
Viséan	Asbian	Border Group	Arbigland Limestone Formation (top not seen)	no strata	Upper Border Group
	Holkerian		Thirlstane Sandstone Member	Rascarrel Formation	Glencartholm Volcanic Beds
			Powillimount Sandstone Formation		Middle Border Group
	Arundian		Gillfoot Sandstone Formation	no strata	
	Chadian		Syringothyris Limestone	Orroland Formation	Harden Beds
			Southerness Limestone Formation		Lower Border Group
			Kirkbean Cementstone Formation (not exposed at coast)	Wall Hill Sandstone Formation	
Tournaisian	Courceyan		Birrenswark Volcanic Formation		Birrenswark Lavas
		Upper Old Red Sandstone (cf. Kinnesswood Formation and Stockiemuir Sandstone Formation of the Midland Valley)			Upper Old Red Sandstone

Notes:

1   This table does not show relative thickness of different groups, formations and members.
2   The tripartite division of Border Group of the Langholm area (Lumsden et al., 1967) is biostratigraphically defined. Lithostratigraphical formations of the Kirkbean area are placed within the Border Group as used by Hughes (1995), BGS (1996) and Smith and McMillan (1996)
3   The Rascarrel Formation, Gillfoot Sandstone Formation and Powillimount Sandstone Formation may be lateral equivalents of the diachronous Fell Sandstone (as originally proposed by Craig, 1956)

strata are exposed (Craig, 1956). The base of the sequence locally comprises a siltstone breccia and conglomerate dominated by greywacke and granite clasts. Above this, typical lithologies are purple-grey, green and red mudstone, red-brown, micaceous siltstone and brownish grey, fine-grained sandstone. In Ladyland Burn, the principal lithology comprises soft, red, micaceous mudstone interbedded with sandstone. Both at Kirkbean Glen and Ladyland Burn, numerous carbonate (cornstone) nodules in beds of red mudstone may be the equivalent of palaeosols recognized elsewhere within the topmost few metres of the Upper Old Red Sandstone strata of the Scottish Borders Basin (Leeder, 1973; 1976).

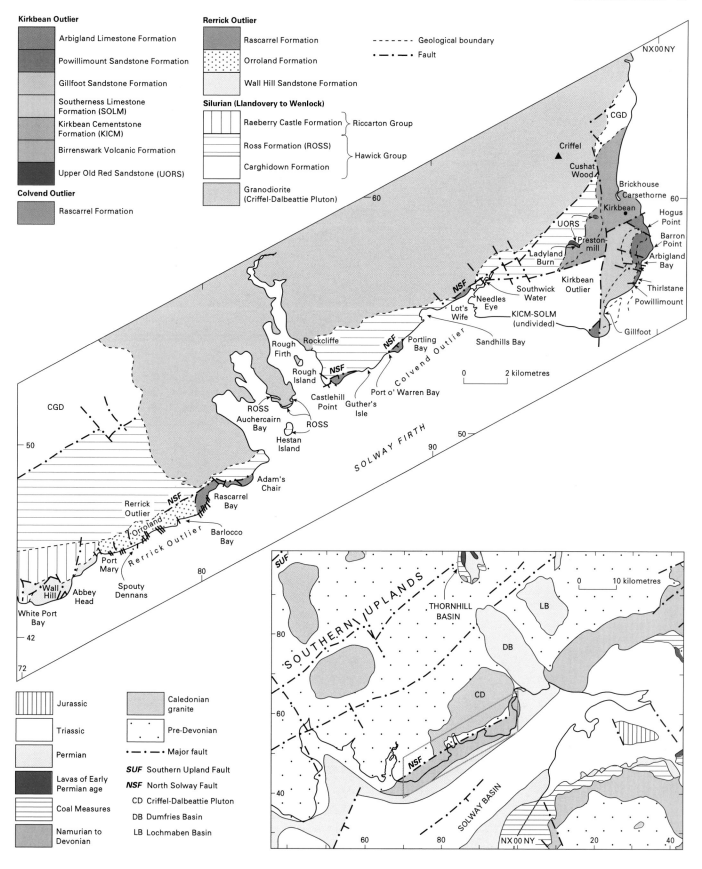

Figure 28 Upper Devonian and Lower Carboniferous outliers on the northern margin of the Solway Basin. Area of detailed map (top) outlined.

Table 13 Formational nomenclature and depositional environment for the Lower Carboniferous Kirkbean Outlier.	Formation	Thickness (metres)	Environment of deposition (after Craig, 1956, and Deegan, 1970)
	Arbigland Limestone Formation	> 300 m	Intertidal and subtidal
	Powillimount Sandstone Formation (including 25 m-thick Thirlstane Sandstone Member)	c. 160 m	Tidal lagoon with occasional parallic intervals
	Gillfoot Sandstone Formation	120–150 m	Marginal marine with strong fluviatile influence
	Southerness Limestone Formation	135 m	Lagoonal, intertidal to subtidal
	Kirkbean Cementstone Formation	> 100 m	Parallic, low rates of sedimentation within estuarine environment
	Birrenswark Volcanic Formation	15 m	Fissure eruption
	Upper Old Red Sandstone	c. 10 m	Alluvial plain, local development of palaeosols

The Kirkbean Glen and Ladyland Burn rocks represent the westernmost extension of the Upper Old Red Sandstone sequence in the Scottish Borders Basin, which is regarded as a wholly fluviatile sequence (Leeder, 1973). Lithological characteristics of the bulk of the succession are similar to those of the Stockiemuir Sandstone Formation of the Midland Valley (Paterson and Hall, 1986). The uppermost part of the sequence, characterised by concretionary carbonates, may be the equivalent of the Kinnesswood Formation of the Midland Valley (Browne et al., 1996). Palaeocurrent data for the basin as a whole indicate persistent stream flow from south-west to north-east. However, at the basin margin a north westerly derivation for the sediments is consistent with palaeocurrents from this direction and is supported by compositional characteristics including pebbles of wacke

and felsic igneous rocks which suggest a local provenance (Leeder, 1973). The presence of cornstone nodules and recognisable carbonate palaeosols was considered by Leeder (1974; 1976) to represent periods of uplift and dissection of the alluvial depositional surface, effected by partial melting in the upper mantle. Subsequent local volcanic activity resulted in partial burial of the palaeosols by lava flows in parts of the basin, followed by the more extensive eruption of basaltic lavas of the Birrenswark Volcanic Formation.

The Kirkbean 'red beds' are considered to be of Tournaisian age. At Langholm, Lumsden et al. (1967) suggested that lithologically similar strata yielding *Holoptychius nobilissimus* may represent a distinctive reddened facies of early Carboniferous age. Age determination of the succeeding basalt lavas from Langholm and Kelso in

Table 14 Revised formational nomenclature and depositional environment for the Lower Carboniferous Colvend and Rerrick outliers.	Formations (formerly groups of Deegan, 1973)	Members (formerly formations of Deegan, 1973)	Environment of deposition (after Deegan, 1973)
	Rascarrel > 360 m	Lochenling c. 60 m	Alluvial fan preceded by piedmont and marginal marine conditions
		Rascarrel Burnfoot c. 210 m	Piedmont
		Castle Muir c. 90 m	Middle to Lower fan, braided channels
	Orroland c. 280 m	Black Neuk c. 100 m	Coarse alluvial fan
		Scar Heugh c. 28 m	Fluvial
		Orroland Lodge c. 9 m	Marginal marine with fluvial incursions
		Barlocco Heugh > 10 m	Marginal marine with fluvial incursions
		Dropping Craig 25 m	Lower fan and piedmont
		Spouty Dennans c. 18 m	Lower fan and piedmont
		Hanged Man c. 90 m	Alluvial fan
	Wall Hill Sandstone c. 360 m	Abbey Head < 40 m	Low sinuosity fluvial system
		Sheep Bught 120 m	Fluvial, meandering system
		White Port 210 m	Low sinuosity fluvial system

the Scottish Borders indicates that eruption probably straddled the Devonian–Carboniferous boundary (see below; De Souza 1982).

CARBONIFEROUS

BORDER GROUP

Kirkbean Outlier

BIRRENSWARK VOLCANIC FORMATION

Resting conformably on the Upper Old Red Sandstone strata is a thin sequence of olivine-basalt lava flows, regarded as the westernmost extension of the Birrenswark lavas of Dumfriesshire (Pallister, 1952) and Langholm (McRobert, 1920; Lumsden et al., 1967) (Tables 12 and 13). The rocks underlie a broad strip of fertile ground along the lowest part of the southern scarp of Criffel. The principal exposure is in Kirkbean Glen where some 15 m of crudely stratified, deeply weathered, dark grey to black, fine-grained, amygdaloidal basalt flows are present. Amygdales, rimmed with chlorite and filled with calcite, up to 1 cm diameter are commonly seen. In thin section, the Fe-rich, finely crystalline groundmass contains laths of subhedral plagioclase and pseudomorphs after olivine, indicative of the macroporphyritic Markle Basalt type of the Midland Valley volcanic province (Cameron and Stephenson, 1985).

In his review of the petrochemistry of Dinantian lavas, Macdonald (1975) classified the Birrenswark lavas as hawaiites and basaltic hawaiites and noted that they are hypersthene ± quartz normative basalts, moderately to strongly enriched in TiO_2. Although there is no evidence of basalt-filled feeder dykes and/or aligned necks, Leeder (1974) proposed that fissures aligned along the length of the outcrop produced the observed north-east-orientated elongate distribution of the lava pile and probably formed as a result of north–south tensional stresses responsible for the generation of the Solway Basin. Such a stress field may have been related to back-arc stretching of the lithosphere as the Rheno-Hercynian seaway closed (Leeder, 1982; 1988).

The lavas of the Birrenswark Volcanic Formation and the broadly contemporaneous Kelso Lavas (Francis, 1991) represent the first magmatic episode in the Scottish Carboniferous volcanic cycle. An olivine basalt flow at Watch Hill near Langholm [NY 435 905] and an aphyric basalt from a plug at Mellerstain Hill, near Kelso [NT 641 397] have been dated by the K–Ar whole-rock method as 361 ± 12 and 361 ± 7 Ma respectively, i.e. close to the Devonian–Carboniferous boundary (De Souza, 1982). Lithostratigraphically, they are defined as forming the base of the Border Group (Table 12).

KIRKBEAN CEMENTSTONE FORMATION

Rocks of the Kirkbean Cementstone Formation are exposed at several inland localities, although their contact with the younger Dinantian strata on the coast is not seen. Termed the Basal Cementstones by Craig (1956), the formation is thought to represent the oldest

Carboniferous strata (of Courceyan age) preserved in the North Solway outliers and to be the equivalent of the cementstone facies within strata of Lower Border Group age in the Langholm area (Lumsden et al., 1967) (Table 12). Lithologically, the strata are similar to the Ballagan Formation of the Midland Valley (Browne et al., 1996). Within the district, based on limited field evidence, the formation is of the order of 100 m thick and rests unconformably on the Birrenswark Volcanic Formation. Locally the sequence oversteps the basalt lavas to lie directly on Wenlock strata and at the north-easternmost extent of outcrop it is downfaulted against granodiorite of the Criffel–Dalbeattie Pluton.

The cementstone facies rocks are best seen in Kirkbean Glen [NX 9759 5912], where fragmentary plant remains but no shelly fauna have been found in a 20 m sequence of carbonaceous siltstones and mudstones with thin cementstone stringers. The strata are faulted against basalt. North of Kirkbean Glen, strata containing *Modiolus latus* and ostracods are found in sections in the Nimbly Burn [9800 6036], near Brickhouse. Exposures in the unnamed streams draining the lower slopes of Criffel in Cushat Wood [974 613] provide short sequences of steeply dipping, hard, pale grey cementstones and interbedded mudstones with scattered fossiliferous horizons containing *Naticopsis* sp., *Modiolus latus* and *Naiadites* sp. (Brand, 1996). The latter is a form, so far undescribed, which also occurs in the upper part of the Lower Border Group sequence of the Langholm area. In Prestonmill Burn [9664 5761], calcareous mudstones rest on an uneven surface of lava. Downstream, dark grey micaceous mudstones have yielded a sparse fauna including *Modiolus latus* and ostracods (Brand, 1996). In the Redbank Burn [9490 5662], algal growths and several bivalves including *Schizodus* cf. *pentlandicus* have been found, a fauna which occurs at or about the biostratigraphical boundary between the Lower and Middle Border groups at Langholm. Strata in a tributary of the Prestonmill Burn [9848 0832] provided a brachiopod fauna including *Antiquatonia* sp., '*Camarotoechia*' cf. *proava* and *Cleiothyridina* cf. *glabistria*, and may represent an horizon in the overlying Southerness Limestone Formation.

The facies of the Kirkbean Cementstone Formation is indicative of deposition of small volumes of fine-grained sediment in shallow, slow-moving water in a predominantly estuarine environment (Table 13). The impure muddy limestones or cementstones probably formed as a result of frequent submergence of mudflats in semi-stagnant saline water.

SOUTHERNESS LIMESTONE FORMATION

The Southerness Limestone Formation is well exposed on the coast to the south-west of the village of Southerness [976 543]. Further west, the strata are concealed by thick deposits of estuarine and glacial drift deposits which occupy the coastal strip of land known as Preston Merse, an area approximately 2 by 6 km extending westwards to the Southwick Water [916 560]. In this area the strata are shown as undivided 'Lower Border Group' on Sheet 5E, (Dalbeattie; BGS, 1993b) and as Border Group on Sheet 6W, (Kirkbean; BGS, 1996).

The type section of the Southerness Limestone Formation (Craig, 1956) occupies a 0.5 km stretch of coast about 400 m west of the lighthouse at Southerness between [968 543] and [973 541]. The strata are deformed by a gently north-east-plunging anticline [9703 5416], within the eastern limb of which are exposed some 135 m of fossiliferous, thin-bedded calcareous mudstones, siltstones and limestones. Four prominent thin beds of well-sorted, calcareous sandstone, averaging 1 m thick, are present. Dips vary from 5° to 45°. At Southerness [9733 5414], a north–south-orientated fault downthrows the succeeding Gillfoot Sandstone Formation against the Southerness Limestone Formation. East of the fault and about 0.5 km to the north of the lighthouse the conformable junction of the Southerness Limestone Formation and the overlying Gillfoot Sandstone Formation is taken at the base of a sandstone with calcareous, rod-shaped concretions (Craig, 1956). The contact with the underlying Kirkbean Cementstone Formation is not seen.

Although a number of east–west-orientated faults disrupt the shore strata of the Southerness Limestone Formation west of Southerness, a reasonably complete section across the eastern limb of the anticline has been measured and described by Deegan (1970, fig 2; Figure 29). Limestones range from light grey, massive, crystalline types to dark grey argillaceous and sandy varieties. They contain an abundant, varied marine fauna mainly comprising molluscs and brachiopods. Within this sequence, the Syringothyris Limestone (Table 12; Figure 29) was estimated by Craig (1956) to be 16.7 m thick. The limestone comprises several beds of argillaceous limestone and calcareous mudstone, and contains a varied marine fauna including *Antiquatonia* cf. *teres*, *Productus* cf. *garwoodi*, *Punctospirifer* cf. *scabricosta*, *Syringothyris cuspidata*, *Naiadites crassus*, *Pteronites* cf. *angustatus*, *Sanguinolites* cf. *roxburgensis* and *Schizodus* cf. *pentlandicus* (Brand, 1996). Faunally there are similarities with the Harden Beds at the base of the Middle Border Group at Langholm (Lumsden et al., 1967, p.91; Brand, 1996), and the biostratigraphy indicates that the Southerness Limestone Formation is for the most part Chadian (as stated by George et al., 1976) but could range into Arundian (Table 12).

Above the Syringothyris Limestone, two distinctive algal stromatolite bands, 1.2 m and 1 m thick, are present within the sequence (Plate 10). Craig (1956) and Frölicher (1977) referred the stromatolite forms to the genus *Somphospongia*. The stromatolite structures resemble the dome type described by Leeder (1975) from the lower part of the Border Group of the Northumberland Basin. Individual domes are up to 30 cm in diameter with a relief of 10 to 15 cm and are set in a calcareous mudstone matrix. They are composed of alternating micritic and detrital laminae. Calcareous algal filaments commonly wrap fragments of shell including gastropods and ostracods. The irregular, nodular exterior of the algal growths indicates limited reworking. Basing his observations on studies of modern stromatolites, Leeder (1975) inferred that domed types formed in a low intertidal to shallow subtidal depositional environment (Table 13).

In the upper part of the Southerness Limestone Formation Deegan (1970) identified a series of sedimentary cycles. Prominent algal horizons are developed at similar positions in two of the three cycles he identified and a composite cycle may be summarised as follows:

> Flaggy sandstone with plant remains
> Interbedded limestone and micaceous mudstones
> Interbedded limestone and calcareous mudstones
> Nodular algal band
> Thin muddy limestone with calcareous mudstone
> Fine-grained, rippled sandstone
> Flaggy, micaceous sandstone with ripple marks and plant remains

The cyclicity reflects varying depositional environments and may be attributed to gradual subsidence and rise in sea level combined with variations in terrigenous sediment input (Deegan, 1970), possibly related to periodic dip-slip movement on basin boundary faults. Each cycle commences with sandstone, probably deposited in a littoral environment, and is succeeded by calcareous beds which were formed under shallow subtidal conditions. Sandy limestones containing oolites indicate that the sediments were affected by wave action. Conversely, the algal beds show little sign of reworking and probably represent slightly deeper water below the wave base (Table 13).

GILLFOOT SANDSTONE FORMATION

Between 120 and 150 m of strata assigned to the Gillfoot Sandstone Formation are exposed on the shore between the fault, 400 m west of the lighthouse at Southerness [9733 5414]and a position south of Powillimount Farm [9880 5620] (Tables 12, 13). To the east of Southerness [980 548], the strata conformably overlie the Southerness Limestone Formation, whereas to the west of the lighthouse they are down-faulted against these rocks. Craig (1956) placed the top of the formation at the base of a grey calcareous breccia, the lowest bed of the succeeding Powillimount Sandstone Formation.

The Gillfoot Sandstone Formation is dominated by white and purplish, flaggy, quartzose sandstones, purple conglomerates with intraformational fragments, red flaggy siltstones and purple mudstones. A few red to grey, thin-bedded sandy limestones with scattered detrital and fossil remains are also present. Conglomerates, which form about 20% of the succession, have a calcareous matrix and contain intraformational fragments in addition to pebbles of vein quartz, turbidite sandstone and 'porphyrite' (porphyritic microdiorite) derived from the Southern Uplands hinterland to the north. Some of the

Figure 29 Generalised lithological logs of Dinantian strata in the Kirkbean Outlier, mainly from sections logged by Deegan (1970). Gillfoot Sandstone Formation not shown. Column width illustrates relative hardness of beds.

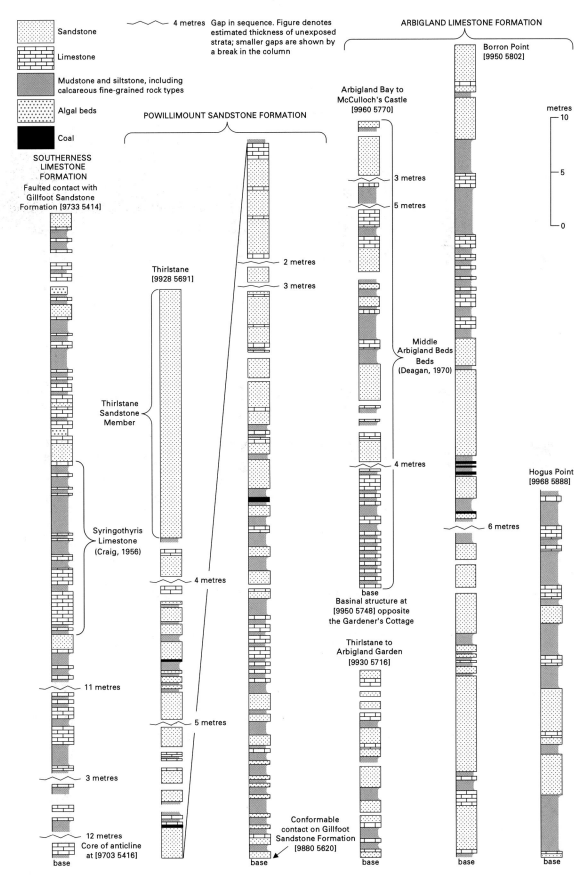

Sandstone

Limestone

Mudstone and siltstone, including calcareous fine-grained rock types

Algal beds

Coal

SOUTHERNESS LIMESTONE FORMATION

Faulted contact with Gillfoot Sandstone Formation [9733 5414]

Thirlstane Sandstone Member

Syringothyris Limestone (Craig, 1956)

11 metres

3 metres

12 metres
Core of anticline at [9703 5416]
base

POWILLIMOUNT SANDSTONE FORMATION

4 metres Gap in sequence. Figure denotes estimated thickness of unexposed strata; smaller gaps are shown by a break in the column

Thirlstane [9928 5691]

4 metres

5 metres

Conformable contact on Gillfoot Sandstone Formation [9880 5620]
base

2 metres

3 metres

base

ARBIGLAND LIMESTONE FORMATION

Borron Point [9950 5802]

Arbigland Bay to McCulloch's Castle [9960 5770]

3 metres

5 metres

Middle Arbigland Beds Beds (Deagan, 1970)

4 metres

base
Basinal structure at [9950 5748] opposite the Gardener's Cottage

Thirlstane to Arbigland Garden [9930 5716]

6 metres

metres
— 10

— 5

— 0

Hogus Point [9968 5888]

base

base

Plate 10   Algal stromatolites from the Southerness Limestone Formation, Southerness
[9722 5413] (D 4482).

more feldspathic bands are dominated by porphyrite debris.

The formation is sparsely fossiliferous. Near the top of the formation east of the lighthouse [9777 5428] a shelly rib yielded a fauna, possibly derived, including *Siphonodendron* cf. *scoticum* and *Punctospirifer scabricosta* amongst other marine fossils (Craig, 1956). Hill (1940, p.173) stated that *S. scoticum* occurs in S$_2$ and D$_1$ zones in Britain, that is, in strata of Arundian to Asbian age. Faunal evidence suggests that the strata of the Gillfoot Sandstone Formation are of Arundian age and biostratigraphically equivalent to the upper part of the Middle Border Group of Langholm (Lumsden et al., 1967; George et al., 1976; Brand, 1996).

The lithologies typical of the Gillfoot Sandstone Formation indicate a more marginal depositional setting than that deduced for the underlying formation. The conglomeratic facies may have been periodically trans-ported from the hinterland and deposited by sheetfloods flowing over low-lying supra-tidal areas (Table 13). Textures in the sandstones indicate extensive wave action in a littoral environment. Shallow subtidal environments may be indicated by the presence of thin, fossiliferous sandy limestones.

POWILLIMOUNT SANDSTONE FORMATION

About 160 m of strata exposed on the shore between Powillimount Bay [9880 5610] and Thirl Stane [9925 5690] are assigned to the Powillimount Sandstone Formation (Craig, 1956, Table 12). The top 25 m comprises the Thirlstane Sandstone Member, a prominent ridge of thick-bedded sandstone with spectacular penecontemporaneous deformation structures (Craig, 1956; Deegan, 1970; Ord et al., 1988). A lithological log of the Powillimount Sandstone Formation, based on Deegan (1970) is given as 2 in Figure 29. The base of the Powillimount

Sandstone Formation is taken at the top of the highest bed of conglomerate associated with purple mudstones. The strata form part of the south-east limb of the major north-east-trending anticlinal structure and, on the coast, are folded about a tight, gently plunging synclinal–anticlinal fold pair, the axial planes of which trend north-north-east.

Lithologies include calcareous and quartzose sandstones, sandy limestones with beds of dark grey fissile mudstone and calcareous mudstone. Locally, thin coals and associated seatearths are present. Sandstone beds are laterally extensive, range in thickness from 0.3 to 3 m and are well sorted with common ripple cross-lamination. They contain abundant carbonaceous plant remains and are extensively burrowed, particularly by *Chondrites*. Limestones range from arenaceous to argillaceous types and contain detrital fossil remains, ooliths and rolled algal nodules. One distinctive oncolite bed, 0.3 m thick, contains rounded algal-coated lithic and fossil fragments, individual oncolites reaching 1 cm diameter (Plate 11). Aspects of the fauna immediately below the Thirlstane Sandstone resemble those of the overlying Arbigland Limestone Formation (Brand, 1996) but overall faunal assemblages indicate biostratigraphical equivalence with strata of Middle Border Group age of Langholm (Lumsden et al., 1967).

The characteristic lithologies together with the presence of rolled algal nodules and detrital fragments point to a shallow-marine environment in which wave action predominated. Deegan (1970) proposed that the sediments were deposited in a tidal lagoon protected from the effects of severe storms by some form of offshore sand barrier. The presence of thin developments of coal and associated seatearth indicates periodic shallowing of lagoonal waters and the development of highly vegetated low-lying supratidal flats (Table 13).

Thirlstane Sandstone Member

This 25 m thick unit at the top of the Powillimount Sandstone Formation forms a prominent sandstone ridge which can be traced from [9908 5645] to Thirl Stane [9928 5691]. The basal 0.75 m of the Thirlstane Sandstone Member comprises a lag deposit of medium- to coarse-grained sandstone containing intraformational red mudstone clasts and large carbonaceous wood fragments. The contact with the underlying strata is sharp and erosive.

Above the basal beds is a continuous sequence of stacked, trough cross bedded, pinkish grey, fine- to medium-grained, moderately to well-sorted, quartzose sandstone. Palaeocurrents indicate flow was predominantly to the west (Maguire et al., 1996). Within the sequence there is evidence for intense penecontemporaneous liquefaction (Plate 12). In a detailed study, Ord et al. (1988) noted that soft sediment deformation structures increased in frequency and magnitude from south to north along the strike of the outcrop and recognised a number of styles of deformation including oversteepened and recumbently folded cross-stratification, domes, sand volcanoes and zones of anastomosing, vertical cracks. Ord et. al. (1988) attributed the magnitude and frequency of the liquefaction structures to allokinetic causes, and deduced the presence of a syndepositionally active fault lying to the north of the present outcrop of the Thirlstane Sandstone.

Deegan (1970) proposed that the Thirlstane Sandstone formed as an offshore sand barrier which initially enabled the inshore lagoonal environment of the Powillimount Sandstone Formation to be developed. A marine origin was also favoured by Barrett (1988), but the absence of marine indicators and the presence of stacked unidirectional bedforms points to deposition within a

Plate 11 Algal oncolites from the Powillimount Sandstone Formation, shore near Powillimount Glen [9894 5630] (D 4485).

Plate 12 Penecontemporaneous liquefaction deformation structures in sandstone beds, Thirlstane Sandstone Member, Thirl Stane, Powillimount [9925 5684] (D 4489).

braided fluvial system (Ord et al., 1988, Maguire et al., 1996).

ARBIGLAND LIMESTONE FORMATION

All the coastal strata exposed between Thirl Stane and Hogus Point [997 589] are assigned to the Arbigland Limestone Formation (Craig, 1956). The top of the formation is not exposed. The base is probably conformable with the Thirlstane Sandstone Member (Smith, 1910). Shifting beach sands often obscure this relationship and the most readily observed contact is a rotated normal fault on the rocky foreshore [9926 5692] (Craig, 1956). Between Thirl Stane and a west-north-west-orientated hinge fault opposite Arbigland Garden [9930 5716], the strata strike parallel to the line of the coast. North of the fault at Arbigland Garden, a narrow zone of disrupted bedding is succeeded by a series of beds striking west-north-west. Across Arbigland Bay the rocks are poorly exposed. North of the bay a small, shallow, periclinal basin structure is present. To the north of this basin the strike of the strata swings from east–west through east-north-east to north-west, to broadly parallel the line of the coast around Borron Point [9950 5802] where locally dips are steep. The northernmost coastal exposures of the formation, which may not necessarily be the highest stratigraphically (cf. Craig, 1956), are present at Hogus Point [9970 5888]. The strata are cut by numerous normal faults of west-north-west and north-west orientation. For this reason, and because of discontinuous exposure, it is not possible to measure a complete section through the Arbigland Limestone Formation. However, according to Craig (1956) and Deegan (1970), the total thickness of exposed strata is probably in excess of 300 m. Lithological logs of representative sections in the Arbigland Limestone Formation are presented as 3–6 in Figure 29.

The sequence is generally more fossiliferous than the Powillimount Sandstone Formation. In particular the section between Arbigland Bay and Borron Point (Middle Arbigland Beds of Deegan, 1970) is richly fossiliferous and contains a fine coral fauna including spectacular massive hemispherical colonies of *Lithostrotion clavaticum,* first recorded by Smith (1910). Some appear to have been overturned and then buried. *Siphonophyllia benburbensis*, which is also present in the fauna, has a long range through the Asbian into strata of Brigantian age (Mitchell, 1989, p.235) but is unknown in earlier strata. Hill (1940) compared the coral fauna at Arbigland with those obtained from S_2 to D_1 zones elsewhere in Britain.

The lithologies in the section between Thirl Stane and Arbigland Garden resemble those of the Powillimount Sandstone Formation and include thick-bedded, bioturbated, calcareous sandstones with coalified plant casts, thin sandy limestones locally with ooliths and algal debris, dark grey carbonaceous mudstones and thin coal partings (3 in Figure 29).

As noted above, exposure is poor across Arbigland Bay but is continuous between the small basinal structure [at 9950 5748] and Borron Point [9950 5802]. Deegan (1970) referred to these rocks as the Middle Arbigland Beds. His measured section between the basin and a position opposite the site of McCulloch's Castle [9960 5770] (4 in Figure 29) shows the sequence to comprise mainly thin argillaceous and sandy limestones interbedded with calcareous mudstones and several prominent thick beds of massive, bioturbated sandstone. Many beds of sandstone and sandy limestone have been extensively and repeatedly reworked by sediment feeders, and burrow forms such as *Chondrites, Diplocraterion* and *Rhizocorallium* are common. The limestones and mudstones have an abundant and diverse fauna including corals, brachiopods, bivalves, gastropods, crinoids, bryozoa and orthocones (Plate 13 and Brand, 1996).

At Borron Point, stratigraphically higher rocks of the Arbigland Limestone Formation are downthrown by two small faults; in the process the strata have been steeply inclined and are locally overturned. The sequence (5 in Figure 29) is characterised by thick-bedded, bioturbated, laminated and ripple cross-laminated, fine-grained sandstone interbedded with calcareous mudstone and a few argillaceous limestones. Shallow sandstone-filled scours and washouts are common.

Shore exposure is reasonably good at Hogus Point [9968 5888] where the strata are disposed about a tight, gently north-east–south-west-plunging anticline-syncline fold-pair. A lithological section is shown as 6 in Figure 29 and comprises thick units of thin-bedded silty, calcareous mudstone, well-bedded sandstone and some thin-bedded sandy limestone. Although Craig (1956) considered the beds at Hogus Point to be the highest in the sequence, the fauna indicates a position no higher than the beds between the Gardener's Cottage and Borron Point and the indications are that the rocks lie on the upthrow side of a north-west orientated normal fault, the trace of which may lie north of Tallowquhairn Farm [993 584]. Faunal equivalence between the Arbigland Limestone

Formation and the Upper Border Group of Langholm of Asbian age (Lumsden et al., 1967), is considered most likely (Brand, 1996).

Lithological characteristics of the sequence between Thirl Stane and Arbigland Garden, together with the sparse, locally detrital fauna, are consistent with a restricted, lagoonal environment in which there was limited reworking of sediment. Overall, however, sedimentary rocks of the Arbigland Limestone Formation were probably deposited within the intertidal to subtidal zone in which current scour was sufficiently strong to disturb coral colonies (Figure 29).

Western outliers

West of Kirkbean, the Rerrick and Colvend outliers comprise isolated, faulted blocks of predominantly coarse-grained strata with sporadic fossiliferous limestone interbeds of Viséan age (Table 12). The rocks occur on the hanging wall of the north-east-trending North Solway Fault. On the basis of faunal content of limestones at Orroland [777 463], Craig and Nairn (1956) were able to correlate the sequence with the Kirkbean Outlier. Deegan (1973) established group and formational nomenclature for the outliers following a detailed stratigraphical and sedimentological study. The strata have been shown to form geographically restricted but mappable units, and formational rank is here accorded to Deegan's (1973) Wall Hill Sandstone, Orroland and Rascarrel groups, and correspondingly, member rank established for his formations (Table 14).

Rerrick Outlier

The Rerrick Outlier comprises coastal exposures between White Port Bay [723 434], south-west of Wall Hill and Barlocco Bay [795 469], and in Rascarrel Bay [807 482] (Figure 28).

WALL HILL SANDSTONE FORMATION

The basal Wall Hill Sandstone Formation, comprising three members (Table 14), is exposed between Port Mary [752 452] and White Port Bay where it rests with angular unconformity on Wenlock strata of the Raeberry Castle Formation. In the absence of fossils no biostratigraphical correlation is possible but on stratigraphical grounds the Wall Hill Sandstone Formation is older than the Orroland Formation. Deegan (1973) estimated the formation to be about 360 m thick. The principal lithologies comprise upward-fining sequences of conglomeratic sandstone, siltstone, marl and mudstone. Sedimentological studies (Deegan, 1973) suggest that the deposits were laid down in a braided fluvial system of low to moderate sinuosity. The coarse-grained sedimentary rocks are considered to have been deposited in channels, whereas the fine-grained rocks are thought to be the product of floodplain deposition. Palaeocurrent data indicate a predominately north and north-westerly source in the Southern Uplands Terrane, including the roof zone of the Criffel–Dalbeattie Pluton. Local but intense development of sediment liquefaction and fluidisation structures

Plate 13 Selected Carboniferous fossils from the district.

a. *Punctospirifer scabricosta redesdalensis* and crinoids, GSE 14807 × 1.5. Shore 90 m S of gardener's cottage, Arbigland [9941 5732]. Upper Border Group.

b. *Linoprotonia* cf. *ashfellensis*, GSE 14803 × 1. Shore between gardener's cottage and Borron Point [9958 5751 to 9976 5778]. Upper Border Group.

c. *Siphonodendron scotica*, GSE 6068 × 1. Arbigland Bay [996 576]. Upper Border Group.

d. *Actinopteria persulcata*, GSE 14761 × 1. Arbigland Bay [996 576]. Upper Border Group.

e. *Antiquatonia* cf. *teres*, GSE 14794 × 1.5. Southerness Shore [973 542]. Middle Border Group.

f. *Stenocisma* cf. *isorhyncha*, GSE 14787 × 1. Arbigland shore [996 576]. Upper Border Group.

g. *Modiolus latus*, GSE 15101 × 1. Nimbly Burn, 130 m ESE of Brickhouse [9800 6025].

h. *Prothyris* cf. *oblonga*, GSE 15102 × 3. Arbigland shore [996 576]. Upper Border Group.

i. *Syringothyris* cf. *cuspidata*, GSE 15103 × 1. Southerness shore [9728 5415]. Middle Border Group.

j. *Productus* cf. *garwoodi*, GSE 14806 × 1.5. Shore 90 m S of gardener's cottage, Arbigland [9941 5732]. Upper Border Group.

k. *Pteronites* cf. *angustatus*, GSE 15104 × 3. Shore at Hogus Point [9970 5890]. Upper Border Group.

is observed at a number of localities in the Sheep Bught and Abbey Head members (Ord et al., 1988).

ORROLAND FORMATION

The Orroland Formation comprises seven members (Table 14) and is confined to the Port Mary–Barlocco Bay coast where about 280 m of strata are exposed. The strata were described by Craig and Nairn (1956) who named them the Orroland Limestone Beds. The rocks comprise mainly red beds formed under subaerial conditions on the margin of the Solway Basin against the synsedimentary active North Solway Fault (Deegan, 1973; Ord et al., 1988). Minor north-west-orientated normal faults separate the various members which consist mainly of upward-fining sequences of con-glomerate, coarse-grained poorly sorted sandstone, red siltstone, marl and cornstone. Detailed sedimentological analysis by Deegan (1973) shows the depositional setting to range from alluvial-fan, lower-fan and piedmont environ-ments to occasional marginal marine conditions including tidal flat and adjacent higher energy littoral environments. The marine phases are represented by greyish red, fossilif-erous, sometimes oolitic, impure limestones within the Barlocco Heugh and Orroland Lodge Members (Table 14). The principal fossiliferous exposures are those on the shore near Orroland House where extensive collections were made by Macconochie of the Geological Survey in 1876, Smith (1910) and Craig and Nairn (1956). The more significant elements in the fauna include *Syringopora ramulosa*, *Antiquatonia* cf. *teres*, '*Camarotoechia*' cf. *proava*, *Syringothyris*?, *Modiolus latus*, *Pteronites* sp. and *Schizodus* cf. *pentlandicus*. All these forms have been recorded from exposures at Southerness and on this basis it is suggested that the horizon may be correlated with part of the South-erness Limestone Formation of Chadian age (Table 12; Brand, 1996). The fauna also includes a variety of gas-tropods, all of which appear to be long ranging forms, though their presence probably reflects a shallow-water depositional environment providing adequate feeding surfaces for this group of molluscs. Wilson (1989, p.117) suggested that the majority of gastropods were epifaunal benthos grazing on weed or algal mats.

RASCARREL FORMATION

The principal outcrop of the three members of the Rascarrel Formation (Table 14) is in Rascarrel Bay where Deegan (1973) estimated a total thickness in excess of 360 m. Lithologies present include arkosic and conglomer-atic sandstone, purple marl and siltstone, with thin mudstones and coals. Plant fragments and a sparse marine fauna collected from thin beds of carbonaceous sandstone within the Lochenling Member north of Rascarrel Burn mouth, have proved nondiagnostic for correlation purposes (Craig and Nairn 1956; Brand, 1996). Sedimen-tological evidence points to the Rascarrel Formation strata having been laid down in braided channels and alluvial-fan piedmont environments (Deegan, 1973; Table 14).

Colvend Outlier

The Colvend Outlier comprises three small isolated coastal outliers between Lot's Wife sea stack [910 557]

and Needle's Eye Cove [914 562], Portling Bay [883 540] and Port o' Warren [879 534] and Castlehill Point [856 525] and Gutcher's Isle [864 527].

The easternmost outlier, Lot's Wife sea stack–Needle's Eye Cove, comprises scattered outcrops of arkosic con-glomerate and sandstone protruding through the modern tidal flats of Southwick Merse [920 560] (Craig and Nairn, 1956). The strata generally dip southwards at angles between 20 and 70°, and are downthrown at their northern margin against Silurian hornfels and porphyritic microdiorite ('porphyrite'). Near the trace of the North Solway Fault, sheared and brecciated rocks are seen both in cliff sections and in tidal flat outcrops. Brecciated contacts observed in the cores of three boreholes sited near Needle's Eye [915 562] indicate a sheared contact dipping at 50°SE between Carboniferous and Silurian strata (Miller and Taylor, 1966). Lithologically, the strata resemble the coarse-grained facies of the Rascarrel Formation. No fossils have been found in these rocks.

More continuous exposure between Portling Bay and Port o' Warren and between Castlehill Point and Gutcher's Isle has enabled some 50 m of section to be measured in each outlier (Craig and Nairn, 1956; Deegan, 1973). The rocks are assigned to the Rascarrel Formation. According to Deegan (1973) they comprise 'a lower series of conglomeratic beds passing upwards into fossiliferous mudstones, sandstones and, at Portling, limestones'. Both outcrops are downfaulted against Silurian turbidites by the North Solway Fault.

In the Portling Bay–Port o' Warren outlier, sequences of poorly sorted conglomeratic sandstone fine upwards into grey siltstone and mudstone. Interbedded thin sandy limestones contain algal fragments and a sparse marine fauna. Low in the sequence Craig and Nairn (1956) recovered *Bevocastria* sp., whilst somewhat higher grey mudstones yielded both *Modiolus* sp. and common orthocone nautiloids. It is not possible to relate this fauna to the Southerness sequence with any certainty, but the admittedly sparse fauna and the presence of algal material suggest a correlation with the Powillimount Sandstone Formation (Table 12; Brand, 1996).

East of Castlehill Point in the sea cliff south-west of Barcloy Hill [857 527], the spectacular Carboniferous/Silurian unconformity is represented by a veneer of carbonate-cemented Carboniferous angular breccia, overlain by conglomerate, clinging to cliffs of Silurian strata. The breccia clasts comprise porphyritic microdior-ite ('porphyrite'), greywacke and mudstone derived from the hinterland to the north. The breccia and conglomer-ate dip seawards at high angles as a result of synsedimen-tary displacement on the North Solway Fault. Within the oversteepened zone, about 10 m wide adjacent to the faulted unconformity, the rocks have been affected by syndepositional seismic activity, as noted by Ord et al. (1988), who observed allokinetic liquefaction structures and extensional faults in both unlithified and semi lithified sediments. The conglomeratic beds are overlain by fossiliferous calcareous sandstones and black shales which contain *Linoprotonia* sp. (Ferguson, 1971) and *Punctospirifer*? together with poorly preserved bivalves (Craig and Nairn, 1956). The general aspect is of a fauna of Viséan age, possibly Holkerian, though the beds may be of early Asbian age (Brand, 1996).

As at Rascarrel Bay, the strata of the Colvend outlier were deposited in an alluvial-fan piedmont environment, influenced by intermittent syndepositional fault activity (Deegan, 1973; Table 14). Local marine incursions are represented by the fossiliferous strata within both the Portling Bay–Port o' Warren and Castlehill Point–Gutcher's Isle outliers.

Crustal shortening and basin inversion took place in late Carbonifeous times resulting in the folding of Lower Carboniferous strata. No rocks of Namurian or Westphalian age are present on the coast. A change from a marine-dominated to a terrestrial desert environment occurred at the end of the Carboniferous and rocks of Lower Palaeozoic to Carboniferous age were unconformably overlain by Permian 'red bed' breccia and sandstone sequences.

PERMIAN

DUMFRIES BASIN

The Dumfries Basin is a synclinal half graben structure bounded to the west by a north-north-west-trending fault, and filled with aeolian sandstones of the Locharbriggs Sandstone Formation and interdigitating breccias of the Doweel Breccia Formation (Brookfield, 1978). Synsedimentary fault movement coupled with relative uplift of the low density crustal block of the Criffel–Dalbeattie Pluton (Bott and Masson Smith, 1960) uplifted the basement rocks to the west and resulted in the deposition of dominantly coarse-grained, fluviatile breccia, the Doweel Breccia Formation, in the western part of the basin. The formation is regarded as partly contemporaneous with, and partly younger than the Locharbriggs Sandstone Formation which predominates in the central and eastern part of the basin.

Thick drift cover precludes field confirmation of the possibility that the breccias unconformably overlap the faulted basin margin. Breccias do, however, crop out on the east shore of the estuary of the River Nith near Glencaple [994 685]. Clasts comprise a variety of locally derived sedimentary rocks of mainly Lower Palaeozoic origin together with porphyritic andesite ('porphyrite') and granodiorite derived from the Criffel–Dalbeattie complex. At Glencaple, geophysical evidence indicates the presence of between 200–400 m of Permian strata (Chapter 3; Bott and Masson Smith, 1960). The maximum thickness modelled for the axial depocentre of the Dumfries Basin is greater than 1.4 km. There is no direct evidence that Permian rocks overlie Carboniferous strata within the basin.

STRUCTURE

The Solway coast preserves a record of late Devonian to Permian sedimentation, which was largely controlled by syndepositional rifting on reactivated north-east-trending Caledonoid structures. The principal basin-bounding structure in the district is the North Solway Fault, which forms the northern margin to the Solway Basin and controlled the deposition of Dinantian strata. Although Leeder (1974) considered that the Upper Old Red Sandstone alluvial-plain sediments were deposited in a pre-rift setting, it is also possible that they accumulated in a series of small linked basins which developed during an earlier phase of crustal extension of limited magnitude (Chadwick et al., 1995). A lengthy cessation of rifting prior to the eruption of lavas of the Birrenswark Volcanic Formation is indicated by the regional development of palaeosols at the top of the Upper Old Red Sandstone sequence. Substantial regional extension during Courceyan to Holkerian times was heralded by the eruption of the lavas. Leeder (1982; 1988) considered that the volcanicity and generation of the sedimentary basin resulted from lithospheric stretching induced in a north–south orientated stress field which was related to the closure of the Rheno-Hercynian back-arc seaway to the south.

The North Solway Fault is the western continuation of a system of en echelon synsedimentary normal faults which are orientated parallel to the north-east–south-west axial strike of the Solway Basin. Dinantian synextensional dislocations oblique to this trend, orientated between north and north-west, can also be identified. Rapid extension-induced subsidence occurred during Courceyan to Chadian times (Chadwick et al., 1995) with coarse clastic sedimentary rocks in the Rerrick and Colvend outliers (Rascarrel Formation) providing evidence of periodic synsedimentary dip slip at the basin margin (Deegan, 1973; Ord et al., 1988). Cyclicity within alluvial-fan deposits of the Rerrick Outlier may be attributed to the interplay between tectonic subsidence and changing sea level. Syndepositional fault deformation of hanging-wall strata increases towards the North Solway Fault. To the east at Kirkbean, where there is little evidence for a major basin margin fault, the fluviatile and marginal marine sedimentary facies of the Kirkbean Outlier show indications of a more stable depositional environment. Locally, however, there is convincing evidence of syndepositional seismic activity (Ord et al., 1988) within the coastal outcrop of the Thirlstane Sandstone Member of the Powillimount Sandstone Formation, of Arundian to Holkerian age.

Basin-wide extensional fault activity waned during the Holkerian and Asbian stages. By Namurian times the dominant structural controls on sedimentation were regional thermal relaxation subsidence and the effects of differential compaction. A major phase of basin shortening and inversion effected by the Variscan Orogeny postdates Westphalian sedimentation and predates the deposition of Permian strata (Leeder and McMahon, 1988; Chadwick et al., 1995). Evidence of structural inversion is well displayed in the Kirkbean Outlier where the Dinantian strata are folded into a series of north-north-east-trending anticlines and synclines. Craig (1956) demonstrated that the coastal strata between Southerness and Hogus Point form the south-east limb of a major north-north-east-plunging anticline whose axial plane strikes between 040° and 030°. Post-depositional reverse movement occurred on reactivated syn-extensional dislocations oblique to the axial trend of the Solway Basin, as exemplified by faults exposed on the Arbigland foreshore.

The onset of continental rifting has been proposed by Holloway (1985) and Glennie (1986) as a mechanism for onshore and offshore subsidence during early Permian times. Caledonian north–south and north-west-trending strike slip faults were reactivated during renewed north-east–south-west extension to produce several half-graben Permian basins in the Southern Uplands (Stone, 1988; Anderson et al., 1995; McMillan and Brand, 1995). In the district, these faults cut the folded Dinantian strata and offset the North Solway Fault and the Criffel–Dalbeattie granodiorite. Sedimentation in the Dumfries Basin may

have been controlled by reactivation of north-north-west-orientated faults bounding the western margin of the basin. Fault movement was probably enhanced by relative uplift of the low density crustal block including the Criffel–Dalbeattie Pluton (Bott and Masson Smith, 1960).

The timing of Mesozoic fault movements is problematical. Uraninite veins within small north-west-orientated tear faults in the footwall of the North Solway Fault near Sandyhills Bay were dated using the U–Pb method at 185 ± 20 Ma (Miller and Taylor, 1966). However the uranium deposits appear to be spatially related to the Caledonian Criffel–Dalbeattie Pluton (Basham et al., 1989; Milodowski et al., 1990), implying that mineralisation may be related to late intrusive processes. No recent confirmation of uraninite ages has been made.

EIGHT

Tertiary

DYKES

A few dolerite dykes of generally north-west–south-east trend crop out on the coast near Knockbrex [576 504 and 592 482], about 8 km south of Gatehouse of Fleet, and around Mullock Bay [710 435], 7 km south-east of Kirkcudbright. They are thought to be members of the Mull or Arran Tertiary dyke swarms.

There is also geophysical evidence (Chapter 3) that the important Cleveland–Armathwaite Dyke, though not exposed, traverses the north-eastern corner of the district.

NINE

Quaternary

Following the original mapping of the Geological Survey in the 1870s, Horne et al. (1896) in their Explanation of the Geology of Sheet 5 emphasised compelling evidence for recent glaciation and marine inundation in Kirkcudbrightshire. During the first half of the 20th century the Quaternary geology of the district received little further attention apart from the researches of Charlesworth (1926) on granite erratic sources. However, during the last thirty years the work of Sissons (for a review see Ballantyne and Gray, 1984) and post-graduate research, in particular by Price (1961), Cornish (1980) and May (1981), has stimulated interest in the late Devensian history of southern Scotland. Concurrently, the research of Jardine (1975; 1980; 1981) has detailed the history of Flandrian sedimentation and relative sea-level change along the North Solway coast. Although the implications of Jardine's interpretations of radiocarbon age determinations have been disputed, particularly in relation to sea-level curves (e.g. Haggart, 1988; 1989; Sutherland, 1984), his work, together with studies of insect assemblages by Bishop and Coope (1977), have thrown light upon the changing depositional environments and fluctuating climate during the early part of the Flandrian.

SUMMARY OF QUATERNARY HISTORY

Biostratigraphical evidence from ocean floor sediments indicates that there have been at least 16 major cold events during the last 1.6 Ma (Bowen, 1978; Price, 1983). It is unlikely that each of these events produced ice sheets and till deposits on the British landmass. In Norway there is evidence for four periods of build-up of major ice sheets during the last 115 Ka (115 000 years)(Larsen and Sevrup, 1990). In Scotland and Ireland, and to a lesser extent in England and Wales, evidence is present for two major ice advances during this period (McCabe, 1987; Bowen, 1989). The earlier glaciation developed at about 70 Ka BP (Before Present) (within the Early Devensian substage) and the second at about 26 Ka BP (at the beginning of Late Devensian substage, c.26–10 Ka BP) (Rose, 1989; Gordon and Sutherland, 1993).

Ice-sheet development during the Late Devensian substage was complex and has been modelled only in general terms (Boulton et al., 1977; Boulton, 1990; Boulton and Payne, 1994). Its effects were to remove or redistribute most deposits of previous Quaternary events in the ice-covered area. Because of this erosive action, only the very latest events since about 26 Ka BP are known with any degree of certainty for southern Scotland. Even during this period the record is incomplete, but, from an assessment of geomorphological,

lithological, biostratigraphical and sedimentological evidence, the glacial and post-glacial history may be constructed with reference to the following climatostratigraphical divisions (Table 15):

Dimlington Stadial (26–13 Ka BP)
Windermere Interstadial* 13–11 Ka BP)
Loch Lomond Stadial (11–10 Ka BP)
Flandrian Stage** (Interglacial) (10 Ka BP to present).

* (equivalent of Lateglacial Interstadial of Gray and Lowe (1977).
** see footnotes on table 15.

Dimlington Stadial

The earlier of the two cold episodes during the Late Devensian substage, the Dimlington Stadial (Table 15), was associated with the build-up of glaciers in both the mountains of the Western Highlands of Scotland and in the western Southern Uplands in response to increasing precipitation and a cooling climate. During the first 3 Ka of the Dimlington Stadial, these centres of ice accumulation nourished radiating patterns of expanding glaciers until Highland ice became confluent with Southern Uplands ice. Thereafter, the whole of the Southern Uplands was overtopped by a single ice sheet. The Dimlington Ice Sheet continued to expand and at its maximum extent some 18 000 years ago covered most of the Scottish landmass and much of England. From theoretical reconstructions, Boulton et al. (1977) estimated that at the time of its maximum extent the relative elevation of the ice-sheet surface over the Southern Uplands may have been in excess of 1700 m.

The pattern of ice movement over Kirkcudbrightshire during the Dimlington Stadial, as evidenced by glacial striae, *roches moutonnées* and drumlin forms, is shown in Figure 30. Although these lines are most likely to confirm the general directions of ice flow during the Dimlington Stadial, it is possible that they record ice movement during earlier glaciations. The pattern from glacial striae across the district is dominantly one of south-easterly and southerly flow emanating from the Galloway hills. Striations on well-preserved *roches moutonnées* indicate ice flow in a predominantly south to south–south-westerly direction west of Kirkcudbright Bay (Horne et al., 1896). Well-formed, streamlined drumlins on the ground between New Galloway and Castle Douglas, particularly to the east of the valley of Loch Ken [720 670], confirm a generally south-easterly flow direction. North of the district in the area between Crocketford and Dumfries, an easterly flow may be attributed to deflection of the ice around the high ground of Criffel (569 m) and adjacent hills, although during the glacial maximum all of the high ground was overtopped. The distribution of erratic

Table 15   Summary of events, deposits and conditions in south-west Scotland during the latter part of the Quaternary.

Approximate age in years before present (BP)	Stage	Substage	Climato-stratigraphical unit	Deposits	Climate	Sea level relative to present OD
Present–10 Ka	Flandrian** (Holocene or Recent)			Alluvial silt, sand and gravel, peat; Carse deposits (marine and estuarine deposits)	Rapid climatic amelioration at end of Loch Lomond Stadial. Climate possibly warmer than that of present day by 9.6 Ka BP	Withdrawal of sea to present coastline began about 5.6 Ka BP. Maximum relative sea level 8–10 m above OD at about 7.2 Ka BP (Jardine, 1980) or 6.6 Ka BP (Haggart, 1989)
10–11 Ka	Devensian	Late Devensian	Loch Lomond Stadial*	Solifluction deposits; peat; freshwater pond deposits	Arctic	Relative sea level below OD
11–c.13 Ka			Windermere Interstadial*	Peat and fluvial deposits; raised beach deposits	Warm climate 13–12.5 Ka BP. Climatic deterioration from 12.5–12 Ka BP	Early eustatic sea level rise. Raised beach deposits 10–25 m above OD
13– c.26 Ka			Dimlington Stadial	Till; morainic deposits; glacial meltwater sand and gravel.	Arctic	Relative sea level below OD

*   the informal term 'Lateglacial' covering the period of the Windermere Interstadial and Loch Lomond Stadial has been long established in Scottish Quaternary literature (see Gray and Lowe, 1977) and has also been applied to raised beach deposits on Geological Survey 1:50 000 Drift Edition maps of the district (IGS, 1980; 1981).

** referred to on Geological Survey 1:50 000 Drift Edition maps of the district as 'Recent'; includes 'Post-glacial Raised Beach deposits' (IGS, 1980; 1981).

blocks and pebbles of granodiorite from the Criffel pluton confirms a pattern of ice flow ranging from a south-easterly direction across the Solway Firth to Cumbria to an easterly flow across eastern Dumfriesshire to Northumberland (Charlesworth, 1926; Sissons, 1967; Taylor et al., 1971).

Till deposits, the product of glacial deposition, are widely distributed on lower hill slopes and within the principal valleys as undulating sheets and glacially moulded drumlins. The deposits comprise sandy and clay-rich diamictons in which both the matrix and clast lithologies vary according to local bedrock types. Thus till covering the Lower Palaeozoic sedimentary rocks tends to be composed of a hard tenacious clay matrix with greywacke and siltstone clasts whereas, in areas of granitic rocks around Bengairn and Criffel, a more gritty, sandy till predominates. Ice-smoothed and striated pebbles and boulders are commonly found within the till. Locally, thin lenses of water-laid sand and gravel may be present within the till but otherwise the deposits are unstratified. Moraine, comprising mounds and ridges of poorly sorted sandy diamicton, sand and gravel, covers

small areas north of Loch Skerrow [605 680] and at Auchenhay [875 580].

During deglaciation, prior to 13 Ka BP, glacial sand and gravel, deposited by meltwaters of the receding Dimlington glaciers, accumulated along the Solway coast and within the principal valleys of the district. Moundy deposits and esker ridges, indicative of ice-contact and sub-glacial deposition, are present at a number of localities summarised below. The distribution of these deposits is shown on Geological Survey 1:50 000 Drift Edition maps (IGS 1980; 1981). Details of sections are described by Goodlet (1970, pp.16–18).

Between Parton [690 700] and Castle Douglas [760 620], extensive moundy spreads of sand and gravel flank Loch Ken and the River Dee. In the valley of the Tarff Water between Laurieston [680 650] and Tongland [690 530], partly terraced kames are composed of stratified sand and fine gravel resting on till. Discontinuous terrace deposits of stratified sand and gravel also flank the Water of Fleet north of Gatehouse of Fleet [600 560]. In the Urr valley, sand and gravel terraces are present between Castle Douglas and Dalbeattie [830 610]. Glaciofluvial deposits are found at elevations up to about 120 m above OD to the north-east of Dalbeattie. North of Criffel, sand and gravel is present around New Abbey [960 660]. To the south, between Caulkerbush [925 570] and Kirkbean [980 590], a series of elongate ridges and terraces trend in a west-north-west to east-south-east orientation.

Windermere Interstadial

Prior to about 13 Ka BP, the pollen record indicates that a varied aquatic and semi-aquatic flora grew in and around pools left in the glacially moulded landscape. Tree cover, however, was very limited. By 13 Ka BP, the record provided by assemblages of beetles (sensitive indicators of climatic change) preserved in organic sediments shows that a rapid amelioration of climate had taken place heralding the beginning of the Windermere Interstadial (Table 15). Beetle collections from organic

lake silts and sands from Bigholm Burn [NY 316 812], Redkirk Point [NY 301 652] in Dumfriesshire east of the district and from other sites in southern Scotland, dating from 13–12.5 Ka BP, are indicative of temperatures similar to those of today (Bishop and Coope, 1977). In contrast, the thermal maximum as shown by the pollen record occurred between 11.8 and 11 Ka BP, an indication that vegetation recolonization at the end of the glaciation lagged behind the climatic changes (Gordon, 1993a). Between 12.5 and 12 Ka BP the first of two stages of rapid cooling is recorded in the coeolopteran record (Bishop and Coope, 1977).

The chronology of relative sea level changes in southern Scotland during the Windermere Interstadial is poorly known. Early rapid eustatic rise in sea level was compensated in due course by the slower process of isostatic recovery of the land. Remnants of Lateglacial raised beach and estuarine deposits, comprising bedded

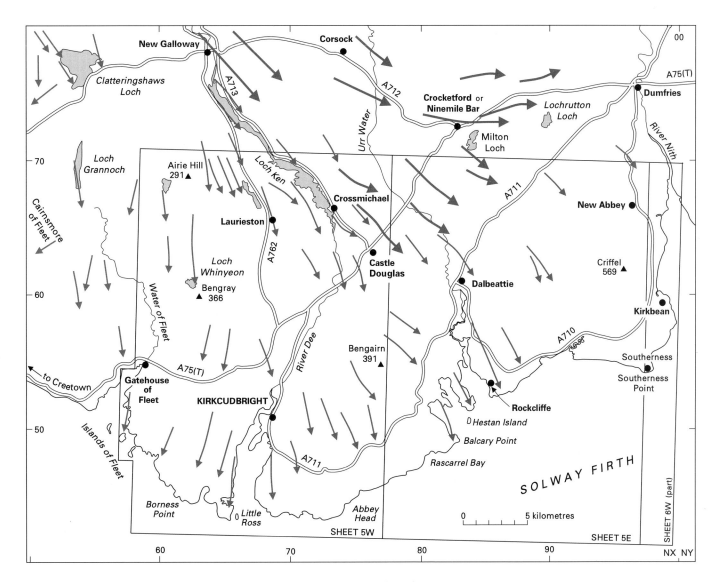

Figure 30 Pattern of ice flow in the district as deduced from glacial striae, *roches moutonnées* and drumlin forms.

silt, well-sorted sand and fine gravel are preserved at elevations between 10 and 25 m along the north Solway coast at several localities in the district (IGS, 1980; 1981). Small isolated pockets of raised beach deposits are found in the vicinity of Gatehouse of Fleet [600 560], the west bank of the Tarff Water [680 540] and River Dee [680 510] north of Kirkcudbright, Balmae Burn [685 440], Auchencairn [800 515], Palnackie [820 570], New Abbey [960 660], and landward of the Preston Merse floodplain [955 555] between Gillfoot and Caulkerbush. At Castle Muir [795 473] in Barlocco Bay, the raised beach deposits are backed by a line of old sea cliffs which were occupied by the Lateglacial sea. It is possible that the cliffs formed during an earlier marine inundation. East of the district at Redkirk Point [NY 301 652] organic and marine sediments preserve evidence for sea-level changes during the Late-glacial and early Flandrian (Bishop and Coope, 1977; Jardine, 1980). Here, the indications are that, prior to 13 Ka BP and throughout almost the whole of the Lateglacial period, sea level was below that of the present day (Gordon, 1993b).

Loch Lomond Stadial

Climatic deterioration culminated in the arctic conditions of the Loch Lomond Stadial (11–10 Ka BP) (Gray and Lowe, 1977). East of the district, evidence from studies of beetles at Bigholm Burn [NY 316 812] and Redkirk Point [NY 301 652] records the second sharp drop in temperatures between 11–10 Ka BP during the Windermere Interstadial (Bishop and Coope, 1977; Gordon, 1993a). In the Southern Uplands, corrie glaciers developed on a limited scale to the north-east of the district between Broad Law and Hart Fell (Price, 1963; May, 1981) and to the north-west of the district in the Galloway hills (Cornish, 1981). Most of the south of Scotland, in common with other areas which remained unglaciated during the Loch Lomond Stadial, suffered severe climatic conditions and was subjected to intense periglacial activity. Fossil frost wedges in glaciofluvial sands and gravels, as at Powfoot [NY 153 656] east of the district (Jardine and Peacock, 1973), and solifluction deposits on hill slopes testify to these effects.

Flandrian

The rapidity of climatic change at the beginning of the Flandrian (10 Ka BP to Present) is clearly recorded in deposits at Brighouse Bay [635 455]. Here, present day intertidal beach deposits overlie peat, yielding a radiocarbon age of 9640 ± 180 years BP, and containing a temperate insect assemblage indicative of a climate as warm or even warmer than that in south-west Scotland today (Bishop and Coope, 1977).

Littoral and estuarine deposits of Flandrian age form low-lying areas adjacent to present high water mark of ordinary Spring tides. These are shown as Post-Glacial Raised Beach Deposits, undivided on published Geological Survey Drift maps (IGS, 1980; 1981). They include two quite separate deposits: fine- to medium-grained sediments of former tidal flat, gulf and estuarine

environments, grouped as 'Carse Deposits' by Jardine (1975; 1980); and recently deposited parallel laminated, fine sands, silts and clays of the present floodplain or saltmarsh of the Solway Firth, locally referred to as 'Merse' (Marshall, 1962; Bridson, 1980) and currently mapped by BGS as 'Tidal river and creek' deposits (Hughes, 1995). All of these deposits may be referred to the Solway Formation as defined by Thomas (in press). In the district, coastal sediments occupy extensive tracts at Carsethorn and Preston Merse near Southerness and smaller areas at the mouth of the Urr Water at Auchencairn, the River Dee at Kirkcudbright and Water of Fleet at Gatehouse. Sequences through them have been interpreted by Jardine (1967; 1975; 1980) and Jardine and Morrison (1976) who identified seven principal environments of deposition: beach, gulf or open bay, estuarine (including tidal flat), lagoonal, coastal bar, coastal dune and coastal marsh.

Several localities along the northern shores of the Solway Firth which provide evidence of relative sea-level change were examined in detail by Jardine (1975; 1980; 1981) and Jardine and Morrison (1976). During and immediately after the Loch Lomond Stadial a relative sea level in the Solway Firth lower than that at present is considered likely (Jardine, 1980; Haggart, 1989). Early Flandrian peat which accumulated in coastal swamps was covered by 'Carse Deposits' formed during the marine inundation of the Main Postglacial (Flandrian) Marine Transgression (Jardine, 1980). Littoral sequences deposited in response to this transgression consist of marine silt and fine sand interbedded with fluvial sand and gravel and terrestrial peat (Jardine, 1980).

In the eastern part of the district, 'Carse Deposits' containing a marine macro- and micro-fauna formed in a number of embayments lying west of the Nith estuary at Kirkconnell Merse [99 69], New Abbey [96 66] and Carsethorn [99 59]. 'Carse Deposits' are also extensively developed west of Southerness [97 54] at Preston Merse. The deposition of the fine- to medium-grained sediments in these areas was succeeded by the formation of gravel ridges and brackish water sediments (Jardine, 1975). The earliest marine sediments were deposited in a small embayment between Kirkbean and Carsethorn; a borehole put down there at South Carse [9883 5944] proved more than 11 m of sand with marine shells resting on a red till surface (Jardine, 1980). Near the base of the sequence a brown layer of organic detritus yielded a radiocarbon date of 9390 ± 130 years BP and the shelly sands were interpreted by Jardine as indicating an early Flandrian rise in sea level. However, Haggart (1989) has noted that the horizon might equally well represent a regressive event.

Jardine (1980) cited the radiocarbon age from basal organic layers from the South Carse Borehole together with ages from localities east of the district at Redkirk Point (about 8.1 Ka BP), at Newbie (c.7.5–7.2 Ka BP) and in the northern part of the 'Lochar Gulf', a 10 km long Flandrian embayment southeast of Dumfries (about 7.4 Ka BP) as evidence for diachronous transgression. According to Jardine (1980), marine waters had reached their maximum lateral extent along the northern coast of the Solway Firth and relative sea level had risen to between 8 and 10 m above OD by about 7.2 Ka BP. The shoreline at this time may have been controlled to some extent by the distribution and orientation of ridges of glacial and fluvioglacial gravel. Thus, for example, the old sea cliff which clearly defines the former Flandrian shoreline at Preston Merse between Southwick Home Farm [938 568] and West Preston [958 558] is probably the edge of a kame-terrace (Jardine, 1980). Alternative interpretation of the available data from index points (Jardine's sample points) indicates that the culmination of the Holocene (Flandrian) rise in relative sea level occurred at about 6.6 Ka BP (Haggart, 1989) which is in accord with the interpretation of Tooley (1980) for Crosscanonby [NY 060 400], Cumbria.

Jardine (1975; 1980) noted that morphological controls such as storm-produced gravel bars may have influenced the position of the coast particularly affecting embayments including those at New Abbey and the 'Lochar Gulf'. The significance of these bars as barriers to the sea has, however, been questioned (Haggart, 1988). Using radiocarbon dates from peat overlying the 'Carse Deposits', Jardine (1980) deduced that the culmination of marine transgression was locally diachronous. By about 6.6 Ka BP, the 'Lochar Gulf' had been abandoned by the sea, whereas at Newbie regression of the sea towards the present coastline did not commence until about 5.6 Ka BP. Evidence of intermittent regression was described at New Abbey Pow, Carsethorn and also near Southwick Bank [915 561] where a 1–2 m high cliff marks an old shoreline formed during a hiatus in sea-level fall. Between Southerness Point and Southwick

Bank, a pause in the regression in late Flandrian time is represented by the deposition of foraminiferal sands which are concealed under peat deposits. The latter, which are locally up to 2 m thick, were dated at 1850 ± 95 years BP (Jardine, 1980). Blown sand covers much of the peat and parts of the area underlain by the 'Carse Deposits' of Preston Merse.

Jardine's interpretations and their implications for the Flandrian sea-level curve were reconsidered by Sutherland (1984) and Haggart (1988; 1989) who have shown that the available evidence does not necessarily conflict with a synchronous maximum for the Main Postglacial Transgression along the north coast of the Solway Firth. However, it is admitted (Haggart, 1988) that small eustatically controlled fluctuations may have occurred during the period covered by the formation of the regional Main Postglacial Shoreline. In his 1989 review of the eastern Solway Firth Holocene (Flandrian) sea-level curve, Haggart (1989) stated that available index (sample) points are largely unsupported by pollen or other micropalaeontological data which could be used to validate dating and aid the determination of hiati in sedimentation and the direction (rise or fall) of sea-level movement.

Alluvial tracts, comprising silt, sand and gravel, occupy the valley floor of the principal rivers and streams in the district, notably the Water of Fleet, River Dee, Tarff Water and Urr Water and New Abbey Pow. Small areas of lake alluvium are also present within enclosed hollows. Peat mosses accumulated during the Late Flandrian at Aucheninnes [853 605] near Dalbeattie, Auchencairn and at a number of localities in the vicinity of Laurieston and Laurieston Forest.

TEN

Mineralisation

Disseminated and vein-type mineralisation of copper, baryte, haematite and uranium was probably emplaced over a considerable period during and following intrusion of various post-tectonic (late Silurian–Devonian) igneous suites (dykes, stocks and plutons). Most of the veins have been known since the late 18th century and were worked by a series of trials and small-scale commercial operations dating mainly from the 1850s. However, the large-scale disseminated 'volcanic porphyry-type' copper mineralisation at Black Stockarton Moor was only discovered within the last 20 years using modern geochemical reconnaissance methods.

BLACK STOCKARTON MOOR

Subvolcanic intrusions of late Silurian to early Devonian age (Chapter 6) delineate a 65 km² oval area centred on Black Stockarton Moor [723 554]. Copper anomalies detected in a primary drainage survey (Leake et al., 1978) were traced by soil and overburden geochemistry to subeconomic but metallogenetically significant occurrences of copper minerals and molybdenite. The mineralisation is associated with enrichment in pyrite which is tracable by geophysical surveys. Small geochemical enrichments of As, Sb and Au were also noted in drill-core from three deep and nine shallow boreholes (Brown et al., 1979; Leake and Brown, 1979). Detailed mapping revealed a multiphase intrusive complex comprising intersecting porphyrite dyke swarms, granodiorite sheets, granodiorite stocks and breccia pipes, now known as the Black Stockarton Moor subvolcanic complex (Table 7; Leake and Cooper, 1983). The host rocks are turbidites of the Carghidown Formation.

Alteration and mineralisation

The main episode of mineralisation and associated hydrothermal alteration is roughly contemporaneous with the intrusion of sheet complexes during the first phase of igneous activity. Second phase dykes cutting these bodies are little mineralised (Leake and Brown, 1979).

An arcuate propylitic zone characterised by chlorite, amphibole, epidote and calcite passes eastwards into a sericitic zone where muscovite, dolomite and quartz are developed. It is possible, though not proven, that the alteration zone, within an arc that subtends an angle of about 90°, represents part of a concentric zone that was subsequently dismembered. Propylitic alteration is best expressed in the host wackes and shales which are typically chloritised and veined by quartz and calcite. Intense alteration of wacke has taken place in the vicinity of chert layers, where sharp changes in lithology have created local

chemical gradients, and is accompanied by the formation of metasomatic veins containing hornblende, actinolite, epidote, calcite and albite. Pyrite and minor chalcopyrite occur in the veins and also in dilational veinlets. In the igneous rocks, propylitisation is expressed by chloritisation of primary mafic silicates, haematitisation of spinels, generation of disseminated epidote, and minor sericitisation of plagioclase. There is geochemical enrichment of Mn, Zn, As and Pb in borehole cores from the propylitic zone. Isolated breccia sections from both the propylitic and sericitic alteration zones display some enrichment of As (100 ppm), Sb (200 ppm) and Au (61 ppb) in association with copper minerals and molybdenite, assays reaching 4400 ppm Cu and 350 ppm Mo.

Fine-grained sericitic alteration has bleached the wackes and produced quartz, dolomite, muscovite and haematite in the igneous rocks. Associated dilational veinlets contain quartz, carbonates and in some cases chlorite, sericite or feldspar. Pyrite is most abundant in the western (outer?) part of the sericitic zone, whereas chalcopyrite and bornite, with rare chalcocite, are more conspicuous further east. Generally, pyrite is disseminated, whereas the copper minerals occur in veinlets, at the margins of which, molybdenite may be present. Chalcopyrite has also been observed in miarolytic cavities, forming up to 5% of some granodiorite sheets. Also present in these small (< 5 mm) cavities are one or more of the minerals quartz, calcite, muscovite, chlorite, dolomite, pyrite and haematite.

Argillite alteration represented by local developments of kaolinitic rock is believed to be later than the propylitic and sericitic phases; in one borehole, a 6 m intersection contains up to 10% by volume of copper sulphides and a minor amount of a silver telluride (R C Leake, oral communication, 1991).

Metallogenesis

The mineralisation at Black Stockarton Moor falls into the volcanic subgroup of the porphyry copper group (Lowell and Guilbert, 1970; Sillitoe, 1973; Sheppard, 1977), in the same way as that elsewhere in south-west Scotland, at Cairngarroch Bay (Allen et al., 1981) and Fore Burn (Allen et al., 1982). Comparisons can also be drawn with the mineralised igneous rocks at Lagalochan (Harris et al., 1988) and Ardsheal in the western Highlands, the Cheviot volcanic-plutonic complex in northern England and the Fore Burn Complex in the Loch Doon district (Sheet 8E) to the north, all of which contain abundant tourmaline. The porphyry systems of south-west Scotland are associated with the earliest phase of late Silurian–early Devonian magmatism rather than with the later dyke swarms or large zoned composite plutons of mainly granodioritic composition (Leake and Cooper, 1983).

OTHER MINERALISATION

Copper

Apart from the Black Stockarton Moor occurrence, numerous other thin veins carrying copper mineralisation are known within the district, almost all within the country rocks along the southern margin of the Criffel–Dalbeattie Pluton. Most localities are known from the coastal cliffs and platforms where the green copper secondary minerals are easily recognised. They are typically breccia veins filled with crushed country rock and containing copper minerals such as chalcopyrite and malachite. Several of them have been worked on a small scale but there are no plans of the workings deposited with BGS, although some details are provided by Wilson (1921).

The largest occurrence is at Enrick [6185 5500], about 2.5 km south-east of Gatehouse of Fleet, where the vein was discovered about 1820. Wilson (1921) reported it to be 1.2 to 1.8 m wide, trending about 105° and cutting wackes of the Kirkmaiden Formation. The workings are quite extensive and include several shafts and five levels, some driven for more that 1000 m along the vein.

A vein with copper mineralisation also occurs on the north side of Hestan Island [838 504], in Auchencairn Bay. Here, the vein trends about 045° and is associated with crushing along a felsic dyke which intrudes the Ross Formation. Several small levels were opened up about 1845, some up to 70 m in length.

At Colvend [868 528], on the coast about 1.7 km south of the village, a vein trending 045° and 0.6 to 1.2 m wide cuts porphyritic microdiorite sheets intruded into wackes of the Ross Formation. The vein was worked on a small scale in the 1770s.

A vein with copper mineralisation is known at Piper's Cove [8893 5454], on the coast about 700 m south of Sandyhills.

The small occurrence of copper mineralisation at Rascarrel Bay [8135 4830], 13 km east-south-east of Kirkcudbright, is associated with baryte on the mine dump and is probably on the western extension of the known baryte vein at Auchencairn (described below).

Baryte

During the late 18th and early 19th centuries, baryte was mined on a commercial scale at Barlocco [785 474], 11 km ESE of Kirkcudbright, and at Auchencairn [816 483] some 3 km further east, and substantial tonnages extracted. Mine plans for Barlocco and Auchencairn were revised in the 1950s and are on deposit with BGS (Information Sources).

At Barlocco, there are two veins 100 m apart, which trend about 098° and cut wackes of the Ross Formation. The more southerly vein reportedly varies between 1 and 2.4 m in width whereas the more northerly is 0.4 to 2.1 m wide (Dines, 1922). The main mining operations lay on the west side of the Barlocco Burn and concentrated on the northern vein. Three levels were driven, the middle being the adit level, and the baryte was worked by stoping. It is reported that about 3000 tonnes of baryte were produced between 1856 and 1920.

Auchencairn mine worked a vein, trending east-north-east and about 0.6 m wide at surface, which cuts coarse red sandstone and conglomerate of the Rascarrel Formation. Dines (1922) reported that about 700 tonnes of baryte were extracted in the 1860s.

A baryte vein is also known at the eastern margin of the Criffel–Dalbeattie Pluton [9730 6190], about 2 km north of Kirkbean, along a structure where the granodiorite is faulted against the Kirkbean Cementstone Formation (Leeder 1971; Smith et al., 1996b). The vein is reported as trending 340° with a visible strike length of about 5 m and a width of up to 3 m.

Haematite

A vein of haematite occurs within the granite near the western margin of the Bengairn Complex at Auchenleck [774 525], some 8 km east of Kirkcudbright. The vein was extensively worked in the early 19th century and it was reported that, in 1845, 50–70 tons of ore per week were then being extracted and sent to Birmingham. The mineralised structure trends about 105° and was reputed to be up to 20 m wide (Macgregor et al., 1920).

Two other small haematite veins are known, both close to the northern margin of the Criffel–Dalbeattie Pluton. The first vein is at Auchenfad [953 697], 4 km north of New Abbey and trends 158°, almost normal to the granite margin. Although its southern limit lies within the granite of the district, for most of its length the vein cuts wackes of the Carghidown Formation in the Thornhill district (Sheet 9E) to the north. Macgregor et al. (1920) reported that some trial workings had been made on this vein. The second vein is at Craigend [925 697], about 2.5 km west of the Auchenfad locality. It trends about 073° and lies entirely within the granite.

Uranium

Natural uranium mineralisation has been detected in vein-breccia deposits associated with faulting along the southern margin of the Criffel–Dalbeattie Pluton at Needle's Eye [915 562] (Miller and Taylor, 1966; Gallagher et al., 1971). This mineralisation has recently been the subject of a detailed study by Basham et al. (1989) into its value as a natural analogue for radionucleide migration in the geosphere. The mineralisation occurs as uraninite (variety pitchblende) and occurs with abundant secondary uranium minerals in several polymetallic-carbonate breccia veins which cross-cut the margin of the granodiorite and the hornfelsed Silurian country rocks. The uraninite has been dated at 185 ± 20 Ma (Triassic–Jurassic) (Miller and Taylor, 1966) but the close association of the mineralisation with the granite pluton (397 ± 2 Ma — Chapter 6) suggests a connection, possibly as a very late stage Caledonian event (Basham et al., 1989).

INFORMATION SOURCES

Further geological information held by the British Geological Survey relevant to the Kirkcudbright–Dalbeattie district is listed below. It includes published material in the form of maps, memoirs and reports and unpublished maps and reports. Also included are other sources of data held by BGS in a number of collections, including borehole records, fossils, rock samples, thin sections, hydrogeological data and photographs.

Searches of indexes to some of the collections can be made on the Geoscience Index System in BGS libraries. This is a developing computer-based system which carries out searches of indexes to collections and digital databases for specified geographical areas. It is based on a geographical information system linked to a relational database management system. Results of the searches are displayed on maps on the screen. At the present time (1998) the datasets are limited and some are incomplete. The indexes which are available are listed below:

- Index of boreholes
- Topographical backdrop based on 1:250 000 scale maps
- Outlines of BGS maps at 1:50 000 and 1:10 000 scale and 1:10 560 scale County Series
- Chronostratigraphical boundaries and areas from BGS 1:250 000 maps
- Geochemical sample locations on land
- Aeromagnetic and gravity data points
- Land survey records

Details of geological information available from the British Geological Survey can be accessed on the BGS Web Home Page at http://www.bgs.ac.uk.

MAPS

GEOLOGY MAPS

1:625 000
United Kingdom (Sheet 1)
  Solid geology, 1979
  Quaternary geology, 1977

1:250 000
Sheet 55N 06W   Clyde
  Solid geology, 1986
  Sea bed sediments and Quaternary, 1986
  Borders (Sheet 55N 04W)
  Solid geology, 1986
Sheet 54N 06W   Isle of Man
  Solid geology, 1982
  Sea bed sediments and Quaternary, 1985
Sheet 54N 04W   Lake District
  Solid geology, 1980
  Sea bed sediments and Quaternary, 1983

1:50 000
Sheets 1 and 3   Rhins of Galloway, Solid, 1992
Sheet 1   Kirkmaiden, Drift, 1982
Sheet 3   Stranraer, Drift, 1982
Sheet 4W   Kirkcowan, Solid, 1992; Drift, 1982
Sheet 4E   Wigtown, Solid, 1992; Drift, 1981

Sheet 5W   Kirkcudbright, Solid, 1993; Drift, 1980
Sheet 5E   Dalbeattie, Solid, 1993; Drift, 1981
Sheet 8W   Carrick, Solid, 1994; Drift, 1981
Sheet 8E   Loch Doon, Solid, 1994; Drift, 1980
Sheet 9W   New Galloway, Solid, 1997; Drift, 1979
Sheet 9E   Thornhill, Solid, 1997; Drift, 1980
Sheet 10W   Lochmaben; Drift, 1983
Sheet 10E   Ecclefechan; Drift, 1982

1:10 000 and 1:10 560
The original geological survey was carried out at the the six-inch to one mile scale by D K Irvine and J Horne and was published at the one inch to one mile scale in 1879. The district was revised between 1879 and 1896 by B N Peach and J Horne and published at the one-inch scale as a combined Solid and Drift edition in 1927. Copies of the fair-drawn maps of these earlier surveys may be consulted at the BGS library in Edinburgh.

Modern maps at 1:10 000 scale wholly or partly included in the 1:50 000 scale sheets 5W and 5E are listed below, together with the surveyors' initials and the dates of the survey. The surveyors were: M C Akhurst, R P Barnes, C Cooper, D J Fettes, D H Land, R C Leake, B C Lintern and A A McMillan.

These maps are not published but are available for consultation in the Library, British Geological Survey, Murchison House, Edinburgh, EH9 3LA, and also at the BGS Keyworth office and the BGS London Information Office in the Natural History Museum, South Kensington, London. Dyeline copies may be purchased from the Sales Desk.

NX 54 NE	BCL	1986
NX 55 NE	RPB, BCL	1987–88
NX 55 SE	RPB, BCL	1985–88
NX 56 NE	BCL	1987
NX 56 SE	RPB, BCL	1987
NX 57 SE	DJF, BCL	1989
NX 64 NW	BCL	1986
NX 64 NE	BCL	1986
NX 64 SW	BCL	1986–87
NX 64 SE	BCL	1986
NX 65 NW	BCL	1987
NX 65 NE	BCL	1987
NX 65 SW	BCL	1987
NX 65 SE	BCL	1987
NX 66 NW	BCL	1987
NX 66 NE	BCL	1987
NX 66 SW	BCL	1987
NX 66 SE	BCL	1987
NX 74 NW	BCL	1989
NX 74 NE	BCL	1988–89
NX 74 SW	DHL, BCL	1986
NX 75 NW	CC, RCL, BCL	1978–90
NX 75 NE	CC, RCL, BCL	1978–89
NX 75 SW	CC, RCL, BCL	1978–90
NX 75 SE	CC, RCL, BCL	1978–89
NX 76 NW	BCL	1987
NX 76 NE	BCL	1987
NX 76 SW	BCL	1987–88
NX 76 SE	BCL	1987–89
NX 84 NW	BCL	1989

NX 85 NW	BCL	1989
NX 85 NE	BCL	1989
NX 85 SW	BCL	1988
NX 85 SE	BCL	1988
NX 86 NW	BCL	1989
NX 86 NE	BCL	1989
NX 86 SW	BCL	1989
NX 86 SE	BCL	1989
NX 87 SW	MCA	1991
NX 87 SE	MCA	1992
NX 95 NW	BCL, AAM	1989
NX 95 NE	AAM	1989
NX 96 NW	AAM	1990
NX 96 NE	AAM	1990
NX 96 SW	AAM	1990
NX 96 SE	AAM	1989
NX 97 SW	MCA	1992

GEOPHYSICAL MAPS

1:1 500 000
Colour shaded relief gravity anomaly map of Britain, Ireland and adjacent areas, 1997
Colour shaded relief magnetic anomaly map of Britain, Ireland and adjacent areas, 1998

1:625 000
United Kingdom (North Sheet)
  Aeromagnetic anomaly, 1972
  Bouguer anomaly, 1981
  Regional gravity, 1981

1:250 000
Sheet 55N 06W   Clyde
  Aeromagnetic anomaly, 1980
  Bouguer gravity anomaly, 1985
Sheet 55N 04W   Borders
  Aeromagnetic anomaly, 1980
  Bouguer gravity anomaly, 1981
Sheet 54N 06W   Isle of Man
  Aeromagnetic anomaly, 1978
  Bouguer gravity anomaly, 1978
Sheet 54N 04W   Lake District
  Aeromagnetic anomaly, 1977
  Bouguer gravity anomaly, 1986

1:50 000
Geophysical information maps; these are plot–on–demand maps which summarise graphically the publicly available geophysical information held for the sheet in the BGS databases. Features include:

- Regional gravity data: Bouguer anomaly contours and location of observations.

- Regional aeromagnetic data: total field anomaly contours and location of digitised data points along flight lines.

- Gravity and magnetic fields plotted on the same base map at 1:50 000 scale to show correlation between anomalies.

- Separate colour contour plots of gravity and magnetic fields at 1:125 000 scale for easy visualisation of important anomalies.

- Location of local geophysical surveys.

- Location of public domain seismic reflection and refraction surveys.

- Location of deep boreholes and those with geophysical logs.

Bouger gravity and aeromagnetic data are held digitally in the National Gravity Databank and the National Aeromagnetic Databank at BGS, Keyworth.

The results of local geophysical surveys conducted at Black Stockarton Moor, Over Linkins, Ben Tudor, Screel Burn, Barcloy–White Hills, Lotus Hill and Kirkbean are held at BGS, Keyworth. Those from Kirkbean are in digital form, while the remainder are in analogue form.

GEOCHEMICAL ATLAS

1:250 000
The Geochemical Baseline Survey of the Environment (G–BASE) is based on the collection of stream sediment and stream water samples at an average density of one sample per 1.5 km^2. The fine (minus 150μm) fractions of stream sediment samples are analysed for a wide range of elements, using automated instrumental methods.

The samples from the Southern Uplands were collected in 1977 and 1981–86. The results (including Ag, As, B, Ba, Be, Bi, CaO, Cd, Co, Cr, Cu, Fe$_2$O$_3$, Ga, K$_2$O, La, Li, MgO, Mn, Mo, Ni, Pb, Rb, Sb, Sn, Sr, TiO$_2$, U, V, Y, Zn and Zr in stream sediments, and pH, conductivity, fluoride, bicarbonate and U for stream waters) are published in atlas form:

British Geological Survey. 1993.   *Regional geochemistry of southern Scotland and part of northern England.*   (Keyworth, Nottingham: British Geological Survey).

The geochemical data, with location and site information, are available as hard copy for sale or in digital form under licencing agreement. The coloured geochemical atlas is also available in digital form (on CD–ROM or floppy disk) under licencing agreement. The British Geological Survey offers a client–based service for interactive GIS interrogation of G-BASE data.

HYDROGEOLOGICAL MAP

1:625 000
Sheet 18 (Scotland) 1988.

GROUNDWATER VULNERABILITY MAP

1:625 000
Scotland

BOOKS

Books, reports and papers relevant to the Kirkcudbright–Dalbeattie district arranged by topic. Some publications are out of print but may be consulted at BGS and other libraries.

GENERAL GEOLOGY

British Regional geology
The South of Scotland, 3rd Edition, 1971

Memoirs
Geology of the Whithorn district, 1989
Geology of the Rhins of Galloway district, 1995
Geology of the Carrick–Loch Doon district, 1998
Geology of the New Galloway–Thornhill district (in preparation)
Geology of the Kirkcowan–Wigtown district (in preparation)

ECONOMIC GEOLOGY AND MINERALISATION

BASHAM, I R, and HYSLOP, E K. 1989.   Uranium location studies at the Needle's Eye Natural Analogue site–a preliminary account.   *British Geological Survey Technical Report*, WG/89/6R.

BASHAM, I R, MILDOWSKI, A E, HYSLOP, E K, and PEARCE, J M. 1989. The location of Uranium in source rocks and sites of secondary deposition at the Needle's Eye natural analogue site, Dumfries and Galloway. *British Geological Survey Technical Report*, WE/89/56.

BROWN, M J, LEAKE, R C, PARKER, M E, and FORTEY, N J. 1979. Porphyry style copper mineralisation at Black Stockarton Moor, south-west Scotland. *Mineral Reconnaissance Programme Report, Institute of Geological Sciences*, No. 30.

DINES, H.G. 1922. Barytes and witherite. *Special Report on the Mineral Resources of Great Britain, Memoir of the Geological Survey*, Vol. 2. (3rd edition).

LEAKE, R C, BROWN, M J, SMITH, T K, and DATE, A R. 1978. A reconnaissance geochemical drainage survey of the Criffel–Dalbeattie granodiorite complex and its environs. *Mineral Reconnaissance Programme Report, Institute of Geological Sciences*, No. 19.

LEAKE, R C, BROWN, M J, SMITH, T K, and DATE, A R. 1978. A geochemical drainage survey of the Fleet granitic complex and its environs. *Mineral Reconnaissance Programme Report, Institute of Geological Sciences*, No. 21.

LEAKE, R C, ROLLIN, K E, and SHAW, M H. 1996. Assessment of the potential for gold mineralisation in the Southern Uplands of Scotland using multiple geological, geophysical and geochemical datasets. *Mineral Reconnaissance Programme Report, British Geological Survey*, No. 141.

MACGREGOR, M, LEE, G W, and WILSON, G V. 1920. The Iron Ores of Scotland. *Special Report on the Mineral Resources of Great Britain, Memoir of the Geological Survey, Scotland*, Vol. 11.

SMITH, R T, and MCMILLAN, A A. 1996. Mineral investigations in the Northumberland Trough: Part 3, Ecclefechan–Waterbeck Area. *British Geological Survey, Mineral Reconnaissance Programme Open File Report*, No. 21.

SMITH, R T, NORTON, G E, WALKER, A S D W, KIMBELL, G S, GIBBERD, A J G, and MCMILLAN, A A. 1996. Mineral investigations in the Northumberland Trough: Part 5, The Kirkbean area, south-west Scotland. *British Geological Survey, Mineral Reconnaissance Programme Open File Report*, No. 23.

WILSON, G V. 1921. The lead, zinc, copper and nickel ores of Scotland. *Special Report on the Mineral Resources of Great Britain, Memoir of the Geological Survey, Scotland*, Vol. 17.

GEOPHYSICAL AND ROCK PROPERTIES

ENTWISLE, D C. 1993. Density and porosity determinations on twelve Palaeozoic rock samples from Southern Scotland. *British Geological Survey, Engineering Geology and Geophysics Laboratory Report*, No. 93/15.

HIPKIN, R G, and HUSSAIN, A. 1983. Regional gravity anomalies. 1 Northern Britain. *Report of the Institute of Geological Sciences*, No. 82/10.

METAMORPHISM

MERRIMAN, R J, and ROBERTS, B. 1993. The low grade metamorphism of Lower Palaeozoic strata on the Rhins of Galloway, SW Scotland. *British Geological Survey Technical Report*, WG/92/40.

BIOSTRATIGRAPHY

There is a collection of internal biostratigraphical reports. Those which include graptolites are listed in Appendix 1.

BULK MINERALS

GOODLET, G A. 1970. Sands and gravels of the southern counties of Scotland. *Report of the Institute of Geological Sciences*, No. 70/4.

CAMERON, I B. 1977. Sand and gravel resources of the Dumfries and Galloway Region of Scotland. *Report of the Institute of Geological Sciences*, No. 77/22.

SMITH, C G, and FLOYD, J D. 1989. Scottish Highlands and Southern Uplands Mineral Portfolio: Hard–rock aggregate resources. *British Geological Survey Technical Report*, WF/89/4.

Regional geochemistry

BRITISH GEOLOGICAL SURVEY. 1993. *Regional geochemistry of southern Scotland and part of northern England.* (Keyworth, Nottingham: British Geological Survey).

HYDROGEOLOGY/GEOCHEMISTRY

DOUBLET, R, JAMET, PH, and SOUBEYRAN, R. 1990. Hydrogeochemistry of the Needle's Eye Site – first interpretation. *British Geological Survey Technical Report*, WE/89/55.

GAUSS, G. 1969. Records of wells in the areas of Scottish one-inch Geological Sheets Kirkmaiden (1), Whithorn (2), Stranraer (3), Wigtown (4), Kirkcudbright (5) and Annan (6). *Water Supply Papers of the Geological Survey of Great Britain, Well Catalogue Series.*

ROBINS, N S. 1990. *Hydrogeology of Scotland.* (London: HMSO for the British Geological Survey).

DOCUMENTARY COLLECTIONS

BOREHOLE RECORD COLLECTION

BGS holds collections of records of boreholes which can be consulted at BGS, Edinburgh, where copies of most records may be purchased. For the Kirkcudbright–Dalbeattie district the collection consists of the sites and logs of about 150 boreholes.

Most were drilled in search of water supplies, with the balance divided between metalliferous mineral exploration and site investigation.

Index information, which includes site references, for these bores has been digitised. The logs are either hand-written or typed and many of the older records are drillers logs.

SITE EXPLORATION REPORTS

This collection consists of site exploration reports carried out to investigate foundation conditions prior to construction. There is a digital index and the reports themselves are held on microfiche. For the Kirkcudbright–Dalbeattie district there are presently (1998) 36 reports.

MINE PLANS

BGS maintains a collection of plans of underground mines for minerals other than coal and oil shale. The following small-scale mines are known to have been worked within the district but only those noted have abandonment plans deposited with BGS.

Mine	Mineral worked	Plan No.
Auchencairn	copper, baryte	AP15154, SP1019, SP1080
Barlocco	baryte	AP15133
Enrick	copper	

Hestan Island	copper	
Rascarrel	copper	
Colvend	copper	
Piper's Cove	copper	
Windmill	baryte	AP15191, SP1081

MATERIAL COLLECTIONS

GEOLOGICAL SURVEY PHOTOGRAPHS

Sixty two photographs illustrating aspects of the geology of the Kirkcudbright–Dalbeattie district are deposited for reference in the libraries at BGS, Murchison House, West Mains Road, Edinburgh EH9 3LA and BGS, Keyworth, Nottingham NG12 5GG; and in the BGS Information Office, Natural History Museum Earth Galleries, Exhibition Road, London SW7 2DE.

Eight of the photographs are black and white and date from 1937–39. They concentrate on the granite sett and kerb making operations at Craignair Quarry, near Dalbeattie. The others are modern colour photographs taken during the recent resurvey. A list of titles can be supplied on request. The photographs can be supplied as black and white or colour prints and 2 × 2 colour transparencies, at a fixed tariff.

PETROLOGICAL COLLECTIONS

The petrological collections for the Kirkcudbright–Dalbeattie district consist of about 500 hand specimens and thin sections. Most of the older samples and thin sections are of the igneous rocks in the district, whereas more recent collections concentrate on the Silurian sedimentary rocks. The collections are indexed on the basis of the 1:50 000 geological maps, but much of the older part of the collection cannot at present be searched by National Grid Reference.

PALAEONTOLOGICAL COLLECTIONS

The collections of biostratigraphical specimens are mostly taken from surface and temporary exposures throughout the district. They are essentially working collections and mainly used for reference. Some locality index data are held on a computer database.

REFERENCES

Most of the references listed below are held in the Libraries of the British Geological Survey at Edinburgh and Keyworth, Nottingham. Copies of the references can be purchased subject to the current copyright legislation.

ALLEN, P M, BIDE, P J, COOPER, D C, PARKER, M E, and HASLAM, H W. 1981. Copper-bearing intrusive rocks at Cairngarroch Bay, south-west Scotland. *Mineral Reconnaissance Programme Report, Institute of Geological Sciences*, No. 39.

ALDRIDGE, R J, and JEPPSSON, L. 1984. Ecological specialists among Silurian conodonts. 141–149 *in* Autecology of Silurian organisms. BASSETT, M G, and LAWSON, J D (editors). *Special Papers in Palaeontology*, No. 32.

ALLEN, P M, COOPER, D C, PARKER, M E, EASTERBROOK, G D, and HASLAM, H W. 1982. Mineral exploration in the area of the Fore Burn igneous complex, south-western Scotland. *Mineral Reconnaissance Report, Institute of Geological Sciences*, No. 55.

ANDERSON, T B. 1987. The onset and timing of Caledonian sinistral shear in County Down. *Journal of the Geological Society of London*, Vol. 144, 817–825.

ANDERSON, T B, PARNELL, J, and RUFFELL, A H. 1995. Influence of basement on the geometry of Permo-Triassic basins in the northwest British Isles. 103–122 *in* Permian and Triassic rifting in Northwest Europe. BOLDY, S A R (editor). *Special Publication of the Geological Society of London*, No. 91.

BALLANTYNE, C K, and GRAY, J M. 1984. The Quaternary geomorphology of Scotland: the research contribution of J B Sissons. *Quaternary Science Reviews*, Vol. 3, 259–289.

BALSLEY, J R, and BUDDINGTON, A F. 1958. Iron-titanium oxide minerals, rocks and aeromagnetic anomalies of the Adirondack area, New York. *Economic Geology*, Vol. 53, 777–805.

BARNES, R P. 1989. Geology of the Whithorn district. *Memoir of the British Geological Survey*, Sheet 2 (Scotland).

BARNES, R P. In preparation. Geology of the Kirkcowan, Wigtown and Whithorn districts. *Memoir of the British Geological Survey*, Sheets 4W, 4E and 2, Scotland.

BARNES, R P, ANDERSON, T B, and McCURRY, J A. 1987. Along-strike variation in the stratigraphical and structural profile of the Southern Uplands Central Belt in Galloway and Down. *Journal of the Geological Society of London*, Vol. 144, 807–816.

BARNES, R P, LINTERN, B C, and STONE, P. 1989. Timing and regional implications of deformation in the Southern Uplands of Scotland. *Journal of the Geological Society of London*, Vol. 146, 905–908.

BARNES, R P, PHILLIPS, E R, and BOLAND, M P. 1995. The Orlock Bridge Fault in the Southern Uplands of SW Scotland: a terrane boundary? *Geological Magazine*, Vol. 132, 523–529.

BARNES, R P, ROCK, N M S, and GASKARTH, J W. 1986. Late Caledonian dyke-swarms in Southern Scotland: new field, petrological and geochemical data for the Wigtown Peninsula, Galloway. *Geological Journal*, Vol. 21, 101–125.

BARRETT, P A. 1988. Early Carboniferous of the Solway Basin: a tectonostratigraphic model and its bearing on hydrocarbon potential. *Marine and Petroleum Geology*, Vol. 5, 271–281.

BARRON, H F. 1988. A palynological investigation of Ordovician and Silurian samples from the northern part of the Kirkcudbright Sheet, Southern Uplands. *British Geological Survey Technical Report*, WH/88/134R.

BASHAM, I R, MILODOWSKI, A E, HYSLOP, E K, and PEARCE, J M. 1989. The location of Uranium in source rocks and sites of secondary deposition at the Needle's Eye natural analogue site, Dumfries and Galloway. *British Geological Survey Technical Report*, WE/89/56.

BEAMISH, D, and SMYTHE, D K. 1986. Geophysical images of the deep crust: the Iapetus suture. *Journal of the Geological Society of London*, Vol. 143, 489–497.

BENTON, M J. 1982. Trace fossils from Lower Palaeozoic ocean-floor sediments of the Southern Uplands of Scotland. *Transactions of the Royal Society of Edinburgh: Earth Sciences*, Vol. 73, 67–87.

BISHOP, W W, and COOPE, G R. 1977. Stratigraphical and faunal evidence for Lateglacial and Early Flandrian environments in South-West Scotland. 61–88 *in* Studies in the Scottish Lateglacial Environment. GRAY, J M, and LOWE, J J (editors). (Oxford: Pergamon Press.)

BOTT, M H P. 1964. Gravity measurements in the north-eastern part of the Irish Sea. *Quarterly Journal of the Geological Society of London*, Vol. 120, 369–396.

BOTT, M H P, and MASSON SMITH, D. 1957. The geological interpretation of a gravity survey of the Alston Block and Durham Coalfield. *Quarterly Journal of the Geological Society of London*, Vol. 113, 93–117.

BOTT, M H P, and MASSON SMITH, D. 1960. A gravity survey of the Criffel granodiorite and the New Red Sandstone deposits near Dumfries. *Proceedings of the Yorkshire Geological Society*, Vol. 32, 317–332.

BOULTON, G S. 1990. Sedimentation and sea level changes during glacial cycles and their control on glacimarine facies architecture. 15–52 *in* Glacimarine Environments: Processes and Sediments. DOWDESWELL, J A, and SCOURSE, J D (editors). *Special Publication of the Geological Society of London*, No. 53.

BOULTON, G S, JONES, A S, CLAYTON, K M, and KENNING, M J (editors). 1977. *A British ice-sheet model and patterns of glacial erosion and deposition in Britain*. (British Quaternary Studies). (Oxford: Clarendon Press.)

BOULTON, G S, and PAYNE, A. 1994. Northern hemisphere icesheets through the last glacial cycle: Glaciological and geological reconstructions. 177–212 *in* Long term climatic changes: data and modelling. (NATO ASI Series). DUPLESSY, J-C (editor). (Stuttgart: Springer.)

BOUMA, A H. 1962. *Sedimentology of some flysch deposits: a graphic approach to interpretation*. (Amsterdam: Elsevier.)

BOWEN, D Q. 1978. *Quaternary Geology*. (Oxford: Pergamon Press.)

BOWEN, D Q. 1989. The last interglacial-glacial cycle in the British Isles. *Quaternary International*, Vol. 3/4, 41–47.

BRAND, P J. 1996. Carboniferous biostratigraphy of the Kirkcudbright–Dalbeattie district. *British Geological Survey Technical Report*, WH/96/49R.

BREWER, J A, and 5 OTHERS. 1983. BIRPS deep seismic reflection studies of the British Caledonides — the WINCH profile. *Nature, London*, Vol. 305, 206–210.

BRIDSON, R H. 1980. Saltmarsh — its accretion and erosion at Caerlaverock National Nature Reserve, Dumfries. *Transactions of the Dumfriesshire and Galloway Natural History and Antiquarian Society*, Vol. 55, 60–80.

BRITISH GEOLOGICAL SURVEY. 1992a. Kirkcowan. Scotland Sheet 4W. Solid geology. 1:50 000. (Keyworth, Nottingham: British Geological Survey.)

BRITISH GEOLOGICAL SURVEY. 1992b. Wigtown. Scotland Sheet 4E. Solid geology. 1:1:50 000. (Keyworth, Nottingham: British Geological Survey.)

BRITISH GEOLOGICAL SURVEY. 1993a. *Regional geochemistry of southern Scotland and part of northern England.* (Keyworth, Nottingham: British Geological Survey.)

BRITISH GEOLOGICAL SURVEY. 1993b. Dalbeattie. Scotland Sheet 5E. Solid geology. 1:50 000. (Keyworth, Nottingham: British Geological Survey.)

BRITISH GEOLOGICAL SURVEY. 1996. Kirkbean. Scotland Sheet 6W. Solid geology. 1:50 000. (Keyworth, Nottingham: British Geological Survey.)

BROOKFIELD, M E. 1978. Revision of the stratigraphy of Permian and supposed Permian rocks of southern Scotland. Vol. 67, 110–149.

BROWN, M J, LEAKE, R C, PARKER, M E, and FORTEY, N J. 1979. Porphyry style copper mineralisation at Black Stockarton Moor, south-west Scotland. *Mineral Reconnaissance Programme Report, Institute of Geological Sciences*, No. 30.

BROWN, P E, MILLER, J A, and GRASTY, R L. 1968. Isotopic ages of late Caledonian granitic intrusions in the British Isles. *Proceedings of the Yorkshire Geological Society*, Vol. 36, 251–276.

BROWNE, M A E, and 5 OTHERS. 1996. A lithostratigraphical framework for the Carboniferous rocks of the Midland Valley of Scotland. *British Geological Survey Technical Report*, WA/96/29/R.

BUSBY, J P. 1987. An interactive FORTRAN 77 program using GKS graphics for 2.5D modelling of gravity and magnetic data. *Computers and Geosciences*, Vol. 13, 639–644.

CAMERON, I B, and STEPHENSON, D. 1985. *British regional geology: the Midland Valley of Scotland.* (3rd edition). (London: HMSO.)

CASEY, D M. 1983. Geological studies in the Central Belt of the Eastern Southern Uplands of Scotland. Unpublished PhD thesis, University of Oxford.

CHADWICK, R A, HOLLIDAY, D W, HOLLOWAY, S, and HULBERT, A G. 1993. The evolution and hydrocarbon potential of the Northumberland–Solway Basin. 717–726 in *Petroleum Geology of Northwest Europe: Proceedings of the 4th Conference.* PARKER, J R (editor). (London: The Geological Society.)

CHADWICK, R A, HOLLIDAY, D W, HOLLOWAY, S, and HULBERT, A G. 1995. The structure and evolution of the Northumberland–Solway Basin and adjacent areas. *Subsurface memoir of the British Geological Survey.*

CHAPPELL, B W, and WHITE, A J R. 1974. Two contrasting granite types. *Pacific Geology*, Vol. 8, 173–174.

CHARLESWORTH, J K. 1926. The glacial geology of the Southern Uplands, west of Annandale and upper Clydesdale. *Transactions of the Royal Society of Edinburgh*, Vol. 55, 1–23.

CLARKSON, C M, CRAIG, G Y, and WALTON, E K. 1975. The Silurian rocks bordering Kirkcudbright Bay, South Scotland. *Transactions of the Royal Society of Edinburgh*, Vol. 69, 313–325.

COOK, D R. 1976. The geology of the Cairnsmore of Fleet granite and its environs, southwest Scotland. Unpublished PhD thesis, University of St Andrews.

COOK, D R, and WEIR, J A. 1979. Structure of the Lower Palaeozoic rocks around Cairnsmore of Fleet, Galloway. *Scottish Journal of Geology*, Vol. 15, 187–202.

COOK, D R, and WEIR, J A. 1980. The stratigraphical setting of the Cairnsmore of Fleet pluton, Galloway. *Scottish Journal of Geology*, Vol. 16, 125–141.

CORNISH, R. 1980. Glacial geomorphology of the west-central Southern Uplands of Scotland, with particular reference to the 'Rogen moraines'. Unpublished PhD thesis, University of Edinburgh.

CORNISH, R. 1981. Glaciers of the Loch Lomond Stadial in the western Southern Uplands of Scotland. *Proceedings of the Geologists' Association*, Vol. 92, 105–114.

COURRIOUX, G. 1987. Oblique diapirism: the Criffel granodiorite/granite zoned pluton (southwest Scotland). *Journal of Structural Geology*, Vol. 9, 313–330.

COWIE, J W, and BASSETT, M G. 1989. International Union of Geological Sciences 1989 Global Stratigraphic Chart. *Episodes*, Vol. 12, No. 2, Supplement.

CRAIG, G Y. 1956. The Lower Carboniferous Outlier of Kirkbean, Kirkcudbrightshire. *Transactions of the Geological Society of Glasgow*, Vol. 22, 113–132.

CRAIG, G Y, and NAIRN, A E M. 1956. The Lower Carboniferous Outliers of the Colvend and Rerrick shores, Kirkcudbrightshire. *Geological Magazine*, Vol. 93, 249–256.

CRAIG, G Y, and WALTON, E K. 1959. Sequence and structure in the Silurian rocks of Kirkcudbrightshire. *Geological Magazine*, Vol. 96, 209–220.

CRAIG, G Y, and WALTON, E K. 1962. Sedimentary structures and palaeocurrent directions from the Silurian rocks of Kirkcudbrightshire. *Transactions of the Edinburgh Geological Society*, Vol. 19, 100–119.

CUNNINGHAM, R H. 1843. Geognostical description of the Stewartry of Kirkcudbrightshire. *Highland Society Transactions*, Vol. 8, New Series, 697.

DAGLEY, P. 1969. Palaeomagnetic results from some British Tertiary dykes. *Earth and Planetary Science Letters*, Vol. 6, 349–354.

DAY, J B W. 1970. Geology of the country around Bewcastle. *Memoir of the Geological Survey of Great Britain*, Sheet 12 (England and Wales).

DE SOUZA, H A F. 1982. Abstract NDS 165. 847–848 in *Numerical dating in Stratigraphy.* ODIN, G S (editor). (Chichester: John Wiley & Sons, Ltd.)

DEEGAN, C E. 1970. The petrology and sedimentology of the Lower Carboniferous rocks between White Port and Kirkbean, Kirkcudbrightshire. Unpublished PhD thesis, University College of Wales (Aberystwyth).

DEEGAN, C E. 1973. Tectonic control of sedimentation at the margin of a Carboniferous depositional basin in Kirkcudbrightshire. *Scottish Journal of Geology*, Vol. 9, 1–28.

DEER, W A, HOWIE, R A, and ZUSSMAN, J. 1963. *Rock–forming minerals.* (London: Longmans.)

DEWEY, J F. 1969. Evolution of the Appalachian/Caledonian orogen. *Nature, London*, Vol. 222, 124–129.

DEWEY, J F. 1971. A model for the Lower Palaeozoic evolution of the southern margin of the early Caledonides of Scotland and Ireland. *Scottish Journal of Geology*, Vol. 7, 219–240.

DICKINSON, W R, and SUCZEK, C A. 1979. Plate tectonics and sandstone compositions. *Bulletin of the American Association of Petroleum Geologists*, Vol. 63, 2164–2182.

DIMBERLINE, A J, BELL, A, and WOODCOCK, N H. 1990. A laminated hemipelagite facies from the Wenlock and Ludlow of the Welsh Basin. *Journal of the Geological Society of London*, Vol. 147, 693–701.

DINES, H G. 1922. Barytes and witherite. (3rd edition). *Special Report on the Mineral Resources of Great Britain, Memoir of the Geological Survey*, Vol. 2.

ENTWISLE, D C. 1993. Density and porosity determinations on twelve Palaeozoic rock samples from Southern Scotland. *British Geological Survey, Engineering Geology and Geophysics Report*, No. 93/15.

ESPERANÇA, S, and HOLLOWAY, J R. 1987. On the origin of some mica-lamprophyres: experimental evidence from a mafic minette. *Contributions to Mineralogy and Petrology*, Vol. 95, 207–216.

FERGUSON, J. 1971. *Linoprotonia*, a new genus of Lower Carboniferous Productoid. *Proceedings of the Yorkshire Geological Society*, Vol. 38, 549–564.

FETTES, D J, and TIMMERMAN, H. 1993. The geology of the Cairnsmore of Fleet Granite. *British Geological Survey Technical Report*, WA/82/89.

FITTON, J G, and HUGHES, D J. 1970. Volcanism and plate tectonics in the British Ordovician. *Earth and Planetary Science Letters*, Vol. 8, 223–228.

FLOYD, J D. 1982. Stratigraphy of a flysch succession: the Ordovician of W Nithsdale, SW Scotland. *Transactions of the Royal Society of Edinburgh: Earth Sciences*, Vol. 73, 1–9.

FLOYD, J D. 1996. Lithostratigraphy of the Ordovician rocks in the Southern Uplands: Crawford Group, Moffat Shale Group, Leadhills Supergroup. *Transactions of the Royal Society of Edinburgh: Earth Sciences*, Vol. 86, 153–165.

FOWLER, M B. 1988. Ach'uaine hybrid appinite pipes: evidence for mantle-derived shoshonitic parent magmas in Caledonian granite genesis. *Geology*, Vol. 16, 1026–1030.

FRANCIS, E H. 1991. Carboniferous-Permian igneous rocks. 400–401 in *Geology of Scotland*. CRAIG, G Y (editor). (3rd edition). (London: The Geological Society.)

FREEMAN, B, KLEMPERER, S L, and HOBBS, R W. 1988. The deep structure of northern England and the Iapetus Suture zone from BIRPS deep seismic reflection profiles. *Journal of the Geological Society of London*, Vol. 145, 727–740.

FRÖLICHER, F J. 1977. The sedimentology and palaeoecology of the Dinantian outlier of Kirkbean, Kirkcudbrightshire, Scotland. Unpublished PhD thesis, University of Edinburgh.

FRÖLICHER, F J. 1984. Dinantian stratigraphy and evolution of the Northumberland Trough near Kirkbean, Scotland. *Transactions of the Dumfriesshire and Galloway Natural History and Antiquarian Society*, Vol. 59, 15–20.

GALLAGHER, M J, MICHIE, U McL, SMITH, R T, and HAYNES, L. 1971. New evidence of uranium and other mineralisation in Scotland. *Transactions of the Institution of Mining and Metallurgy (Section B: Applied earth science)*, Vol. 80, B150–173.

GARDINER, C I, and REYNOLDS, S H. 1937. The Cairnsmore of Fleet Granite and its metamorphic aureole. *Geological Magazine*, Vol. 74, 289–300.

GEOLOGICAL SURVEY OF GREAT BRITAIN. 1879. Scotland Sheet 5. Solid geology. 1:63 360. (Southampton: Ordnance Survey for Geological Survey of Great Britain.)

GEORGE, T N, and 6 OTHERS. 1976. A correlation of Dinantian rocks in the British Isles. *Special Report of the Geological Society of London*, No. 7.

GILL, J B. 1981. *Orogenic Andesites and Plate Tectonics.* (Berlin: Springer.)

GLENNIE, K W. 1986. Early Permian — Rotliegend. 63–85 in *Introduction to the petroleum geology of the North Sea*. GLENNIE, K W (editor). (2nd edition). (Oxford: Blackwell Scientific Publications.)

GOODLET, G A. 1970. Sands and gravels of the southern counties of Scotland. *Report of the Institute of Geological Sciences*, No. 70/4.

GORDON, J E. 1993a. Bigholm Burn. 596–599 in *Quaternary of Scotland*. (Geological conservation review series: 6). GORDON, J E, and SUTHERLAND, D G (editors). (London: Chapman and Hall.)

GORDON, J E. 1993b. Redkirk Point. 599–602 in *Quaternary of Scotland*. (Geological conservation review series: 6). GORDON, J E, and SUTHERLAND, D G (editors). (London: Chapman and Hall.)

GORDON, J E, and SUTHERLAND, D G. (editors) 1993. *The Geological Conservation Review Series 6: The Quaternary of Scotland* (London: Chapman and Hall.)

GRAY, D R. 1981. Cleavage-fold relationships and their implications for transected folds: an example from southwest Virginia, USA. *Journal of Structural Geology*, Vol. 3, 265–277.

GRAY, J M, and LOWE, J J. 1977. Introduction. xi–xiii in *Studies in the Scottish Lateglacial Environment*. GRAY, J M, and LOWE, J J (editors). (Oxford: Pergamon Press.)

GREIG, D C. 1971. *British regional geology: the South of Scotland*. (3rd edition). (Edinburgh: HMSO for British Geological Survey.)

HAGGART, B A. 1988. A review of radiocarbon dates on peat and wood from Holocene coastal sedimentary sequences in Scotland. *Scottish Journal of Geology*, Vol. 24, 125–144.

HAGGART, B A. 1989. Variations in the pattern and rate of isostatic uplift indicated by comparison of Holocene sea-level curves from Scotland. *Journal of Quaternary Science*, Vol. 4, 67–76.

HALLIDAY, A N. 1984. Coupled Sm-Nd and U-Pb systematics in late Caledonian granites and the basement under northern Britain. *Nature, London*, Vol. 307, 229–233.

HALLIDAY, A N, STEPHENS, W E, and HARMON, R S. 1980. Rb-Sr and O isotopic relationships in 3 zoned Caledonian granitic plutons, Southern Uplands, Scotland: evidence for varied sources and hybridization of magmas. *Journal of the Geological Society of London*, Vol. 137, 329–348.

HARKNESS, R. 1850. On the Silurian rocks of Dumfriesshire and Kirkcudbrightshire. *Quarterly Journal of the Geological Society of London*, Vol. 7, 46–58.

HARKNESS, R. 1853. On the Silurian rocks of Kirkcudbrightshire. *Quarterly Journal of the Geological Society of London*, Vol. 9, 181–186.

HARKNESS, R. 1856. On the lowest sedimentary rocks of the South of Scotland. *Quarterly Journal of the Geological Society of London*, Vol. 12, 238–245.

HARRIS, M, KAY, E A, WIDNELL, M A, JONES, E M, and STEELE, G B. 1988. Geology and mineralisation of the Lagalochan intrusive complex, western Argyll, Scotland. *Transactions of the Institution of Mining and Metallurgy (Section B: Applied earth science)*, Vol. 97, B15–21.

HATCH, F H, WELLS, A K, and WELLS, M K. 1972. *Petrology of the igneous rocks.* (13th edition). (London: Murby.)

HENNEY, P J. 1991. The geochemistry and petrogenesis of the minor intrusive suite associated with the Late Caledonian Criffel–Dalbeattie pluton, SW Scotland. Unpublished PhD thesis, University of Aston, Birmingham.

HENNEY, P J, EVANS, J A, HOLDEN, P, and ROCK, N M S. 1989. Granite-lamprophyre associates in the Scottish Caledonides: trace element and isotopic evidence for mantle involvement in Caledonian granite genesis. *TERRA abstracts*, Vol. 1, 285–286.

HILL, D. 1940. A monograph of Carboniferous Rugose corals of Scotland. *Monographs of the Palaeontographical Society*, 115–204.

HOLDEN, P, HALLIDAY, A N, and STEPHENS, W E. 1987. Neodynium and strontium isotope content of microdiorite enclaves point to mantle input to granitoid production. *Nature, London*, Vol. 330, 53–56.

HOLLOWAY, S. 1985. The Permian. 26–30 in *Atlas of onshore sedimentary basins in England and Wales: post-Carboniferous tectonics and stratigraphy.* WHITTAKER, A (editor). (Glasgow: Blackie and Son.)

HORNE, J, PEACH, B N, and TEALL, J J H. 1896. Explanation of Sheet 5, Kirkcudbrightshire. *Memoir of the Geological Survey, Scotland.*

HUGHES, R A. 1995. A synoptic account of the revision of the Scottish 1:50 000 series Sheet 6W (Kirkbean), with a summary of the Flandrian history. *British Geological Survey Technical Report*, WA/95/21.

HUTTON, D H W. 1982. A tectonic model for the emplacement of the main Donegal granite, N.W. Ireland. *Journal of the Geological Society of London*, Vol. 139, 615–632.

HUTTON, D H W. 1987. Strike-slip terranes and a model for the evolution of the British and Irish Caledonides. *Geological Magazine*, Vol. 124, 405–425.

HUTTON, D H W, DEMPSTER, T J, BROWN, P E, and BECKER, S M. 1990. A new mechanism of granite emplacement: intrusion in active extensional shear zones. *Nature, London*, Vol. 343, 452–455.

INSTITUTE OF GEOLOGICAL SCIENCES. 1972. Aeromagnetic Map of Great Britain. (Southampton: Ordnance Survey.)

INSTITUTE OF GEOLOGICAL SCIENCES. 1980. Kirkcudbright. Scotland Sheet 5W. Drift geology. 1:50 000. (Southampton: Ordnance Survey for Institute of Geological Sciences.)

INSTITUTE OF GEOLOGICAL SCIENCES. 1981. Dalbeattie. Scotland Sheet 5E. Drift geology. 1:50 000. (Southampton: Ordnance Survey for Institute of Geological Sciences.)

JACKSON, D I, and 5 others. 1995. *United Kingdom offshore regional report: the Geology of the Irish Sea.* (London: HMSO for British Geological Survey.)

JAMESON, R. 1814. Notes on the Geognosy of Criffel, Kirkbean, and the Needles Eye, in Galloway. *Memoirs of the Wernerian Natural History Society*, Vol. 4, 541–547.

JARDINE, W G. 1967. Sediments of the Flandrian transgression in south-west Scotland: terminology and criteria for facies distinction. *Scottish Journal of Geology*, Vol. 3, 221–226.

JARDINE, W G. 1975. Chronology of Holocene marine transgression and regression in south-western Scotland. *Boreas*, Vol. 4, 173–196.

JARDINE, W G. 1980. Holocene raised coastal sediments and former shorelines of Dumfriesshire and Eastern Galloway. *Transactions of the Dumfriesshire and Galloway Natural History and Antiquarian Society*, Vol. 43, 1–59.

JARDINE, W G. 1981. Holocene shorelines in Britain: recent studies. 297–304 in Quaternary geology: a farewell to A J Wiggers. VAN LOON, A J (editor). *Geologie en Mijnbouw*, Vol. 60.

JARDINE, W G, and MORRISON, A. 1976. The archaeological significance of Holocene coastal deposits in south-western Scotland. 175–195 in *Geoarchaeology: Earth Science and the Past.* DAVIDSON, D A, and SHACKLEY, M L (editors). (London: Duckworth.)

JARDINE, W G, and PEACOCK, J D. 1973. Scotland. 53–59 in A correlation of Quaternary deposits in the British Isles. MITCHELL, G F, PENNY, L F, SHOTTON, F W, and WEST, R G (editors). *Special Report of the Geological Society of London*, No. 4.

JOLLY, W. 1869. Notes on the geology of Southerness, Kirkcudbrightshire. *Transactions of the Edinburgh Geological Society*, Vol. 1, 278–284.

KAFAFY, A M, and TARLING, D H. 1985. Magnetic fabric in some granitic aureoles, Southern Uplands, Scotland. *Journal of the Geological Society of London*, Vol. 142, 1007–1014.

KELLING, G. 1961. The stratigraphy and structure of the Ordovician rocks of the Rhins of Galloway. *Quarterly Journal of the Geological Society of London*, Vol. 117, 37–75.

KELLING, G, DAVIES, P, and HOLROYD, J. 1987. Style, scale and significance of sand bodies in the Northern and Central belts, southwest Southern Uplands. *Journal of the Geological Society of London*, Vol. 144, 787–805.

KEMP, A E S. 1985. The later (Silurian) sedimentary and tectonic evolution of the Southern Uplands accretionary terrain. University of Edinburgh PhD thesis (unpublished).

KEMP, A E S. 1986. Tectonostratigraphy of the Southern Belt of the Southern Uplands. *Scottish Journal of Geology*, Vol. 22, 241–256.

KEMP, A E S. 1987a. Tectonic development of the Southern Belt of the Southern Uplands accretionary complex. *Journal of the Geological Society of London*, Vol. 144, 827–838.

KEMP, A E S. 1987b. Evolution of Silurian depositional systems in the Southern Uplands, Scotland. Chapter 7 in *Marine Clastic Sedimentology.* LEGGETT, J K, and ZUFFA, G G (editors). (London: Graham & Trotman.)

KEMP, A E S, OLIVER, G J H, and BALDWIN, J R. 1985. Low-grade metamorphism and accretion tectonics: Southern Uplands terrain, Scotland. *Mineralogical Magazine*, Vol. 49, 335–344.

KEMP, A E S, and WHITE, D E. 1985. Silurian trench sedimentation in the Southern Uplands, Scotland: implications of new age data. *Geological Magazine*, Vol. 122, 275–277.

KIMBELL, G S. 1991. Magnetic anomalies and the deep structure of the Iapetus Convergence Zone [Abstract]. *Geophysical Journal International*, Vol. 104, 687.

KIMBELL, G S, CHADWICK, R A, HOLLIDAY, D W, and WERNGREN, O C. 1989. The structure and evolution of the Northumberland Trough from new seismic reflection data and its bearing on modes of continental extension. *Journal of the Geological Society of London*, Vol. 146, 775–787.

KIMBELL, G S, and STONE, P. 1995. Crustal magnetization variations across the Iapetus Suture Zone. *Geological Magazine*, Vol. 132, 599–609.

KING, B C. 1937. The minor intrusives of Kirkcudbrightshire. *Proceedings of the Geologists' Association*, Vol. 48, 282–306.

KISCH, H J. 1991. Illite crystallinity; recommendation on sample preparation, X-ray diffraction settings, and interlaboratory samples. *Journal of Metamorphic Geology*, Vol. 9, 665–670.

KNELLER, B, EDWARDS, D, MCCAFFREY, W, and MOORE, R. 1991. Oblique reflection of turbidity currents. *Geology*, Vol. 14, 250–252.

KNELLER, B C, SCOTT, R W, SOPER, N J, JOHNSON, E W, and ALLEN, P M. 1994. Lithostratigraphy of the Windermere Supergroup, Northern England. *Geological Journal*, Vol. 29, 219–240.

KNIPE, R J, CHAMBERLAIN, M I, PAGE, A, and NEEDHAM, D T. 1988. Structural histories in the SW Southern Uplands, Scotland. *Journal of the Geological Society of London*, Vol. 145, 679–684.

KNIPE, R J, and NEEDHAM, D T. 1986. Deformation processes in accretionary wedges — examples from the SW margin of the Southern Uplands, Scotland. 51–65 *in* Collision Tectonics. Coward, M P, and Ries, A C (editors). *Special Publication of the Geological Society of London*, No. 19.

LAPWORTH, C. 1878. The Moffat Series. *Quarterly Journal of the Geological Society of London*, Vol. 34, 240–346.

LAPWORTH, C. 1889. On the Ballantrae rocks of the south of Scotland and their place in the upland sequence. *Geological Magazine*, Vol. 26, 20–24, 59–69.

LAPWORTH, C, and WILSON, J. 1971. On the Silurian rocks of the counties of Roxburgh and Selkirk. *Geological Magazine*, Vol. 8, 456–464.

LARSEN, E, and SEVRUP, H P. 1990. Weichselian land-sea interactions: Western Norway–Norwegian Sea. *Quaternary Science Reviews*, Vol. 6, 85–97.

LE MAITRE, R W (editor). 1989. *A Classification of Igneous Rocks and Glossary of Terms. Recommendations of the International Union of Geological Sciences Subcommission on the Systematics of Igneous Rocks.* (Oxford, London, Edinburgh, Boston, Melbourne: Blackwell Scientific Publications.)

LEAKE, B E. 1990. Granite magmas: their sources, initiation and consequences of emplacement. *Journal of the Geological Society of London*, Vol. 147, 579–589.

LEAKE, R C, and BROWN, M J. 1979. Porphyry-style copper mineralization at Black Stockarton Moor, southwest Scotland. *Transactions of the Institution of Mining and Metallurgy (Section B: Applied earth science)*, Vol. 88, B177–181.

LEAKE, R C, BROWN, M J, SMITH, T K, and DATE, A R. 1978. A reconnaissance geochemical drainage survey of the Criffel–Dalbeattie granodiorite complex and its environs. *Mineral Reconnaissance Report, Institute of Geological Sciences*, No. 19.

LEAKE, R C, and COOPER, C. 1983. The Black Stockarton Moor subvolcanic complex, Galloway. *Journal of the Geological Society of London*, Vol. 140, 665–676.

LEE, M K. 1982. Regional geophysics of the Cheviot area. *Report of the Environmental Protection Unit, Institute of Geological Sciences, ENPU*, No. 82–2.

LEE, M K. 1989. Upper crustal structure of the Lake District from modelling and image processing of potential field data. *British Geological Survey Technical Report*, WK/89/1.

LEEDER, M. 1971. Aspects of the geology of the south-eastern part of the Criffell intrusion and its associated dykes. *Transactions of the Dumfriesshire and Galloway Natural History and Antiquarian Society*, Vol. 48, 1–11.

LEEDER, M R. 1973. Sedimentology and palaeogeography of the Upper Old Red Sandstone in the Scottish Border Basin. *Scottish Journal of Geology*, Vol. 9, 117–144.

LEEDER, M R. 1974. Origin of the Northumberland Basin. *Scottish Journal of Geology*, Vol. 10, 283–296.

LEEDER, M R. 1975. Lower Border Group (Tournaisian) stromatolites from the Northumberland basin. *Scottish Journal of Geology*, Vol. 11, 207–226.

LEEDER, M R. 1976. Palaeogeographic significance of pedogenic carbonates in the topmost Upper Old Red Sandstone of the Scottish Border Basin. *Journal of Geology*, Vol. 11, 21–28.

LEEDER, M R. 1982. Upper Palaeozoic basins of the British Isles: Caledonide inheritance versus Hercynian plate margin processes. *Journal of the Geological Society of London*, Vol. 139, 479–491.

LEEDER, M R. 1988. Recent developments in Carboniferous geology: a critical review with implications for the British Isles and NW Europe. *Proceedings of the Geologists' Association*, Vol. 99, 73–100.

LEEDER, M R, and MCMAHON, A H. 1988. Upper Carboniferous (Silesian) basin subsidence in northern Britain. 43–52 *in* Sedimentation in a synorogenic basin complex: the Upper Carboniferous of northwest Europe. BESLY, B M, and KELLING, G (editors). (Glasgow and London: Blackie and Son.)

LEGGETT, J K. 1987. The Southern Uplands as an accretionary prism: the importance of analogues in reconstructing palaeogeography. *Journal of the Geological Society of London*, Vol. 144, 737–752.

LEGGETT, J K, MCKERROW, W S, and CASEY, D M. 1982. The anatomy of a Lower Palaeozoic accretionary forearc: the Southern Uplands of Scotland. 495–520 *in* Trench-forearc geology: sedimentation and tectonics on modern and ancient active plate margins. LEGGETT, J K (editor). *Special Publication of the Geological Society of London*, No. 10.

LEGGETT, J K, MCKERROW, W S, and EALES, M H. 1979. The Southern Uplands of Scotland: a Lower Palaeozoic accretionary prism. *Journal of the Geological Society of London*, Vol. 136, 755–770.

LOVELL, J P B. 1974. Sand volcanoes in the Silurian rocks of Kirkcudbrightshire. *Scottish Journal of Geology*, Vol. 10, 161–162.

LOWELL, J D, and GUILBERT, J M. 1970. Lateral and vertical alteration-mineralisation zoning in porphyry ore deposits. *Economic Geology*, Vol. 65, 373–408.

LUMSDEN, G I, TULLOCH, W, HOWELLS, M F, and DAVIES, A. 1967. The geology of the neighbourhood of Langholm. *Memoir of the Geological Survey, Scotland*, Sheet 11.

MACDONALD, R. 1975. Petrochemistry of the early Carboniferous (Dinantian) lavas of Scotland. *Scottish Journal of Geology*, Vol. 11, 269–314.

MACDONALD, R, ROCK, N M S, RUNDLE, C C, and RUSSELL, O J. 1986. Relationships between late Caledonian lamprophyric, syenitic and granitic magmas in a differentiated dyke, southern Scotland. *Mineralogical Magazine*, Vol. 50, 547–557.

MACDONALD, R, WILSON, L, THORPE, R S, and MARTIN, A. 1988. Emplacement of the Cleveland Dyke: evidence from geochemistry, mineralogy and physical modelling. *Journal of Petrology*, Vol. 29, 559–583.

MACGREGOR, M. 1937. The western part of the Criffell–Dalbeattie igneous complex. *Quarterly Journal of the Geological Society of London*, Vol. 93, 457–486.

MACGREGOR, M. 1938. The evolution of the Criffell–Dalbeattie quartz-diorite: a study in granitisation. *Geological Magazine*, Vol. 75, 481–496.

MACGREGOR, M, LEE, G W, and WILSON, G V. 1920. The iron ores of Scotland. *Special Report on the Mineral Resources of Great Britain, Memoir of the Geological Survey, Scotland*, Vol. 11.

MAGUIRE, K, THOMPSON, J, and GOWLAND, S. 1996. Dinantian depositional environments along the northern margin of the Solway Basin. 163–182 *in* Recent advances in Lower

Carboniferous geology. STROGEN, P, SOMERVILLE, I D, and JONES, G L (editors). *Special Publication of the Geological Society of London*, No. 107.

MANSFIELD, J, and KENNETT, P. 1963. A gravity survey of the Stranraer sedimentary basin. *Proceedings of the Yorkshire Geological Society*, Vol. 34, 139–151.

MARSHALL, J R. 1962. The physiographic development of Caerlaverock Merse. *Transactions of the Dumfriesshire and Galloway Natural History and Antiquarian Society*, Vol. 39, 102–123.

MAUGER, R L. 1988. Ocelli: transient disequilibrium features in a Lower Carboniferous minette near Concord, North Carolina. *The Canadian Mineralogist*, Vol. 26, Session 117–131.

MAY, J. 1981. The glaciation and deglaciation of upper Nithsdale and Annandale. Unpublished PhD thesis, University of Glasgow .

MCCABE, A M. 1987. Quaternary deposits and glacial stratigraphy in Ireland. *Quaternary Science Reviews*, Vol. 6, 259–299.

MCCAFFREY, W D. 1991. Silurian turbidite provenance in north-west England. Unpublished PhD thesis, University of Leeds.

MCKERROW, W S, LAMBERT, R S-J, and COCKS, L R M. 1985. The Ordovician, Silurian and Devonian periods. 73–79 *in* The Chronology of the Geological Record. SNELLING, N J (editor). *Memoir of the Geological Society of London*, No. 10.

MCKERROW, W S, LEGGETT, J K, and EALES, M H. 1977. Imbricate thrust model of the Southern Uplands of Scotland. *Nature, London*, Vol. 267, 237–239.

MCMILLAN, A A. In press. Geology of the New Galloway and Thornhill district. Memoir of the British Geological Survey, Sheets 9W and 9E, Scotland.

MCMILLAN, A A, and BRAND, P J. 1995. Depositional setting of Permian and Upper Carboniferous strata of the Thornhill Basin, Dumfriesshire. *Scottish Journal of Geology*, Vol. 31, 43–52.

MCROBERT, R W. 1920. Igneous rocks of Teviot and Liddesdale. *Transactions of the Edinburgh Geological Society*, Vol. 11, 86–103.

MERRIMAN, R J, and ROBERTS, B. 1990. Metabentonites in the Moffat Shale Group, Southern Uplands of Scotland: geochemical evidence of ensialic marginal basin volcanism. *Geological Magazine*, Vol. 127, 259–271.

MERRIMAN, R J, and ROBERTS, B. 1993. The low grade metamorphism of Lower Palaeozoic strata on the Rhins of Galloway, SW Scotland. *British Geological Survey Technical Report*, WG/92/40.

MERRIMAN, R J, ROBERTS, B, PEACOR, D R, and HIRONS, S R. 1995. Strain-related differences in crystal growth of white mica and chlorite: a TEM and XRD study of pelite fabrics from the Southern Uplands of Scotland. *Journal of Metamorphic Geology*, Vol. 13, 559–576.

MILLER, J M, and TAYLOR, K. 1966. Uranium mineralization near Dalbeattie, Kirkcudbrightshire. *Bulletin of the Geological Survey of Great Britain*, No. 25, 1–18.

MILODOWSKI, A E, and 5 OTHERS. 1990. Uranium-mineralised microorganisms associated with uraniferous hydrocarbons in southwest Scotland. *Nature, London*, Vol. 347, 465–467.

MITCHELL, M. 1989. Biostratigraphy of Visean (Dinantian) rugose coral faunas from Britain. *Proceedings Yorkshire Geological Society*, Vol. 47, 233–247.

MORRIS, J H. 1987. The Northern Belt of the Longford-Down Inlier, Ireland and Southern Uplands, Scotland: an Ordovician back-arc basin. *Journal of the Geological Society of London*, Vol. 144, 773–786.

MURPHY, F C, and HUTTON, D H W. 1986. Is the Southern Uplands of Scotland really an accretionary prism? *Geology*, Vol. 14, 354–357.

MUSSETT, A E, DAGLEY, P, and SKELHORN, R R. 1988. Time and duration of activity in the British Tertiary Igneous Province. 337–348 *in* Early Tertiary volcanism and the opening of the NE Atlantic. MORTON, A C, and PARSON, L M (editors). *Special Publication of the Geological Society of London*, No. 39.

NAKAMURA, N. 1974. Determination of REE, Ba, Fe, Mg, Na and K in carbonaceous and ordinary chondrites. *Geochimica at Cosmochimica Acta*, Vol. 38, 757–775.

NEEDHAM, D T. 1993. The structure of the western part of the Southern Uplands of Scotland. *Journal of the Geological Society of London*, Vol. 150, 341–354.

NEEDHAM, D T, and KNIPE, R J. 1986. Accretion and collision related deformation in the Scottish Southern Uplands. *Geology*, Vol. 14, 303–306.

OLIVER, G J H, and LEGGETT, J K. 1980. Metamorphism in an accretionary prism: prehnite-pumpellyite facies metamorphism of the Southern Uplands of Scotland. *Transactions of the Royal Society of Edinburgh: Earth Sciences*, Vol. 71, 235–246.

ORD, D M, CLEMMEY, H, and LEEDER, M R. 1988. Interaction between faulting and sedimentation during Dinantian extension of the Solway basin, SW Scotland. *Journal of the Geological Society of London*, Vol. 145, 249–259.

PALLISTER, J W. 1952. The Birrenswark Lavas, Dumfriesshire. *Transactions of the Edinburgh Geological Society*, Vol. 14, 336–348.

PARSLOW, G R. 1964. The Cairnsmore of Fleet granite and its aureole. Unpublished PhD thesis, University of Newcastle upon Tyne.

PARSLOW, G R. 1968. The physical and structural features of the Cairnsmore of Fleet granite and its aureole. *Scottish Journal of Geology*, Vol. 4, 91–108.

PARSLOW, G R. 1971. Variations in mineralogy and major elements in the Cairnsmore of Fleet granite, S W Scotland. *Lithos*, Vol. 4, 43–55.

PARSLOW, G R, and RANDALL, B A. 1973. A gravity survey of the Cairnsmore of Fleet granite and its environs. *Scottish Journal of Geology*, Vol. 9, 219–231.

PATCHETT, P J. 1980. Thermal effects of basalt on continental crust and crustal contamination of magmas. *Nature, London*, Vol. 283, 559–561.

PATERSON, I B, and HALL, I H S. 1986. Lithostratigraphy of the late Devonian and early Carboniferous rocks in the Midland Valley of Scotland. *Report of the British Geological Survey*, Vol. 18, No. 3.

PEACH, B N, and HORNE, J. 1899. The Silurian rocks of Britain, Vol. 1: Scotland. *Memoir of the Geological Survey of the United Kingdom*.

PEACH, B N, and HORNE, J. 1903. The Canonbie Coalfield: its geological structure and relations to the Carboniferous rocks of the north of England and central Scotland. *Transactions of the Royal Society of Edinburgh*, Vol. 40, 835–877.

PEARCE, J A. 1983. Role of the sub-continental lithosphere in magma genesis at active continental margins. 230–249 *in* Continental Basalts and Mantle Xenoliths. HAWKESWORTH, C J, and NORRY, M J (editors). (Nantwich, Cheshire: Shiva.)

PEDLEY, R C. 1991. *GRAVMAG – Interactive 2.5D gravity and magnetic modelling program. User Manual, Integrated Geophysical Services.* (Keyworth, Nottingham: British Geological Survey.)

PHILLIPS, E R. 1992. Microfabric analysis of a series of sheared metasandstones exposed within the Moniaive Shear Zone, Southern Uplands, Scotland. *British Geological Survey Technical Report,* WG/92/45.

PHILLIPS, E R, BARNES, R P, BOLAND, M P, FORTEY, N J, and McMILLAN, A A. 1995. The Moniaive Shear Zone: a major zone of sinistral strike-slip deformation in the Southern Uplands of Scotland. *Scottish Journal of Geology,* Vol. 31, 139–149.

PHILLIPS, W J. 1955. The metasomatic rocks associated with the Criffel–Dalbeattie granodiorite. *Geological Magazine,* Vol. 92, 1–20.

PHILLIPS, W J. 1956a. The Criffell-Dalbeattie granodiorite complex. *Quarterly Journal of the Geological Society of London,* Vol. 112, 221–239.

PHILLIPS, W J. 1956b. Minor intrusive suite associated with the Criffel–Dalbeattie granodiorite complex. *Proceedings of the Geologists' Association,* Vol. 67, 103–121.

PHILLIPS, W J, FUGE, R, and PHILLIPS, N. 1981. Convection and crystallisation in the Criffell–Dalbeattie pluton. *Journal of the Geological Society of London,* Vol. 138, 351–366.

PICKERING, K T, STOW, D A V, WATSON, M P, and HISCOTT, R N. 1986. Deep water facies, processes and models : a review and classification scheme for modern and ancient sediments. *Earth Science Reviews,* Vol. 23, 75–174.

PIDGEON, R T, and AFTALION, M. 1978. Cogenetic and inherited zircon U–Pb systems in granites: Palaeozoic granites of Scotland and England. 183–220 *in* Crustal Evolution in northwestern Britain and adjacent areas. BOWES, D R, and LEAKE, B E (editors). *Geological Journal Special Issue,* No. 10.

POWELL, D W. 1970. Magnetised rocks within the Lewisian of Western Scotland and under the Southern Uplands. *Scottish Journal of Geology,* Vol. 6, 353–369.

PRICE, R J. 1961. The deglaciation of the Tweed drainage area west of Innerleithen. Unpublished PhD thesis, University of Edinburgh.

PRICE, R J. 1963. The glaciation of a part of Peebles-shire, Scotland. *Transactions of the Edinburgh Geological Society,* Vol. 19, 326–348.

PRICE, R J. 1983. *Scotland's environment during the last 30 000 years.* (Edinburgh: Scottish Academic Press.)

PRINGLE, J. 1948. *British regional geology: the South of Scotland.* (2nd edition). (Edinburgh: HMSO for Geological Survey and Museum.)

RICKARDS, R B. 1967. The Wenlock and Ludlow succession in the Howgill Fells (north-west Yorkshire and Westmorland). *Quarterly Journal of the Geological Society of London,* Vol. 123, 215–249.

RICKARDS, R B. 1969. Wenlock graptolite zones in the English Lake District. *Proceedings of the Yorkshire Geological Society,* No. 1654, 61.

RICKARDS, R B. 1976. The sequence of Silurian graptolite zones in the British Isles. *Geological Journal,* Vol. 11, 153–188.

ROBERTS, B, MERRIMAN, R J, and PRATT, W. 1991. The influence of strain, lithology and stratigraphical depth on white mica (illite) crystallinity in mudrocks from the vicinity of the Corris Slate Belt, Wales: implications for the timing of metamorphism in the Welsh Basin. *Geological Magazine,* Vol. 128, 633–645.

ROCK, N M S. 1984. The nature and origin of lamprophyres: minettes, vogesites, kersantites and spessartites. *Transactions of the Royal Society of Edinburgh: Earth Sciences,* Vol. 74, 193–227.

ROCK, N M S. 1987. The nature and origin of lamprophyres: an overview. 191–226 *in* Alkaline igneous rocks. FITTON, J G, and UPTON, B G J (editors). *Special Publication of the Geological Society of London,* No. 30.

ROCK, N M S. 1991. *Lamprophyres.* (Glasgow: Blackie.)

ROCK, N M S, COOPER, C, and GASKARTH, J W. 1986a. Late Caledonian subvolcanic vents and associated dykes in the Kirkcudbright area, Galloway, south-west Scotland. *Proceedings of the Yorkshire Geological Society,* Vol. 46, 29–37.

ROCK, N M S, GASKARTH, J W, and RUNDLE, C C. 1986b. Late Caledonian dyke-swarms in southern Scotland: a regional zone of primitive K-rich lamprophyres and associated vents. *Journal of Geology,* Vol. 94, 505–522.

ROSE, J. 1989. Stadial type sections in the British Quaternary. 45–67 *in Quaternary type sections: imagination or reality?* ROSE, J, and SCHLUCHTER, C (editors). (Rotterdam: Balkema.)

RUSHTON, A W A, and STONE, P. 1991. Terrigenous input to the Moffat Shale sequence, Southern Uplands. *Scottish Journal of Geology,* Vol. 27, 167–169.

RUSHTON, A W A, STONE, P, and HUGHES, R A. 1996. Biostratigraphical control of thrust models for the Southern Uplands of Scotland. *Transactions of the Royal Society of Edinburgh: Earth Sciences,* Vol. 86, 137–152.

RUST, B R. 1965. The stratigraphy and structure of the Whithorn area of Wigtownshire, Scotland. *Scottish Journal of Geology,* Vol. 1, 101–133.

SANDERSON, D J, ANDERSON, T B, and CAMERON, T D J. 1985. Strain history and the development of transecting cleavage, with examples from the Caledonides of the British Isles (Abstract). *Journal of Structural Geology,* Vol. 7, 498.

SCOTT, K M. 1967. Intra-bed palaeocurrent variations in a Silurian flysch sequence, Kirkcudbrightshire, Southern Uplands of Scotland. *Scottish Journal of Geology,* Vol. 3, 268–281.

SHEPPARD, S M F. 1977. Identification of the origin of ore forming solutions by the use of stable isotopes. 25–41 in *Volcanic processes in ore genesis.* (London: IMM and Geological Society.)

SILLITOE, R H. 1973. Geology of the Los Pelambres porphyry copper deposit, Chile. *Economic Geology,* Vol. 69, 1–10.

SISSONS, J B. 1967. *The Evolution of Scotland's Scenery.* (Edinburgh & London: Oliver & Boyd.)

SMITH, I F, and ROYLES, C P. 1989. The digital aeromagnetic survey of the United Kingdom. *British Geological Survey Technical Report,* No. WK/89/5.

SMITH, J. 1910. Carboniferous rocks of the Solway, Scotland. *Transactions of the Geological Society of Glasgow,* Vol. 14, 30–59.

SMITH, R T, and McMILLAN, A A. 1996. Mineral investigations in the Northumberland Trough: Part 3, Ecclefechan–Waterbeck area. *British Geological Survey, Mineral Reconnaissance Open File Report,* No. 21.

SMITH, R T, and 5 others. 1996. Mineral investigations in the Northumberland Trough: Part 5, The Kirkbean area, south-west Scotland. *British Geological Survey, Mineral Reconnaissance Open File Report,* No. 23.

SOPER, N J, ENGLAND, R W, SNYDER, D B, and RYAN, P D. 1992. The Iapetus suture zone in England, Scotland and eastern

Ireland: a reconciliation of geological and deep seismic data. *Journal of the Geological Society of London,* Vol. 149, 697–700.

STEPHENS, W E. 1972. The geochemistry of the Dalbeattie granodiorite complex and associated rocks. Unpublished PhD thesis, University of Wales, Aberystwyth.

STEPHENS, W E. 1992. Spatial, compositional and rheological constraints on the origin of zoning in the Criffell Pluton, Scotland. 191–199 *in* The second Hutton symposium on the origin of granites and related rocks; proceedings. BROWN, P E, and CHAPPELL, B W (editors). Transactions of the Royal Society of Edinburgh: Earth Sciences, Vol. 83. (also *Geological Society of America Special Paper,* No. 272.)

STEPHENS, W E, and HALLIDAY, A N. 1980. Discontinuities in the composition surface of a zoned pluton, Criffell, Scotland. *Bulletin of the Geological Society of America,* Vol. 91, 165–170.

STEPHENS, W E, WHITLEY, J E, THIRLWALL, M F, and HALLIDAY, A N. 1985. The Criffell zoned pluton: correlated behaviour of rare earth element abundances with isotopic systems. *Contributions to Mineralogy and Petrology,* Vol. 89, 226–238.

STEVENSON, T. 1843. Remarks on the geology of the island of Little Ross, Kirkcudbrightshire. *Edinburgh Philosophical Journal,* Vol. 35, 83–88.

STONE, P. 1988. The Permian successions at Ballantrae and Loch Ryan, south-west Scotland. *Report of the British Geological Survey,* Vol. 19, No. 2, 13–18.

STONE, P. 1995. Geology of the Rhins of Galloway district. *Memoir of the British Geological Survey,* Sheets 1 and 3 (Scotland).

STONE, P. 1996. *Geology in south-west Scotland: an excursion guide.* (Keyworth, Nottingham: British Geological Survey.)

STONE, P, COOK, J M, McDERMOTT, C, ROBINSON, J J, and SIMPSON, P R. 1995. Lithostratigraphic and structural controls on the distribution of As and Au in the SW Southern Uplands, Scotland. *Transactions of the Institution of Mining and Metallurgy (Section B: Applied earth science),* Vol. 104, B111–B119.

STONE, P, FLOYD, J D, BARNES, R P, and LINTERN, B C. 1986. A back-arc thrust-duplex model for the Southern Uplands of Scotland (abstract). *Newsletter of the Geological Society of London,* Vol. 15, No. 1, 5.

STONE, P, FLOYD, J D, BARNES, R P, and LINTERN, B C. 1987. A sequential back-arc and foreland basin thrust duplex model for the Southern Uplands of Scotland. *Journal of the Geological Society of London,* Vol. 144, 753–764.

STONE, P, GREEN, P M, LINTERN, B C, SIMPSON, P R, and PLANT, J A. 1993. Regional geochemical variation across the Iapetus Suture zone: tectonic implications. *Scottish Journal of Geology,* Vol. 29, 113–121.

STONE, P, KIMBELL, G S, and HENNEY, P J. 1997. Basement control on the location of strike-slip shear in the Southern Uplands of Scotland. *Journal of the Geological Society of London,* Vol. 154, 141–144.

STRINGER, P, and TREAGUS, J E. 1980. Non-axial planar S$_1$ cleavage in the Hawick Rocks of the Galloway area, Southern Uplands, Scotland. *Journal of Structural Geology,* Vol. 2, 317–331.

STRINGER, P, and TREAGUS, J E. 1981. Asymmetrical folding in the Hawick Rocks of the Galloway area, Southern Uplands. *Scottish Journal of Geology,* Vol. 17, 129–147.

SUTHERLAND, D G. 1984. The Quaternary deposits and landforms of Scotland and the neighbouring shelves: a review. *Quaternary Science Reviews,* Vol. 3, 157–254.

TAYLOR, B J, and 5 OTHERS. 1971. *British regional geology: Northern England.* (London: HMSO.)

THIRLWALL, M F. 1988. Geochronology of late Caledonian magmatism in northern Britain. *Journal of the Geological Society of London,* Vol. 145, 951–967.

THIRLWALL, M F, MAYNARD, J, STEPHENS, W E, and SHAND, P. 1989. Calc-alkaline magmagenesis in the Scottish Southern Uplands forearc: a Pb-Sr-Nd isotope study. *TERRA abstracts,* Vol. 1, 178.

THOMAS, G S P. in press. Northern England. *in* A correlation of the Quaternary rocks of the British Isles. BOWEN, D Q (editor). *Geological Society of London Special Report.*

TOOLEY, M J. 1980. Crosscanonby. 74–77 *in* Field Guide to Western Scotland and Northwestern England. JARDINE, W G (editor). *INQUA Subcommission on shorelines of north-western Europe, field meeting September 1980.*

VERNIERS, J, and 5 OTHERS. 1995. A global Chitinozoa biozonation for the Silurian. *Geological Magazine,* Vol. 132, 651–666.

WALTON, E K. 1955. Silurian greywackes in Peeblesshire. *Proceedings of the Royal Society of Edinburgh,* Vol. 65, Section B, 327–357.

WALTON, E K. 1968. Some rare sedimentary structures in the Silurian rocks of Kirkcudbrightshire. *Scottish Journal of Geology,* Vol. 4, 355–369.

WALTON, E K, and OLIVER, G J H. 1991. Lower Palaeozoic— stratigraphy, structure and palaeogeography. 161–228 in *The Geology of Scotland.* CRAIG, G Y (editor). (3rd edition). (London: The Geological Society.)

WARD, J (editor). 1995. Early Dinantian evaporites from the Easton-1 well in the Solway Basin, Cumbria. *The Petroleum Geology of the Irish Sea and adjacent areas,* No. 29.

WARREN, P T. 1964. The stratigraphy and structure of the Silurian rocks southeast of Hawick, Roxburghshire. *Quarterly Journal of the Geological Society of London,* Vol. 120, 193–218.

WATSON, J V. 1984. The ending of the Caledonian orogeny in Scotland. *Journal of the Geological Society,* Vol. 141, 193–214.

WEIR, J A. 1968. Structural history of the Silurian rocks of the coast west of Gatehouse, Kirkcudbrightshire. *Scottish Journal of Geology,* Vol. 4, 31–52.

WEIR, J A. 1974. The sedimentology and diagenesis of the Silurian rocks on the coast west of Gatehouse, Kirkcudbrightshire. *Scottish Journal of Geology,* Vol. 10, 165–186.

WHITE, D E, BARRON, H F, BARNES, R P, and LINTERN, B C. 1992. (for 1991). Biostratigraphy of late Llandovery (Telychian) and Wenlock turbiditic sequences in the SW Southern Uplands, Scotland. *Transactions of the Royal Society of Edinburgh: Earth Sciences,* Vol. 82, 297–322.

WILSON, G V. 1921. The lead, zinc, copper and nickel ores of Scotland. *Special Report on the Mineral Resources of Great Britain, Memoir of the Geological Survey, Scotland,* Vol. 17.

WILSON, R B. 1989. A study of the Dinantian marine macrofossils of central Scotland. *Transactions of the Royal Society of Edinburgh: Earth Sciences,* Vol. 80, 91–126.

WOOD, D A, JORAN, J L, TREUIL, M, NORRY, M, and TARNEY, J. 1979. Elemental and Sr isotope variations in basic lavas from Iceland and the surrounding ocean floor. *Contributions to Mineralogy and Petrology,* Vol. 70, 319–339.

APPENDIX 1

Graptolite biostratigraphical data for the Kirkcudbright–Dalbeattie district.

A   List of Ordovician graptolite localities in the district

B   Ordovician graptolites from each locality, with author citation

C   Zonal ranges of Ordovician graptolites recorded in the district

D   List of Llandovery graptolite localities in the district

E   Llandovery graptolites from each locality, with author citation

F   Zonal ranges of Llandovery graptolites recorded in the district

G   List of Wenlock graptolite localities in the district

H   Wenlock graptolites from each locality, with author citation

I   Zonal ranges of Wenlock graptolites recorded in the district

A.   LIST OF ORDOVICIAN GRAPTOLITE LOCALITIES IN THE DISTRICT.

No.	Locality	NGR [NX]	Report No. & section	Zone(s)	Overlying turbidite unit
1	Kilnotrie	c. 751 673	90/67.1	*clingani*-low *linearis*	Gala 7
2	Kilnotrie	c. 751 673	90/67.2	*peltifer* or *wilsoni*	Gala 7
3	Trowdale Glen	7645 6885	89/57.1,2	?*clingani*	Gala 7
4	Trowdale Glen	7640 6868	89/57.3	?*clingani*	Gala 7
5	Tottlehams Glen	7769 6985	89/41.1	*gracilis*	Gala 7
6	Tottlehams Glen	7766 6973	89/41.3	uncertain	Gala 7
7	Tottlehams Glen	7762 6969	89/41.4	*clingani-linearis*	Gala 7
8	Tottlehams Glen	7723 6949	89/41.6	*gracilis*	Gala 7
9	Old Bridge of Urr	7622 6848	89/57.4	*gracilis*	Gala 7
10	Old Bridge of Urr	7622 6848	89/57.5	uncertain	Gala 7
11	Old Bridge of Urr	7656 6862	89/57.6	*gracilis*	Gala 7
12	Bellymack	6909 6456	88/43.7	*clingani-linearis*	Gala 7
13	Bellymack	6909 6456	88/43.8	*linearis*	Gala 7
14	Bellymack	6909 6456	88/43.9	?*linearis*	Gala 7
15	Bellymack	6909 6456	88/43.10,11	*clingani*	Gala 7
16	Bellymack	6909 6456	88/43.12	uncertain	Gala 7
17	Bellymack	6909 6456	88/43.13	*clingani*	Gala 7
18	Dinnance	6740 6424	88/22.4	uncertain	Gala 7
19	Dinnance	6743 6422	88/22.5	*wilsoni-clingani*	Gala 7
20	Barlay Burn	c.625 585	88/98.5	?*anceps*	Cairnharrow Formation

B.   ORDOVICAN GRAPTOLITES COLLECTED AT EACH LOCALITY, WITH AUTHORS.

Locality number	1	2	3	4	5	6	7	8	9	10	11	12	13	14	15	16	17	18	19	20
Amphigraptus sp.													+							
Amplexograptus sp.		?																		
Climacograptus antiquus Lapworth, 1873				?			?													
Climacograptus bicornis bicornis (Hall, 1847)	+																		+	
Climacograptus dorotheus Riva, 1976															?	+				
Climacograptus spiniferus Ruedemann, 1908																+				
Climacograptus tubuliferus Lapworth, 1876			+																	
Climacograptus sp.	+		+	+		+		+			+		+	+	+	+		+		+
Corynoides curtus Lapworth, 1876															+					
Corynoides incurvus Hadding, 1915					+															
Corynoides sp.			+																?	
Dicellograptus divaricatus (Hall, 1859)					+			+												
Dicellograptus divaricatus rigidus Lapworth, 1880								+												
Dicellograptus elegans (Carruthers, 1867)													+	?			?			
Dicellograptus flexuosus Lapworth, 1876															+	+				
Dicellograptus intortus Lapworth, 1880											+									
Dicellograptus morrisi Hopkinson, 1871	+												?	+		+				
Dicellograptus pumilus Lapworth, 1876							+									+				
Dicellograptus sextans exilis Elles & Wood, 1904								cf.												
Dicellograptus sp.										+										?
Dicranograptus clingani Carruthers, 1868																+				
Didymograptus superstes Lapworth, 1876											+									
Ensigraptus caudatus (Lapworth, 1876)										cf.										
Glyptograptus sp.			+																	
Hallograptus bimucronatus (Nicholson, 1869)					+															
Leptograptus flaccidus (Hall, 1865)			?																	
Leptograptus flaccidus macer Elles & Wood, 1903													+							
Nemagraptus gracilis (Hall, 1847)									+		+									
Nemagraptus sp.				?																
Normalograptus minimus (Carruthers, 1868)							+												?	
Normalograptus mohawkensis (Ruedemann, 1912)	cf.																			
Orthograptus calcaratus (Lapworth, 1876)	+															+				
Orthograptus calcaratus group																				
Orthograptus truncatus abbreviatus Elles & Wood, 1907						cf.													+	
Orthograptus truncatus intermedius Elles & Wood, 1907																			+	
Orthograptus truncatus pauperatus Elles & Wood, 1907				+											+					
Orthograptus truncatus (Lapworth, 1877) s.l.						cf.														
Orthograptus sp.											+		?							
Plegmatograptus sp.																	?			
Pleurograptus sp.							?													

+ fossil identified   ? uncertain identification   cf. comparable form recorded

C.   ZONAL RANGES OF ORDOVICIAN GRAPTOLITES RECORDED IN THE DISTRICT.

ORDOVICIAN	gracilis	peltier	wilsoni	clingani	linearis	complanat	anceps	persculpt
Amphigraptus sp.								
Amplexograptus sp.				?				
Climacograptus antiquus	?			?				
Climacograptus bicornis bicornis								
Climacograptus dorotheus								
Climacograptus spiniferus								
Climacograptus tubuliferus								
Climacograptus sp.								
Corynoides curtus								
Corynoides incurvus								
Corynoides sp.								
Dicranograptus clingani								
Dicellograptus divaricatus								
Dicellograptus divaricatus rigidus								
Dicellograptus elegans								
Dicellograptus flexuosus								
Dicellograptus intortus								
Dicellograptus morrisi								
Dicellograptus pumilus								
Dicellograptus sextans exilis	cf							
Dicellograptus sp.							?	
Didymograptus superstes								
Ensigraptus caudatus	?cf							
Glyptograptus sp.								
Hallograptus bimucronatus								
Leptograptus flaccidus				?				
Leptograptus flaccidus macer								
Nemagraptus gracilis								
Nemagraptus sp.	?							
Normalgraptus minimus			?					
Normalograptus mohawkensis			–cf–					
Orthograptus calcaratus								
Orthograptus calcaratus group								
Orthograptus truncatus abbreviatus								
Orthograptus truncatus intermedius								
Orthograptus truncatus pauperatus								
Orthograptus truncatus s.l.								
Orthograptus sp.					?			
Plegmatograptus sp.				?				
Pleurograptus sp.				–?–	–?–			

D.   LIST OF LLANDOVERY GRAPHOLITE LOCALITIES IN THE DISTRICT.

No.	Locality	NGR [NX]	Report No. & section	Zone(s)
Localities in Moffat Shales underlying Gala 4 tectonostratigraphical unit (Gillespie Burn Line)				
21	Hensol House	c 678 699	90/67.4	*acuminatus*
22	Hensol House	c 678 699	90/67.3	*acinaces-cyphus*
23	River Dee, Parton	c 670 702	90/67.6	*acinaces-cyphus*
24	River Dee, Parton	c 685 703	90/67.5	?*cyphus*
25	Loch Ken viaduct	6850 7040	88/23.2	mid-*acuminatus*
26	Loch Ken viaduct	6850 7040	88/23.3	*atavus*
27	Loch Ken viaduct	6850 7040	88/23.4	probably *atavus*
28	Loch Ken viaduct	6850 7040	88/23.1	?*atavus* or younger
Localities in Moffat Shales underlying Gala 7 tectonostratigraphical unit (Laurieston Line)				
29	Tottlehams Glen	7758 6964	89/41.5	mid-*acuminatus*
30	Tottlehams Glen	7758 6964	88/21.1	upper *acuminatus*
31	Tottlehams Glen	7766 6973	89/41.2	?*atavus-acinaces*
32	Bellymack	6909 6456	88/43.6	*acuminatus-?atavus*
33	Bellymack	6909 6456	88/43.4	?*acuminatus-atavus*
34	Bellymack	6909 6456	88/43.3	?*atavus-cyphus*
35	Bellymack	6909 6456	88/43.5	poss. *cyphus*
36	Cullernoch	6678 6450	88/43.16	prob. *gregarius-?convolutus*
37	Barlue	6739 6543	88/43.17	*convolutus*
38	Gatehouse Burn (west)	6685 6377	88/22.1	?*cyphus*
39	Gatehouse Burn	6696 6407	88/22.2	*convolutus*
40	Gatehouse Burn (east)	6685 6377	88/18.14	*sedgwickii*
41	Dinnance	6740 6410	88/22.3	prob. lower *atavus*
42	Dinnance	6744 6419	88/22.6	*atavus*
43	Quintinespie	6898 6446	88/22.7	prob. *cyphus*
Localities in Moffat Shales underlying the Cairnharrow Formation				
44	Barlay Burn	6218 5846	89/284.1,2	?
45	Barlay Burn	622 585	88/98.3	*acuminatus-cyphus*
46	Barlay Burn	622 585	88/98.4	prob. *atavus*
47	Barlay Burn	622 585	88/98.1	*acinaces*-lower *cyphus*
48	Barlay Burn	622 585	88/98.2	*convolutus*
Localities within the Cairnharrow Formation				
49	Edgarton	6718 6309	88/43.1a,2	*turriculatus*
50	Trowdale	c 770 690	88/18.16	*turriculatus* or *crispus*
51	Tarff Glen	6735 6130	87/418.1	*turriculatus* or *crispus*
Localities in Moffat Shales underlying the Kirkmaiden Formation				
52	Barstobrick	6861 6011	89/283	mid-*acuminatus*
53	Barstobrick	6861 6011	88/22.8	prob. *atavus-acinaces*
Localities within the Kirkmaiden Formation				
54	Waterside	6654 5868	88/18.15	uncertain (*griestoniensis-crenulata*)

E.   LLANDOVERY GRAPTOLITES FROM EACH LOCALITY, WITH AUTHOR CITATION.

Locality number	21	23	25	27	29	31	33	35	37	39	41	43	45	47	49	51	53
Atavograptus atavus (Jones, 1909)		+	+	?				+									?
Atavograptus gracilis Hutt, 1975			+				?				+						
Atavograptus sp.								?				?	+				
Climacograptus innotatus Nicholson, 1869					cf.						cf.						
Climacograptus trifilis Manck, 1923			+														
Climacograptus sp.		+	+		?	+	+		+		+		+	+	+		+	+
Coronograptus cirrus Hutt, 1975		?															
Coronograptus cyphus (Lapworth,1876)	?	+		?	?		?	?	cf.			+					
Coronograptus cyphus praematurus (Toghill,1968)			cf.														
Coronograptus gregarius (Lapworth, 1876)		+						+				+					
Coronograptus sp.														?			
Cystograptus penna (Hopkinson, 1869)								cf.									
Cystograptus vesiculosus (Nicholson, 1868)	+	+		?	+	+	+	+				?	?	?	+		
Dimorphograptus confertus (Nicholson, 1868) s.s.		+															
Dimorphograptus elongatus Lapworth, 1876											cf.						
Dimorphograptus erectus Elles & Wood, 1908							+	cf.									
Dimorphograptus decussatus Elles & Wood, 1908											?						
Dimorphograptus longissimus (Kurck, 1882)	cf.										cf.						
Dimorphograptus sp.				?									+				
Diplograptus modestus Lapworth, 1876											?cf.						
diplograptids indet.										+				+	+		+
Glyptograptus serratus Elles & Wood, 1907									+	cf.							
Glyptograptus sinuatus (Nicholson, 1869)		cf.															
Glyptograptus tamariscus (Nicholson, 1868)	+	cf.						gp.	sl.								
Glyptograptus tenuis (Rickards, 1970)			cf.														
Glyptograptus sp.	?									?							
Lagarograptus acinaces (Törnquist, 1899)		+	?														
Lagarograptus tenuis (Portlock, 1843)											+						
Monoclimacis crenularis (Lapworth, 1880)										+							
Monoclimacis sp.																	
Monograptus capis Hutt, 1975										+							
Monograptus clingani (Carruthers, 1867)										+							
Monograptus convolutus (Hisinger, 1837)														?			
Monograptus decipiens Törnquist, 1899														+			
Monograptus denticulatus Törnquist, 1899										+							
Monograptus limatulus Törnquist, 1892									+					+			
Monograptus lobiferus (McCoy, 1850)									+	cf.	+						

+ fossil identified   ? uncertain identification   cf. comparable form recorded   gp. member of species-group present   sl. sensu lato

E.   ....*continued*

Locality number	21	23	25	27	29	31	33	35	37	39	41	43	45	47	49	51	53
Monograptus marri Perner, 1897															?		
Monograptus planus (Barrande, 1850)															aff.		
Monograptus proteus (Barrande, 1850)																+	
Monograptus revolutus Kurck, 1882									?								
Monograptus spiralis (Geinitz, 1842)															cf.	?	
Monograptus triangulatus (Harkness, 1851) group									+								
Monograptus aff. *tullbergi* Bouček, 1931																	+
Monograptus sp.								+								+	
Normalograptus medius Törnquist, 1897						cf.			cf.				?	+			
Normalograptus miserabilis Elles & Wood, 1906				cf.							cf.						
Normalograptus normalis Lapworth, 1877				+		+					+						
Normalograptus rectangularis (McCoy, 1850)		+	+	+	+	+	+	+	+	+	?	+					
Normalograptus scalaris (Hisinger, 1837)									?								
'Orthograptus' bellulus (Törnquist, 1891)									+	cf.							
'Orthograptus' mutabilis Elles & Wood, 1907						cf.											
Orthograptus sp.		+			?	?											
Paradiversograptus capillaris (Carruthers, 1867)															?		
Paradiversograptus runcinatus Lapworth, 1876											cf.						
Parakidograptus acuminatus (Nicholson, 1867)	+		+	+	+	+											
Petalolithus altissimus Elles & Wood, 1908															+		
Petalolithus palmeus (Barrande, 1850)									+								
Petalolithus tenuis (Barrande) (or *P. wilsoni* Hutt, 1974)															?		
Pribylograptus incommodus (Törnquist, 1899)			aff.					?									
Pribylograptus sandersoni (Lapworth, 1876)		?							+								
Pristiograptus regularis (Törnquist, 1899)										cf.							
Pristiograptus sp.									?	+	+	+					
Rastrites hybridus Lapworth, 1876										+							
Rastrites longispinus Perner, 1897								+									
Rastrites peregrinus Barrande, 1850										+							
Rhaphidograptus extenuatus (Elles & Wood, 1908)			+	?			+					?	?				
Rhaphidograptus toernquisti (Elles & Wood, 1906)	+	+															
Stimulograptus halli (Barrande, 1850)															cf.		
Stimulograptus sedgwickii (Portlock, 1843)											+						
Streptograptus exiguus exiguus																	
Streptograptus cf. *plumosus* (Bailey, 1871)															+		
Aptychopsis sp.															+		
'Dawsonia' campanulata Nicholson, 1873	+																

+ fossil identified   ? uncertain identification   cf. comparable form recorded   aff. affinity

F.   RANGE OF LLANDOVERY GRAPTOLITES AND OTHER FOSSILS RECORDED IN THE DISTRICT.

Taxon	acuminatus	atavus	acinaces	cyphus	triangulatus	magnus	leptotheca	convolutus	sedgwickii s.l.	turriculatus s.l.	crispus	griestoniensis	crenulata s.l.
Atavograptus atavus		───	---	---									
Atavograptus gracilis		───											
Atavograptus sp.			---	---	---	---	---	---					
'Climacograptus' innotatus		-cf-											
Climacograptus trifilis	─												
Climacograptus sp.	────	────	────	────	────	────	────	────					
Coronograptus cirrus				?									
Coronograptus cyphus		?	?	---									
Coronograptus cyphus praematurus		cf											
Coronograptus gregarius				---	---	---	---	---					
Coronograptus sp.			-?-										
Cystograptus penna				?									
Cystograptus vesiculosus		---	---	---									
Dimorphograptus confertus s.s.		---	---	---									
Dimorphograptus elongatus		cf											
Dimorphograptus erectus		---											
Dimorphograptus decussatus		?											
Dimorphograptus longissimus		cf	---	---									
Dimorphograptus sp.		?											
Diplograptus modestus		cf?											
Diplograptids indet.								───					
Glyptograptus serratus								───	cf				
Glyptograptus sinuatus				cf?									
Glyptograptus tamariscus		---	---	---	---	---	---	---					
Glyptograptus tenuis		cf											
Glyptograptus sp.			?	?				?					
Lagarograptus acinaces			---	---									
Lagarograptus tenuis									─				
Monoclimacis crenularis								───					
Monograptus capis								───					
Monograptus clingani								───					
Monograptus convolutus								?					
Monograptus decipiens								───					
Monograptus denticulatus								───					
Monograptus limatulus								───					
Monograptus lobiferus								───					
Monograptus marri										?			
Monograptus nodifer										aff.			
Monograptus proteus										─			
Monograptus revolutus				?									
Monograptus spiralis										cf			
Monograptus triangulatus group								───					
Monograptus tullbergi													---
Monograptus sp.					---	---	---	---		───			
Normalograptus medius		---	---	---									
Normalograptus miserablis		?											
Normalograptus normalis	────	────	---	---									
Normalograptus rectangularis	────	────	────	────									
Normalograptus scalaris								?					
'Orthograptus' bellulus								───					
'Orthograptus' mutabilis		?	?										
Orthograptus sp.	?		---										
Paradiversograptus capillaris										───			
Paradiversograptus runcinatus										cf			
Parakidograptus acuminatus	─												
Petalolithus altissimus										───			
Petalolithus palmeus								───					
Petalolithus tenuis (or *P. wilsoni*)										?			
Pribylograptus incommodus	?aff.			?									
Pribylograptus sandersoni			-?-	-?-									
Pristiograptus regularis								cf					
Pristiograptus sp.				---	---	---	---	───					
Rastrites hybridus								───					
Rastrites longispinus					---	---	---	---					
Rastrites peregrinus								cf					
Rhaphidograptus extenuatus		---	---										
Rhaphidograptus toernquisti			---	---									
Stimulograptus halli										cf			
Stimulograptus sedgwickii									───				
Streptograptus cf. *plumosus*										---	---		
Streptograptus exiguus exiguus										───			
Aptychopsis sp. Nautiloid operculum										───			
'Dawsonia' campanulata Trilobita			---	---									

G.   LIST OF WENLOCK GRAPTOLITE LOCALITIES IN THE DISTRICT.

No.	Locality	NGR [NX]	Report No. & section	Zone(s)
1	Fauldbog Bay	6428 4453	88/20.1	*centrifugus*
2	Fauldbog Bay	6442 4427	88/20.2	*centrifugus*
3	Meikle Ross	6445 4393	88/20.3	mid *riccartonensis*
4	Meikle Ross	6448 4392	88/20.4	mid *riccartonensis*
5	Meikle Ross	6440 4370	88/20.5	mid *riccartonensis*
6	Meikle Ross	6442 4366	88/20.6	mid *riccartonensis*
7	Meikle Ross	6455 4355	88/20.7	mid *riccartonensis*
8	Meikle Ross	6532 4326	88/20.8	upper *riccartonensis?*
9	Meikle Ross	6537 4331	88/20.9	upper *riccartonensis?*
10	Meikle Ross	6552 4376	88/20.10	*riccartonensis?*
11	Meikle Ross	6562 4394	88/20.11	*riccartonensis?*
12	Ross (Balmangan) Bay	6545 4437	88/20.12	mid *riccartonensis*
13	Ross (Balmangan) Bay	6543 4444	88/20.13	mid *riccartonensis*
14*	Long Robin to Witchwife's Haven	6735 4586	88/135.1	*centrifugus*
15	Long Robin to Witchwife's Haven	6733 4586	88/135.2	*centrifugus*
16	Long Robin to Witchwife's Haven	6735 4582	88/135.3	*centrifugus*
17	Long Robin to Witchwife's Haven	6732 4570	88/135.4	*centrifugus*
18	Long Robin to Witchwife's Haven	6731 4569	88/135.5	*centrifugus*
19	Long Robin to Witchwife's Haven	6732 4566	88/135.6	uncertain
20	Long Robin to Witchwife's Haven	6732 4565	88/135.7	*centrifugus*
21	Long Robin to Witchwife's Haven	6729 4554	88/135.8	*riccartonensis*
22	Long Robin to Witchwife's Haven	6729 4549	88/135.9	upper *riccartonensis*
23	Long Robin to Witchwife's Haven	6731 4542	88/135.10	mid *riccartonensis*
24	Long Robin to Witchwife's Haven	6731 4539	88/135.11	mid *riccartonensis*
25	Long Robin to Witchwife's Haven	6729 4537	88/135.12	mid *riccartonensis*
26	Long Robin to Witchwife's Haven	6731 4531	88/135.13	mid *riccartonensis*
27	Long Robin to Witchwife's Haven	6731 4526	88/135.14	mid *riccartonensis*
28	Long Robin to Witchwife's Haven	6729 4521	88/135.15	uncertain
29	Long Robin to Witchwife's Haven	6729 4521	88/135/16	upper *riccartonensis?*
30	Torrs Point to Balmae Haven	6730 4486	88/135.17	upper *riccartonensis?*
31	Torrs Point to Balmae Haven	6740 4474	88/135.18	upper *riccartonensis?*
32	Torrs Point to Balmae Haven	6772 4442	88/135.19	mid *riccartonensis?*
33	Torrs Point to Balmae Haven	6773 4441	88/135.20	lower *riccartonensis*
34	Torrs Point to Balmae Haven	6774 4439	88/135.21	lower *riccartonensis*
35	Torrs Point to Balmae Haven	6774 4439	88/135.22	lower *riccartonensis*
36	Torrs Point to Balmae Haven	6774 4436	88/135.23	lower *riccartonensis*
37	Torrs Point to Balmae Haven	6780 4428	88 Report 135.24	upper *riccartonensis*
38	Torrs Point to Balmae Haven	6787 4425	88/135.25	upper *riccartonensis*
39	Torrs Point to Balmae Haven	6785 4422	88/135.26	upper *riccartonensis*
40	Torrs Point to Balmae Haven	6785 4419	88/135.27	*riccartonensis*
41	Torrs Point to Balmae Haven	6785 4416	88/135.28	uncertain
42	Torrs Point to Balmae Haven	6785 4414	88/135.29	mid *riccartonensis*
43	Torrs Point to Balmae Haven	6792 4406	88/135.30	mid *riccartonensis*
44	Torrs Point to Balmae Haven	6799 4405	88/135.31	mid *riccartonensis*
45	Balmae Haven to Gypsy Point	6799 4402	88/135.32	post *riccartonensis?*
46	Balmae Haven to Gypsy Point	6799 4400	88/135.33	post *riccartonensis?*
47	Balmae Haven to Gypsy Point	6803 4400	88/135.34	upper *riccartonensis?*
48	Balmae Haven to Gypsy Point	6803 4400	88/135.35	*antennularius?*
49	Balmae Haven to Gypsy Point	6808 4398	88/135.36	post *riccartonensis*
50	Balmae Haven to Gypsy Point	6825 4398	88/135.37	*antennularius*
51	Balmae Haven to Gypsy Point	6826 4397	88/135.38	*antennularius* or *rigidus*
52	Balmae Haven to Gypsy Point	6834 4388	88/135.39	uncertain
53	Balmae Haven to Gypsy Point	6835 4378	88/135.40	*linnarssoni*

G. ......*continued*

No.	Locality	NGR [NX]	Report No. & section	Zone(s)
54	Gypsy Point	6851 4359	88/135.41	top *riccartonensis* or younger
55*	Gypsy Point	6850 4361	88/135.42-44	uncertain and upper *riccartonensis – ellesae*
56	Port Muddle, (east side)	6883 4360	88/135.45	*antennularius*
57	Port Muddle, (east side)	6883 4360	88/135.46	uncertain
58*	Port Muddle, (east side)	6889 4355	88/135.47-51	*riccartonensis* and *antennularius*
59	Howell Bay to Little Raeberry	6945 4385	88/135.52	upper? *riccartonensis*
60	Howell Bay to Little Raeberry	702 437	88/135.53	*rigidus*
61*	Howell Bay to Little Raeberry	7063 4356	88/135.54-60	*rigidus* and ?*lundgreni*
62	Mullock Bay to White Port	7091 4360	88/135.61	*lundgreni*
63	Mullock Bay to White Port	7100 4390	88/135.62	*rigidus*
64	Mullock Bay to White Port	7114 4393	88/135.63	*lundgreni*
65	Mullock Bay to White Port	7142 4379	88/135.64	uncertain
66	Mullock Bay to White Port	7142 4377	88/135.65	uncertain
67	Mullock Bay to White Port	7148 4373	88/135.66	*lundgreni*
68*	Mullock Bay to White Port	7166 4364	88/135.67	*lundgreni*
69	Mullock Bay to White Port	7185 4340	88/135.68	*lundgreni*
70	Mullock Bay to White Port	7218 4340	88/135.69	uncertain (no younger than *lundgreni*)

H.   WENLOCK GRAPTOLITES FROM EACH LOCALITY WITH AUTHOR CITATION.

Locality number	1	2	3	4	5	6	7	8	9	10	11	12	13	14	15	16	17	18	19	20	21	22	23	24	25	26	27	28	29	30
Barrandeograptus? bornholmensis (Laursen, 1940)		+																												
Cyrtograptus centrifugus Bouček, 1931													?					cf.												
Cyrtograptus aff. *insectus* Bouček, 1931													?	+																
Cyrtograptus linnarssoni Lapworth, 1880																														
Cyrtograptus cf. *rigidus cautleyensis* Rickards, 1967																														
Cyrtograptus cf. *rigidus rigidus* Tullberg, 1883																														
Cyrtograptus spp.																+	+	+	+											
cf. *Lapworthograptus grayae* (Lapworth, 1876)		+																												
Mediograptus cautleyensis (Rickards, 1965)															+		+													
Monoclimacis flumendosae kingi Rickards, 1965																														
Monoclimacis flumendosae (Gortani, 1923) s.l.								+																						
Monoclimacis vomerina basilica (Lapworth, 1880)		+													cf.	+	cf.	cf.	+			cf.					+		+	
Monoclimacis vomerina vomerina (Nicholson, 1872)	+														+															
Monoclimacis vomerina (Nicholson, 1872) s.l.		+												+		+		+	+	+		+						+		
Monoclimacis spp.									+					+																
'Monograptus' antennularius (Meneghini, 1857)																														
Monograptus firmus sedberghensis Rickards, 1965								?													?	+						cf.	cf.	
Monograptus flemingii flemingii (Salter, 1852)																														
Monograptus flemingii (Salter, 1852) s.l.																														
Monograptus flexilis aff. *belophoros* (Meneghini, 1857)																														
Monograptus aff. *flexilis belophorus* (Meneghini. 1857)																														
Monograptus flexilis aff. *flexilis* Elles, 1900																														
Monograptus flexilis cf. *flexilis* Elles, 1900														+			+													
Monograptus priodon (Bronn, 1835)		+												+	+	+	+	+	+	+	?		+						cf.	
Monograptus radotinensis inclinatus Rickards, 1965																							cf.							
Monograptus remotus Elles & Wood, 1913																				+										
Monograptus riccartonensis Lapworth, 1876			+	+	+	+	+	?		?	?	+	+								cf.	+	+	+	+	+	+			
Monograptus sp.																														
Plectograptus? bouceki Rickards, 1967																														
Pristiograptus dubius dubius (Suess, 1851)																														
Pristiograptus dubius (Suess, 1851) s.l.																														
Pristiograptus dubius group																												+		
Pristiograptus dubius aff. *latus* (Bouček, 1932)																														
Pristiograptus meneghinii (Gortani, 1923)																							cf.							
Pristiograptus pseudodubius Bouček, 1932																														
Pristiograptus sp.																														
Retiolites geinitzianus angustidens Elles & Wood, 1908														+																
Retiolites geinitzianus geinitzianus (Barrande, 1850)																	+													

+ fossil identified   ? uncertain identification   cf. comparable form recorded

H. ....*continued*

31	32	33	34	35	36	37	38	39	40	41	42	43	44	45	46	47	48	49	50	51	52	53	54	55	56	57	58	59	60	61	62	63	64	65	66	67	68	69	70
																						+																	
																						+								+									
																														?							?		+
																								?						+	cf.	cf.			+	cf.			
															+			+		+	aff.	+		cf.		+		cf.		+									
			+		+						+		+									+																	
		cf.						cf.			cf.																												
		+		+						+			+																										
																																							+
															+	cf.		+							+	+				+									
cf.						cf.	+	+																		cf.									+	+		+	
																						+								+	+		+	+					
																											+	+											
																				+						+		+		+	?								
		+	+	+	+											cf.																							
		cf.					?	cf.								cf.										+													
cf.	+	+	+		cf.	+	+	+		+	+	+			+											+	+												
																							+																
												+								+										?	+	+							
+					cf.					+												+				cf.													+
						+											+	+				+		+	cf.	+				+				+	+	+		
																						+																	

+ fossil identified   ? uncertain identification   cf. comparable form recorded   aff. affinity

I.   ZONAL RANGES OF WENLOCK GRAPTOLITES RECORDED IN THE DISTRICT.

	centrifugus	[murchisoni]	riccartonensis L.	riccartonensis M.	riccartonensis U.	antennularius	rigidus	linnarssoni	[ellesae]	lundgreni
Barrandeograptus ? bornholmensis										
Cyrtograptus centrifugus	cf.									
Cyrtograptus aff. insectus										
Cyrtograptus linnarssoni										
Cyrtograptus cf. rigidus cautleyensis										
Cyrtograptus cf. rigidus				cf.	?					
Cyrtograptus spp			cf.	cf.	?		cf.			?
cf. Lapworthograptus grayae										
Monoclimacis flumendosae kingi										
Monoclimacis flumendosae kingi s.l.										
Monoclimacis vomerina basilica										
Monoclimacis vomerina vomerina										
Monoclimacis vomerina s.l.										
Monoclimacis spp										
"Monograptus" antennularis										
Monograptus firmus sedberghensis										
Monograptus flemingii flemingii										
Monograptus flemingii s.l.										
Monograptus flexilis aff. belophorus										
Monograptus aff. flexilis belophorus				cf.	cf.?					
Monograptus flexilis aff. flexilis										
Monograptus flexilis cf. flexilis										
Monograptus minimus cautleyensis										
Monograptus priodon										
Monograptus radotinensis inclinatus				?	cf.		cf.			
Monograptus remotus										
Monograptus riccartonensis										
Monograptus sp.										
"Plectograptus" bouceki oucek										
Pristiograptus dubius dubius										
Pristiograptus dubius s.l.										
Pristiograptus dubius group										
Pristiograptus dubius aff. latus										
Pristiograptus meneghini										
pseudodubious sp.										
Pristiograptus sp.										
Retiolites geinitzianus angustidens										
Retiolites geinitzianus geinitzianus										

APPENDIX 2

Modal composition of wackes in the Kirkcudbright–Dalbeattie district

Group	Formation etc.	Specimen	Qtz	Plag	K-feld	Tot. feld	Px	Hbl	Mica	Opaq	Acid	And	Basic	Tot. ign	Met	Sed	Matrix	NGR
Gala	GALA 5	S 78257	50			11.3			2.2	10.5	5.5	0.4			2.8	2.6	14.6	6830 6837
	GALA 5	S 78259	22			12			1.7	0.5	5	2.1	0.4		5.5	1.9	49	6745 6894
	GALA 5	S 78319	43			21.1			1.3	0.5	11.9	0.9			2.1	0.2	18.5	6592 6798
	GALA 5	S 78278	38			12.5			5.1	0.6	10.4		0.2		5.6	3.1	24.8	6560 6880
	GALA 7 cg	S 78252	56			15.4			4.9	3	8	0.3	0.5		2.2	1.1	9	6970 6701
	GALA 7 cg	S 78260	39			14.9			3.3	1.9	15	2.7	0.5		4.8	7.1	10.6	6903 6813
	GALA 7 cg	S 78262	48			13.7			6.1	4	11.5	0.5	0.1		2.6	3	10.9	7034 6678
	GALA 7 cg	S 78272	46			11.9			9.9	2.3	9.8	1.7	0.5		4.5	4.9	8.2	7390 6903
	GALA 7 cg	S 78274	48			12.5			6.4	5.4	8.4	0.3	1.5		2.5	1.6	13	7353 6963
	GALA 7 cg	S 78306	43			16			3.8	3.9	3.8	0.2			1.8	1.6	26.2	6889 6506
	GALA 7	S 80376	44			10.2			3.9	1.4	8.9		0.2			0.8	30.8	6067 6266
Hawick	CNW	S 78284	52			11.8			4.3	2.3	9.6	1	0.2		5.2	0.6	13.1	6252 6007
	KMN	S 78291	57			11			4.8	0.6	13.3	0.6			1.3	2.5	8.9	6344 5768
	CGD	S 78177	34			14.1			1.7	2.1	10.7	0.8	0.5		1.4	1.6	33	6155 4493
	CGD	S 78181	26			8.6			1.2	1.6	14.7	1.7	0.9		2.7	2.7	39.7	6168 4466
	CGD	S 78182	32			8.2		0.1	1.4	0.7	16.7	0.4	0.1		2.7	1.1	36.4	6254 4446
	CGD	S 78207	33			8.3		0.1	2.9	4.5	12.9	0.5	0.3		1.8	1.5	34.7	6561 4598
	CGD	S 78229	22			5.5			1.5	3	23.9	6.9	3.2		4.4	2.1	27.7	6617 4894
	ROSS	S 78239	32			7.3	0.4		0.7	2.9	8.3	1.3	0.7		2.5	0.5	43.8	6727 4490
	ROSS	S 78244	29			8			2	1.1	10.2	0.5	0.2		1	1	46.6	6436 4362
	ROSS	S 78193	33			6			1.9	1.1	7		0.1		0.6	0.5	50.3	6439 4412
	ROSS	S 78202	27			9.5			5.7	1.2	7.5				4.2	1	43.8	6496 4439
	ROSS	S 78203	29			8.3		0.1	2.6	2.1	6.3	1	0.5		3.4	2	44.9	6510 4483
Riccarton	RBC (GP)	S 78219	57	3	6				1					2	4	6	21	6915 4366
	RBC (RA)	S 78216	67	1	5									1	4	5	15	6988 4373
	RBC (MB)	S 78212	68	1	6				2					4	2	3	16	7176 4355

1000 points were counted in each thin section.
Data for Riccarton Group supplied by W D McCaffrey.

CGD Carghidown Formation; CNW Cairnharrow Formation;
GP Gipsy Point Member; KMN Kirkmaiden Formation;
MB Mullock Bay Member; RA Raeberry Member;
RBC Raeberry Castle Formation; ROSS Ross Formation.

cg coarse grained facies
S 78257 BGS registered thin section number
Qtz mono and polycrystalline quartz, excluding quartzite
Plag plagioclase feldspar
K-feld K-feldspar

Tot. feld total feldspar
Px pyroxene
Hbl hornblende
Mica micas
Opaq opaque minerals
Acid acidic igneous rock clasts
And andesitic rock clasts
Basic all other basic igneous rock clasts
Tot. ign total igneous rock clasts
Met metamorphic clasts
Sed sedimentary rock clasts
Matrix interstitial material and grains < 0.01 mm diameter
NGR National grid reference

AUTHOR CITATIONS FOR FOSSIL SPECIES

To satisfy the rules and recommendations of the international codes of botanical and zoological nomenclature, authors of cited species are listed below.

This lists includes only the fossils which are not in Appendix IB, E and H.

ORDOVICIAN–SILURIAN

Acritarchs

Ammonidium listeri Smelor 1986
Domasia limaciformis (Stockmans and Willière, 1963) Cramer

Graptolites

Streptograptus plumosus (Baily, 1871)

Chitinozoans

Cingulochitina cingulata (Eisenack, 1937) Paris, 1981

Conodonts

Dapsilodus praecipuus Barrick, 1977

DEVONIAN–LOWER CARBONIFEROUS

Fish

Holoptychius nobilissimus Agassiz in Murchison, 1839.

CARBONIFEROUS

Bivalves

Actinopteria persulcata (McCoy, 1851)
Modiolus latus (Portlock, 1843)
Naiadites crassus (Fleming, 1828)
Prothyris cf. *oblonga* Wilson, 1961
Pteronites cf. *angustatus* McCoy, 1844
Sanguinolites cf. *roxburgensis* Hind, 1900
Schizodus cf. *pentlandicus* (Rhind, 1838)

Brachiopods

Antiquatonia cf. *teres* (Muir-Wood, 1928)
'Camarotoechia' cf. *proava* (Phillips, 1836)
Cleiothyridina cf. *glabistria* (Phillips, 1836)
Linoprotonia cf. *ashfellensis* Ferguson, 1971
Productus cf. *garwoodi* Muir-Wood, 1928
Punctospirifer redesdalensis North, 1920
Stenoscisma cf. *isorhyncha* (McCoy, 1844)
Syringothysis cuspidata (J. Sowerby, 1816)
Syringothyris cf. *cuspidata* (J. Sowerby, 1816)

Corals

Lithostrotion clavaticum Thomson, 1883
Siphonodendron scoticum (Hill, 1940)
Siphonophyllia benburbensis (Lewis, 1927)
Syringopora ramulosa Goldfuss, 1826

GENERAL INDEX

See also Contents (p.v) for principal headings and lithological units.

BRITISH GEOLOGICAL SURVEY

Keyworth, Nottingham NG12 5GG
0115 936 3100

Murchison House, West Mains Road, Edinburgh EH9 3LA
0131 667 1000

London Information Office, Natural History Museum
Earth Galleries, Exhibition Road, London SW7 2DE
020 7589 4090

The full range of Survey publications is available through the Sales Desks at Keyworth and at Murchison House, Edinburgh, and in the BGS London Information Office in the Natural History Museum (Earth Galleries). The adjacent bookshop stocks the more popular books for sale over the counter. Most BGS books and reports can be bought from The Stationery Office and through Stationery Office agents and retailers. Maps are listed in the BGS Map Catalogue, and can be bought together with books and reports through BGS-approved stockists and agents as well as direct from BGS.

The British Geological Survey carries out the geological survey of Great Britain and Northern Ireland (the latter as an agency service for the government of Northern Ireland), and of the surrounding continental shelf, as well as its basic research projects. It also undertakes programmes of British technical aid in geology in developing countries as arranged by the Department for International Development and other agencies.

The British Geological Survey is a component body of the Natural Environment Research Council.

Published by The Stationery Office and available from:

The Stationery Office
(mail, telephone and fax orders only)
PO Box 29, Norwich, NR3 1GN
Telephone orders/General enquiries 0870 600 5522
Fax orders 0870 600 5533

www.the-stationery-office.com

The Stationery Office Bookshops
123 Kingsway, London WC2B 6PQ
020 7242 6393 Fax 020 7242 6412
68–69 Bull Street, Birmingham B4 6AD
0121 236 9696 Fax 0121 236 9699
33 Wine Street, Bristol BS1 2BQ
0117 926 4306 Fax 0117 929 4515
9–21 Princess Street, Manchester M60 8AS
0161 834 7201 Fax 0161 833 0634
16 Arthur Street, Belfast BT1 4GD
028 9023 8451 Fax 028 9023 5401
The Stationery Office Oriel Bookshop
18–19 High Street, Cardiff CF1 2BZ
029 2039 5548 Fax 029 2038 4347
71 Lothian Road, Edinburgh EH3 9AZ
0870 606 5566 Fax 0870 606 5588

The Stationery Office's Accredited Agents
(see Yellow Pages)

and through good booksellers